Decentralizing the State

Elections, Parties, and Local Power in the Andes

This book explores the location and dynamics of power within the state, focusing on a recent wave of decentralizing reforms that have swept across both developed and developing countries in recent years. Variation in the timing of reform across countries only vaguely relates to the genesis of an international consensus pushed by big lenders and development banks or the reemergence of democracy in decentralizing countries. Moreover, many of these reforms were enacted from the top, which appears to contradict one of political science's central tenets: that politicians seek to maximize (or at least maintain) control over political and fiscal resources. This book develops a theory linking decentralization's adoption to the electoral concerns of political parties: Decentralization represents a desirable strategy for parties whose support at subnational levels appears more secure than their prospects in national elections. The book examines this argument against experiences in Bolivia, Colombia, Ecuador, Peru, and Venezuela and speculates on how recent political changes may affect decentralization's shape and extent in coming years.

Acknowledgments

This project began as my Ph.D. dissertation, then blossomed into a book manuscript as time and feedback drew out the key points of this project. As a result, there are more people to thank than I can possibly name; if you do not find your name listed in these brief pages, I hope that you will know that your support and input were, indeed, appreciated.

First, and foremost, I want to acknowledge the unflagging support of my parents. Without their support, this project never would have been brought to fruition.

I also want to thank my dissertation committee and several other advisers and colleagues without whose help this book would be much less coherent and cohesive than it is. Jorge I. Domínguez deserves special recognition for reading each chapter at least three times and providing detailed comments on each new draft. His work and his encouragement have been invaluable. Rather than ending with the successful defense of the dissertation manuscript, Jorge's work merely began there, and he has continued to provide support and advice right up to the final stages of this project. Robert H. Bates and Dani Rodrik supplied much food for thought in the development of this project and brought up fresh points I had not considered that became important building blocks in the development of my argument. As an unofficial adviser, Jeffry Frieden also provided invaluable help and encouragement along the way. As a reviewer of this manuscript, John Carey made several key suggestions that substantially improved this project. A special acknowledgment must be made to Ricardo Godoy for introducing me to fieldwork in the backlands of Honduras and for introducing me to the politics of Bolivia – a country I have come to enjoy both intellectually and on a much more personal level, as well.

A special thanks is due to my colleagues at Cornell University's government department. This collegial department provided a nurturing environment for my first years as an assistant professor and offered the space and resources that allowed this project to go from dissertation to manuscript. I especially want to thank Christopher Way, Valerie Bunce, Sidney Tarrow, Jonathan Kirshner, Jonas Pontusson, Richard Bensel, Elizabeth Sanders and the Katzensteins for their encouragement, support, and friendship during my term there.

The input of my graduate school colleagues was probably the most critical in the process of writing this book; although I indulge in naming a few individuals, the broader graduate student intellectual community I found in my last years of graduate school still stands unrivaled as the most intellectually alive and generous of any I have experienced, and so I thank everyone who participated in it. I want to single out Ashley Timmer for spending a good deal of her time helping me to develop the formal model in Chapter 2. Mike Tomz provided the invaluable service of challenging my methodology and my argument in ways that forced me to improve and extend them. Mala Htun, Gary Bass, and Kanchan Chandra also provided important input on the argument and organization of the book at key points. Donna Lee Van Cott shared freely from her own research to fill gaps in mine, in addition to sharing critical contact information from her fieldwork in both Bolivia and Colombia. Seminar groups at Harvard and Cornell that allowed me to share my work and that generated lively discussions of my project's weaknesses and limitations have also earned a heartfelt thanks.

I also thank the Institute for Electoral Studies in Washington, D.C., for graciously allowing me to root around in their extensive library of electoral statistics to fill the gaps in my data.

My list of thanks would not be complete without acknowledging the help of those who made my fieldwork in Bolivia and Colombia possible, fruitful, and enjoyable. I gratefully acknowledge the Harvard Institute for International Development, the David Rockefeller Center for Latin American Studies, and the Weatherhead Center for International Affairs for providing funds that made my travels possible. I also warmly thank those in both countries who hosted me: the University of the Andes in Bogotá, Colombia; the Federation for Development (Fedesarrollo) in Bogotá, Colombia; and the Entity for Political and Social Research in La Paz, Bolivia (Unidad de Análisis Política Social). I also thank those who contributed to the effectiveness of my research in both countries and all those who graciously submitted to my interviews in somewhat less than fluent Spanish. My sincerest gratitude goes to the Salas family for generously welcoming me into their home during my several visits to Bogotá, Colombia, and for showing me the best of Colombia – both in its historic scenery and in the warmth of its people.

PART I

ELECTORAL THEORY AND COMPARATIVE EVIDENCE

1

Introduction

From Bolivia to India, and from the United Kingdom and Spain to Uganda, national governments are giving away their power. A revolution of local empowerment has quietly swept both developed and developing nations alike in the closing decades of the twentieth century.

Perhaps nowhere has this trend reshaped the political landscape more dramatically than in Latin America – a region more likely to call to mind highly centralized governments run by military strongmen, civilian dictators, or one-party rule (Véliz 1980). In 1980, only half of Latin America's governments held democratic elections at the national level; by 1997, all but one elected both national and regional and/or local governments (Inter-American Development Bank 1997: 99). Even more stunning, many countries have bolstered local political empowerment by increasing the financial independence of subnational governments by apportioning real fiscal resources to elected officials.

Have national politicians all gone mad? Surprisingly, few scholars[1] have paused to probe the puzzling question of why politicians are giving power away. Instead, a great deal of intellectual activity has been devoted to two other questions: Has fiscal decentralization increased economic gains?[2] And have more elections improved democratic

---

[1] Recently, scholarship addressing this question has begun to emerge, especially Willis, Haggard, and Garman (1999), Grindle (2000), Barr (2001), and Garman, Haggard, and Willis (2001). I discuss these contributions more thoroughly in the next chapter.

[2] Several scholars have assessed whether fiscal federalism as practiced in Latin America has generated the efficiency gains promised in economic theory (Tiebout 1956;

quality?[3] Determining what motivates decentralization seems a necessary and prior question to determining what its consequences may be; it is a missed step that can throw the best analysis of consequences awry. Exploring the why and the when of decentralization is the heart of this project. Unfortunately, the answer is not obvious. In most cases, decentralization has not been adopted as a response to pressures from below; rather, it has been initiated by the national governments most likely to be hurt by decentralizing reforms. For these reasons, decentralization poses a thorny puzzle for political scientists who assume that political actors seek to gain and hold on to power.

In some countries, especially the Southern Cone countries of Argentina and Brazil, but also Chile to some extent, decentralization might be written off as merely a return to the pre-authoritarian power-sharing relationship that had been established between central and subnational governments.[4] The more fascinating – and puzzling – cases are those in which both political and fiscal powers were devolved simultaneously and for the first time. In the Andean region of Latin America, comprised of Bolivia, Colombia, Ecuador, Peru, and Venezuela, decentralization generally meant an unprecedented devolution of power from national to local governments.

Musgrave 1959; Rubinfeld 1987; Bird 1990; Oates 1998; Bardhan 2002). Many have found the results disappointing (Bahl and Linn 1994; Tanzi 1994; Prud'homme 1995; Munin 1998; Rodden 2000). Others, most notably Tendler (1997), Faguet (2001), and Campbell (2003), have explored some of the many success stories where decentralization has created pockets of innovative governance.

[3] These scholars have sought to understand decentralization's potential for improving democracy's quality and sustainability in the region. Here, most analysts trumpet decentralization for increasing democratic practice (Fox 1994), providing an entry point into the political arena for ethnic groups and opposition parties (Dahl 1971; Diamond 1999), encouraging policy experimentation (Tocqueville 1843), creating new career paths for ambitious or high-quality political candidates (O'Neill 2002; Escobar-Lemmon and Moreno 2003), as well as simply empowering citizens at the local level. Some observers find fault, however. Dahl (1971) warns that decentralization may prove inimical to a state's democratic consolidation if regionalism itself provides a salient political cleavage or if issues divide society along regional lines. In Latin America, specific concerns have been raised that decentralization may simply legitimate the power of local bosses, create subnational authoritarian enclaves (Cornelius 1999), engender new forms of clientelism (García-Guadilla and Pérez 2002), or, in Colombia particularly, empower agents supported by guerrilla movements, right-wing paramilitary units, and the narcotics trade (Gaitán Pavía and Moreno Ospina 1992).

[4] For an excellent analysis of these countries, and why their decentralizing experiences do not merely represent a return to the status quo before authoritarianism, see Eaton (2004).

In addition to being unitary states (although Venezuela is nominally federal), these countries also provide an ideal set of comparative cases because they share the same cultural and regional context, have achieved broadly similar levels of economic development, and yet differ widely in the pace and extent of decentralization adopted. They also differ substantially along the range of explanatory factors expected to account for differences in decentralization's adoption.

Understanding why administrations in the Andes chose to decentralize and why they chose to decentralize at particular moments in their democratic trajectories is the main task of *Decentralizing the State*. Decentralizing reforms are complex and highly varied policy initiatives, making it highly unlikely that a single logic can explain their adoption; however, I make the case that political – and particularly electoral – motivations play a critical and overlooked role in many decentralizing reforms. By focusing on the political party as the key decision-making unit and by examining its electoral motives, this project finds a solution that reconciles seemingly irrational political action with the drive for political survival. The central argument of *Decentralizing the State* is that administrations are more likely to favor decentralization when their party is likely to benefit from electoral contests for subnational positions. This is most likely when the party in power believes it cannot hold on to power that is centralized in the national government but believes it has a good chance of winning a substantial portion of decentralized power through subnational elections. Decentralization distributes power at one moment in time to the venues where a party's political allies are most likely to win it in future contests. Thus, decentralization can be seen as an electoral strategy to empower political parties with reasonably long time horizons.

While Chapter 2 devotes a good deal of attention to deriving and developing this theory, the underlying logic can be gleaned from a simple thought experiment. Imagine that you are the head of a party that controls the presidency in a highly centralized governing system. Thinking ahead to the next presidential contest, you can compete under the same centralized system or you might choose to use your power to decentralize the system prior to the election. A win yields another term of centralized rule; a loss may mean nearly complete exclusion from power for several years. A decentralized system, in contrast, offers contesting parties a somewhat less attractive presidency but several opportunities to gain footholds of power at subnational levels. Before you cast your lot with the decentralizers, consider that decentralization comes at a cost. To compete in a decentralized system in the future, the administration must give up some of its power now, when its hold on national power is already assured for the term. The benefits of competing under a decentralized system in the future must outweigh the cost of lost power in the present. In this calculation, decentralization will be most attractive when a party's national support is weak (it is unlikely to win the next presidency), when subnational electoral chances look good (it is likely to win subnational contests under a decentralized system), and when the party values the future (since costs are incurred now and benefits accrue in the future).

How does a party have weak national support and strong subnational support? Another thought experiment could illustrate. Imagine a country with 100 states, where the president is selected by majority rule and population is spread evenly across the states. The current president won 60 percent of the vote. In scenario one, this 60 percent was evenly spread across the 100 states, so 60 percent of voters in each state cast their votes for the winning candidate. In scenario two, this 60 percent came from 100 percent of the voters in sixty states voting for the victor and 100 percent of the voters in the remaining forty states voting against the victor. If national support is expected to fall to 40 percent in the next election and if the ruling party expects support to be distributed as in the past, then the party will win 40 percent of the vote in each of the states in scenario one and 100 percent of the vote in forty states in scenario two. If decentralization means that each of the states would elect a governor based on majority rule, the ruling party could expect to lose not only the national election but also all of the state elections in scenario one. Decentralization in scenario two would mean winning state elections in forty states. National support for the party as a whole declines in both scenarios (the party loses the presidency), but subnational electoral prospects look remarkably better in the second scenario. To find an example of a party that is nationally weak but subnationally strong, one need look no further than the Republican party in the United States in 1996; though its candidate faced insuperable odds of winning the presidency, many of its members won or maintained gubernatorial positions throughout the country. Thus, decentralization will not become attractive to a party whose national support is falling, if its electoral possibilities at the subnational level are also in precipitous decline. Likewise, a party that is highly uncertain about its future electoral prospects or that is under-institutionalized may heavily discount the future, also making decentralization unlikely.

While the body of scholarship on decentralization remains incipient, political scientists have developed large bodies of scholarship on federalism and delegation, two areas that would seem to be rich sources of theoretical insight into this wave of reform. No mere extension of the theories developed to explain federalism or delegation seems to explain recent decentralizing reforms in Latin America, however; instead, the study of decentralization promises to add to both literatures.

Federalism and decentralization are closely related: Both refer to systems in which subnational units enjoy a degree of autonomy from central policy makers. Federalism traditionally differs from decentralization in that states or regions play the primary role in federal systems, whereas decentralization often skips the regional level altogether, directing resources toward local governments; in addition, (successful) federal systems usually include a bicameral legislature in which one house is elected to represent territorial interests. Despite these differences, federal and decentralized systems have much in common. Perhaps theories of federalism may shed some light on decentralization, as well.

The most oft-cited scholar of federalism, William Riker, theorizes that federalism results from "a bargain between prospective national leaders and officials of constituent governments for the purpose of aggregating territory, the better to lay taxes and raise armies" (Riker 1964: 11). Prospective national leaders seek to expand territorial control in the face of military or diplomatic threats (or opportunities) and seek confederation because either they cannot conquer the territory or they find conquest distasteful. Although he relies heavily on the U.S. case, his analysis includes the federal states of Switzerland, Germany, the USSR, India, Pakistan, Argentina, and Brazil. As the instances of decentralization studied here begin with a unitary state devolving powers to its constituent units, this theory does not seem appropriate.

After the collapse of communism, a new wave of scholarship on federalism emerged, exploring the role of federal institutions in forestalling or encouraging the decomposition of states (Roeder 1991; Bunce 1999; Solnick 1999). This literature has spread beyond Eastern Europe to include Indonesia (Ferrazzi 2000), Nigeria (Suberu 2001), and Spain

(Moreno 2002), to name a few. Though geographically and culturally disparate, these studies have in common a primary focus on the tensions between a central state and its ethno-territorial components.

Mindful of this wave of case-specific explorations of federalism, Stepan (1999, 2000a, 2000b, 2001) has attempted to amend Riker's theory, arguing that Riker's theory of confederation describes only one of several paths through which countries adopt a federal system. Stepan adds two other categories to the "coming-together" federalism discussed by Riker: "holding-together" federalism and "putting-together" federalism. The latter involves the coercion of units into a federal arrangement (as with some states in the formation of the USSR), while the former occurs when a unified state trades increased autonomy to subunits for their acquiescence in remaining within the broader union of states. This latter is particularly interesting from the perspective of decentralization, as it involves the transfer of power from the center to constituent units; however, "holding-together" federalism is a bargain struck by the center with subunits that are threatening to secede.[5] Even this amended federal literature cannot account for the Latin American cases of decentralization: devolution of power to regions or localities in the absence of anything like secessionist demands from subunits. An exploration of decentralization thus goes beyond the literature on federalism, seeking reasons for the empowerment of subnational units in the absence of secessionist threats. While federal and decentralized governments look similar in practice, the literature addressing federalism's adoption provides little guidance when one attempts to understand the adoption of decentralization in Latin America.

Perhaps decentralization better approximates delegation than federalism; certainly, the literature on delegation begins with the same motivating question: If politicians seek access to political and fiscal resources, why do they give power away? A rich literature probes this question, focusing on delegation of authority by legislatures to the bureaucracy, by parties to legislative committees, and by elected governments to independent agencies.

Lowi (1969) pioneered in this subject matter when he observed an increasing bureaucratization of policy making in the United States. He argued that Congress was abdicating its duties to the bureaucracy,

---

[5] Key examples include Spain in 1975 and India in 1948.

leaving policy open to the influence of special interests that could, and often did, "capture" their regulators. Later, Fiorina (1977) argued a slightly different form of the abdication hypothesis: that members of Congress delegated authority knowing there would be problems, expecting to intervene to address egregious errors and, thereby, boost their support.

An opposing theoretical view argued that delegation, whether by parties to committees (Cox and McCubbins 1993) or by the Congress to the bureaucracy (Kiewiet and McCubbins 1991), did not represent a significant abdication of authority after all. They argued that delegators retained a great deal of control over the committees or bureaucracy through powers of appointment in the latter case and various forms of oversight in the former.

A third theoretical approach draws on the insights of transactions cost analysis in economics. Epstein and O'Halloran (1999) hypothesize that legislators compare the likely policy outcome on each issue from not delegating (i.e., the relevant committee's most preferred outcome) with the likely outcome from delegation and choose the method most likely to get them re-elected. This leads to several testable hypotheses: On issues where the relevant committee's preferences closely approximate the legislature's preferences, delegation is not likely; when the executive's preferences closely approximate the legislature's preferences, delegation is more likely; and when the issue to be decided is more informationally intensive and/or less distributive in nature, delegation is more likely.

Finally, scholars exploring why administrations sometimes attempt to institutionalize their policy preferences by delegating important policy areas to independent agencies (i.e., central banks) provide yet another perspective on the question of giving power away. McCubbins, Noll, and Weingast (1987), Horn and Shepsle (1989), Moe (1990), and Boylan (2001) theorize that outgoing administrations face incentives to institutionalize their policies to protect their interests from incoming opposition.

None of these theories of delegation, which focus on the delegation of authority to appointed officials, quite explains decentralization, which allows for popular elections at subnational levels. Still, several insights can be gleaned from this body of work. In contrast to what the shirking hypothesis would predict, the instances of decentralization studied here[6] involved a substantial devolution of real fiscal resources along with broad policy-making authority. Likewise, the idea that institutional constraints effectively limit the degree of delegation occurring in these cases also does not fit with the nature of these decentralizing reforms, which allow for the popular election of subnational officials and give them broad policy making authority backed by significant fiscal resources that are not distributed purely at the central government's discretion.[7]

The logic of the transactions cost and institutional insulation arguments suggests that decentralization should occur when the delegator's policy preferences are more closely approximated by the workings of a decentralized rather than a centralized system. This basic insight is also the bedrock of this volume's analysis; however, the transactions cost and institutional insulation hypotheses are insufficient to give a full explanation of decentralization. The transactions cost approach, for example, suggests that certain policy areas are more susceptible to delegation than others: those that are more informationally intense and less distributive in nature. This does not seem to fit these cases of decentralization, where policy making in such highly distributive areas as education, health, and local infrastructure was devolved to subnational governments. The work on institutional insulation adds the important component of comparing the preferences of the current administration with an incoming administration, which will prove essential to explaining decentralization, but this comparison remains rooted at the central government level. Because decentralization leads to changes in policy-making authority not just between pieces of the national government, but also across levels of government, one must also look at the likely composition of incoming administrations throughout the country at subnational levels. Furthermore, because decentralization is costly in the current period, one is forced to consider the extent to which potential decentralizers value the future since the benefits will occur in future time periods, though the costs will be incurred in the

---

[6] There are certainly instances of devolving responsibilities without resources (unfounded mandates), but these are not classified as "decentralizing reforms" as the term is used here.

[7] Decentralizing reforms in which the central government keeps tight control over the distribution of funds or sets policies that subnational governments merely carry out are also not considered decentralizing reforms in this volume's definition.

current administration. While the delegation literature does provide some insight into the incentives to decentralize, it provides an incomplete framework for analysis. Exploring decentralization, a policy with clear affinities to both federalism and delegation, may lead to a better understanding of these other fields as well.

On a smaller level, this volume's theory that decentralizing reforms respond to electoral considerations has implications for explaining not just the timing of decentralizing reforms, but also their content and the evolution of decentralizing – and perhaps recentralizing – reforms over time, across successive administrations. In addition, this work contributes to a growing body of work that takes political parties seriously in Latin America's policy-making arenas. The analysis of decentralization suggests the importance of party institutionalization for the enactment of policies with long-term effects. More importantly, this work demonstrates the need to look beyond the nature of party systems to explain reform; instead, it is necessary to look at the structure of individual parties at specific moments in time to understand the incentives that they face when initiating or joining policy debates. Finally, at the individual party level, this work emphasizes that a party's aggregate support is an insufficient metric by which to judge some aspects of its behavior; many important aspects of party behavior depend not just on the overall strength of party support, but on its geographic distribution across electoral boundaries.[8] A political geography approach is crucial to understanding the impetus to decentralize; it may also be important for understanding a number of other political reforms, particularly those that affect changes in electoral rules.

METHODOLOGY AND PLAN OF THE BOOK

Decentralizing the State is a theoretically informed, comparative analysis exploring the causes of decentralization in five Latin American countries: Bolivia, Colombia, Ecuador, Peru, and Venezuela. It spans at least two decades in each country, focusing on the period from 1980 to 2000, when the bulk of decentralizing reforms was passed in these countries. This study combines a variety of analytic methods including

---

[8] See Jones and Mainwaring (2003) for an empirical treatment of this concept across Latin America.

formal modeling, simulation, regression analysis, and in-depth case studies informed by field work, archival research, and interviews with policy makers at central and local levels of government to develop and test its central argument. By bringing these various methodologies to bear on the question, Why decentralize?, I am able to gain greater leverage than would be afforded by a single methodological approach (Tarrow 1995).

I employ formal modeling in my analysis for two reasons. First, this framework allows me to state my argument most concisely and to identify the specific pieces of evidence that will be required to prove my theory's worth. What is more, decentralizing reform fits well into the domain for which rational choice theories appear to be most appropriate. According to Tsebelis (1990: 31–39), the assumptions of rational choice are most likely to obtain when decisions are being made by a select few individuals (party elites, in this case) who interact repeatedly (here, through repeated elections) and for whom the issues at stake are particularly salient. Second, using a deductive theory that follows from basic assumptions about the motives of political actors can prove extremely useful for understanding classes of behavior such as decentralization, where the individuals involved may have strong incentives to misrepresent the reasons for their actions. In this instance, it seems unlikely that politicians will admit to decentralizing for the electoral benefits it might provide their party; instead, politicians are likely to extol decentralization's contribution to increasing economic efficiency or deepening democratic participation.

In testing the theory, the combination of statistical analysis with in-depth qualitative analysis allows me to bolster the weaknesses of each individual methodology by leaning on the strengths of the other. The limitations of statistical comparability constrain the statistical analysis to retrospective data on party support even though ample qualitative evidence exists on party support throughout each presidential administration. Because they are not comparable across countries, prospective data of this sort cannot be included in the statistical data set. At the same time, statistical analysis adds to the rigor of the comparative analysis, assuring that the same standards are required for each of the cases explored. If the results of both analyses point in the same direction, then the case for an electoral theory of decentralization is doubly strong.

Decentralizing the State is divided into three parts. The first formally derives an electoral theory of decentralization, explores the implications of loosening the major assumptions behind this theory, discusses alternative explanations for decentralizing reforms, and tests the electoral theory and some of its alternatives using a statistical model. The second takes a more in-depth look at the evolution of decentralizing reforms across administrations within each of the Andean countries, paying particular attention to the experiences of Colombia and Bolivia, where the text draws on fieldwork carried out in both countries. This section allows for the inclusion of many data that were not included in the statistical analysis and, therefore, provides a second rigorous test of the electoral theory and its alternatives. The final section synthesizes the conclusions of the large, statistical comparison in Part I with the insights gained from the more in-depth country studies in Part II. It also discusses limitations to the theory and some extensions that go beyond understanding the origins of decentralization in the Andes, looking at reforms in other countries, as well as decentralization's future development within and outside the region.

An epilogue sketches political developments since 2000 that bear on decentralization's trajectory. In a word, the trend is troubling. As this book argues, decentralization is championed and defended by far-sighted, stable, political parties. In 2004, all five Andean countries are headed by presidents from non-traditional parties. Debates over the fiscal and democratic benefits that decentralization might bring may soon become a quaint memory as the forces underpinning decentralization dissipate. The analysis in this volume suggests that decentralization – and other kinds of reform that depend on the long planning horizons of responsible and accountable parties – may already have reached and passed its high point in the region.

2

A Political Theory of Decentralization

INTRODUCTION

As decentralization became more widespread throughout the world in the 1980s and 1990s, it ignited a great deal of scholarship. Economists and professionals within the development research community dominated the discussion of decentralization, focusing on outcomes and the implementation of reforms. Indeed, both the Inter-American Development Bank and the World Bank featured detailed discussions of fiscal and political decentralization in their annual reports (Inter-American Development Bank 1994, 1997; World Bank 1997), and both institutions, along with the U.S. Agency for International Development (USAID), have funneled significant funds into decentralizing reforms in the region.[1] These reports ask questions such as: Does decentralization improve service delivery? Does it increase responsiveness to local needs? Does it improve schools? Health care? Poverty? Corruption?

---

[1] USAID has pro-decentralization programs running in Colombia, Ecuador, and Peru. In 2001, the Inter-American Development Bank issued a $4.8 million loan for decentralization in Ecuador, $20 million to strengthen financial management in Bolivia's municipalities, and a $400 million loan to support the fiscal stability of Colombia's subnational governments; in 2003 the Inter-American Development Bank and Peru signed a $28 million agreement for modernization and decentralization of Peru's government. Likewise, the World Bank put $39 million into a water and sewerage decentralization project in the state of Monagas, Venezuela, in 1996, issued a $60 million credit to support decentralization in Bolivia in 2001, and pledged $16.6 million to support Peru's decentralization in 2004. (These facts are available as press releases on the respective Web sites of each of these organizations.)

While these are all critical questions, the equally important and prior questions – why and when do countries decentralize – received much less attention.

The focus on outcomes reflects the priorities of international institutions and the theoretical framework from which economists begin their inquiries. Economists often begin by assuming a welfare-maximizing government, leaving them few tools for exploring the political motives behind decentralizing reforms. Because it peers deeply into the incentives of policy makers, political science is uniquely equipped to explore the question of decentralization's preconditions. As I argued in the last chapter, however, the existing political scholarship on the related topics of federalism and delegation does not yield a compelling theory to explain the actual range of decentralizing experiences.

Empirically, political and fiscal decentralization is neither absent nor ubiquitous, leaving much to be theorized. Attempts to shift power from the central to more local levels of government can be found in several regions and time periods. Kenya, Tanzania, Liberia, Ethiopia, Uganda, Nigeria, Côte d'Ivoire, Ghana, and Zimbabwe experimented with greater decentralization in the 1980s (Barkan 1998; Crook and Manor 1998); China (Shirk 1993; Hao and Zhimin 1994; Montinola, Qian, and Weingast 1995), India, and Pakistan (Shah 1998) have experienced periods of greater and lesser devolution of power to more local levels of government. Currently, the former Soviet republics and much of Eastern Europe face the challenge of determining the correct mix of central and local power (Solnick 1995, 1999; Treisman 1999a, and b). In South America within the last twenty years, decentralizing reforms of one type or another have been adopted in Argentina, Bolivia, Brazil, Chile, Colombia, Ecuador, Peru, Paraguay, Uruguay, and Venezuela.

A political science perspective thus adds an important dimension to the debate: If economists and public policy experts can tell us whether decentralization *should* be adopted, political science can contribute insight into *when* its adoption is likely.

Political parties and their representatives play a key role in answering this question. My theory assumes that parties maximize their political and economic resources through winning elected positions. The central argument is this: Parties that find themselves in the executive of a strong, centralized government may rationally choose to decentralize power if they do not expect to retain the executive[2] indefinitely and if they can expect to gain a significant percentage of power at the level(s) of government to which power is distributed. Parties give today in order to receive tomorrow.

This chapter begins by briefly defining decentralization. It then advances a predictive theory for the executive proposal of decentralizing reforms. Testable implications of this theory are derived from the model, and its dynamics are demonstrated through simulation techniques. A discussion of alternative theories follows. Finally, the chapter discusses case selection and closes by anticipating the kinds of evidence that will be marshaled to evaluate this theory in subsequent chapters.

DEFINITIONS

Before developing a theory of decentralization, it is necessary to introduce several key terms and concepts that will play a role in what follows. What constitutes a strong centralized system of government? What is meant by effective decentralization, and how does it differ from federalism? This analysis focuses on the transition from a centralized to a decentralized system of government; what do these terms mean?

Centralization is the relative concentration of power at the national level of government. This term has no implications for the relative importance of different branches of government at the national level, although the cases discussed here possess strong executives and weaker legislatures. A centralized government is characterized by the concentration of power at the national level.

Decentralization resists simple definitions. Several studies by Rondinelli et al. (1984, 1989) replace "decentralization" with a series of more specific terms such as deconcentration, delegation, and devolution. This exercise attempts to distinguish between the many ways that power can be reallocated within a political system. An executive that delegates decision-making powers to a series of ministries within the executive branch is "decentralizing" (deconcentrating); a government that sells off state industries is also "decentralizing" (delegating or privatizing); a government that transfers funds and responsibilities to

---

[2] We might imagine that the dynamics would differ in parliamentary systems where a coalition of parties controls executive power.

FISCAL

POLITICAL	Centralized	Decentralized
Centralized	*Centralization*	*Delegation*
Decentralized	*Devolution*	*Decentralization*

FIGURE 2.1: Defining decentralization.

appointed state governors also "decentralizes" (delegates or devolves). All three examples include the transference of power away from the national level. Nevertheless, none of these examples qualifies as "effective decentralization" as it is explored here.

Effective decentralization requires a transfer of both political and fiscal power to subnational levels of government. The transfer of fiscal resources to appointed subnational officials – delegation – ensures that local officials spend a significant amount of the public budget, but presidential appointment guarantees their primary loyalty to the national government, not local constituents. The election of subnational officials in the absence of real fiscal and policy-making power – devolution – keeps local officials electorally accountable to their constituents but maintains their financial dependence on the beneficence of national officials. The decentralization of either fiscal or political power alone can have a significant impact on local outcomes, and I believe further study of these variations will reveal different reform motives. This book, however, focuses on the truly revolutionary reforms that devolve both fiscal and political power. Only when local officials are elected and can count on non-discretionary financial transfers from the central government, local taxes, or both is power truly decentralized. Autonomy *and* access to financial resources are the hallmarks of effective decentralization.

Figure 2.1 collapses the range of decentralization along each dimension into two categories, to distinguish roughly how decentralization differs from some of its relatives. Decentralization will be used to refer to that class of reforms that moves a state toward the bottom, right-hand corner of Figure 2.1.[3]

---

[3] It is worth pointing out here that other forms of decentralization (purely fiscal or purely political) may be explained in different ways. The concluding chapter takes up the discussion of these issues.

The Intuition

Decentralizing power requires a calculation of trade-offs. Essentially, the party in power must weigh giving up some of the power it holds in the present for the opportunity to compete for decentralized power in the future. If the party does not expect to compete strongly at the national level under a centralized system but expects to do well in subnational elections in a decentralized system, then it faces powerful incentives to decentralize. This incentive is strengthened if parties care more about the future; parties that do not care much about the next election would rather retain their monopoly of power in the current period than chance decentralization. Parties will also attempt to minimize the portion of the current term in which power is decentralized to enjoy their monopoly on power for as long as possible. These four factors – national level support, subnational level support, time preference, and timing of decentralization – figure prominently in the formal model developed below.

A FORMAL MODEL OF DECENTRALIZATION

This theory considers decentralization the rational act of political parties seeking to maximize their electoral possibilities in presidential systems. The model begins from the somewhat artificial baseline of perfect centralization: The national government (particularly the executive) monopolizes power. This model assumes that parties are primarily motivated by the drive to win access to political power. I consider what happens when these assumptions are relaxed later in the chapter.

The first stage of the game is the election itself. Elections provide the arena in which parties compete for power; the prize for winning election to the presidency is 100 percent of power.[4] In each election, parties calculate:

$$p(W) + (1 - p)(L)$$

---

[4] In a parliamentary system this assumption would not hold. Elections in those systems are rarely zero-sum, as they may be in presidential systems with very centralized power structures.

where W is the prize for winning and L is the prize for losing. Since $W = 1$ and $L = 0$ (this is a zero-sum game), the lottery becomes:

$$p(1) + (1 - p)(0) = p$$

The variable p is subjectively determined based on the party's information about electoral support.[5] Past electoral support plays an important informational role in predicting future elections.[6]

Parties with sufficiently long time horizons can attempt to predict a series of such lotteries when making policy. The decision to decentralize can be examined within this framework. Essentially, this leads to a two-stage game, which is indefinitely repeated. It is worth pointing out that these calculations are based on expected values of future outcomes; given limited information, parties are likely to miscalculate in many cases, leading to unanticipated consequences.[7]

On taking office, victorious parties initiate policies. Among the many policies over which the party may decide is the future structure of the political system. Both stages in this process play a crucial role in the decentralization decision: elections, because they provide information not just on parties' electoral support at the national level, but also at regional and local levels, and terms in office, because they furnish the power to act. Most models that consider elections and office holding begin with elections because they focus on strategies used in the election phase to gain office. This model considers the implications of reversing these stages: Power can be exercised during the term of office in order to maximize future access to office, given expectations about future elections (Ames 1987).

Abstracting from the many ways in which decentralization might occur, this simple model views decentralization as a dichotomous choice.[8]

---

[5] This means that parties can be wrong about their predictions and decentralize, expecting support that never materializes. The test of this theory lies not in the party's ability actually to win elections, but whether or not the party rationally expected to win elections, given the information available at the time of decision making.

[6] In reality, the probability of winning election is a function of the party's expected support. It should be noted that this function is non-linear. I will continue to use p as a simplification, but return to this point later.

[7] For more on unanticipated consequences of decentralizing, see Eaton 2004.

[8] This assumes that the levels to which power can be decentralized are exogenous. Because subnational jurisdictions already exist (states, provinces, etc.), decentralization will occur along these already existing lines. To imagine the choice between

In the single-shot version of this game, the victorious party will never decentralize because, once in power, policy makers face no incentive to relinquish power in such a way that it could be captured by their rivals in democratic, subnational elections. It is only the promise of future gains at the subnational level, coupled with a likely loss of the presidency, that creates the incentive to decentralize.

In the first period, one party controls all policy-making power and decides whether or not to decentralize. At the end of the period, elections are held and electoral victories translate into political office. If the regime remains centralized, all policy-making power accedes to the victor; if decentralization occurs, power is parceled out accordingly. If decentralization is chosen, it may be implemented immediately, depriving the victor of some share of his power in the present term. In a two-term version of the model, the decision to retain the centralized system results in the following payoff for the party in office:

Centralized Payoffs
Period 1: 1
Period 2: δp_1

Note that the subscript 1 will always refer to the probability of winning the presidency.

In words, the first term represents the payoff from controlling centralized policy-making power during the present term of executive office. In this case, that value is 1, reflecting the president's monopoly on power. The second period payoff is the discounted (discount factor $0 < \delta < 1$) value of winning the next election (with probability p_1).

Decentralization changes the equation substantially. In the first period, the party faces a reduction in policy-making power. For some portion of the first period $(1 - \phi)$, the party monopolizes power; for the remainder, the party enjoys the power still invested in the presidency (q_1) and a share of the decentralized power, depending on subnational election outcomes. In the second period, the party no longer calculates its probability of winning a single election; instead, it calculates its ability to win a percentage of the decentralized power. In the equation

decentralizing to the regional or local level, one need only compare the centralized system with each subnational system and choose the level of decentralization that provides the most benefit.

above there is only one election to consider; in a decentralized system, there could be thousands. A formal version of the model considers N elections under the decentralized scheme; that is, elections now determine the holders of N offices. N is indexed by $I = 1 \ldots N$.

Decentralized Payoffs
Period 1:

$$(1 - \phi) + \phi \left(q_1 + \sum_{i=2}^{N} p_i q_i \right)$$

Period 2:

$$\delta \sum_{i=1}^{N} p_i q_i$$

Probabilities of winning election are specific to each office; these probabilities are represented by p_i, $i = 1 \ldots N$. Similarly, each office entitles its holder to some share of political and economic power; this share is represented by q_i, $i = 1 \ldots N$. The probability of winning the presidency in the second period is still non-zero and represented by p_1 in this equation.

Comparing these two expected payoffs, decentralization will occur when:

$$(1 - \phi) + \phi \left(q_1 + \sum_{i=2}^{N} p_i q_i \right) + \delta \sum_{i=1}^{N} p_i q_i > 1 + \delta p_1$$

A few important conditions:

(1) $0 \leq p_i \leq 1$, $\forall_i$
(2) $0 \leq q_i \leq 1$, $\forall_i$
(3) $\sum_{i=1}^{N} q_i = 1$
(4) $q_i = q_j \; \forall_{i,j \neq 1}$

The first condition says that the probability of winning any particular election lies between zero and one; the second condition limits the share of political and economic power in any elected office to less than or equal to the total power in the system; the third condition requires that the power allocated to each office in the system sum to one. Finally, the fourth condition states that decentralization must be equal across subnational governments so that the central government cannot allow the popular election of subnational officials in selected areas.

With some algebraic manipulation, the inequality becomes:

$$\frac{\sum_{i=2}^{N} p_i}{(N-1)} > \frac{\delta p_1 + \phi}{\delta + \phi}$$

The left-hand side represents the party's average probability of winning a subnational election. The right hand side represents the party's probability of winning the presidency, combined with measures of its time preference and the timing of decentralization. Examining a special case clarifies this condition.

Imagine that decentralization can be enacted on the very last day of the current term (an ideal situation for the decentralizer), so that $\phi = 0$. In this case, the decision to decentralize hinges on the relationship between the party's probability of winning in the average subnational contest and its probability of winning the presidency; where the first outweighs the second, decentralization will occur.

Comparative statics help to illuminate how the probability of decentralization changes as each variable changes, holding all the others constant. From the above equation, the probability of decentralization increases as:

(1) $p_{i \neq 1}$ increases
(2) p_1 decreases
(3) δ increases[9]
(4) ϕ decreases[10]

In words, decentralization is more likely as subnational electoral chances increase, national electoral prospects decrease, parties care more about the future, and decentralization can be implemented

---

[9] The derivative of the right-hand side with respect to δ is:

$$\phi(p_1 - 1)/(\delta + \phi)^2$$

the denominator of which is positive and the numerator of which is negative, since $p_1 < 1$. This means that, as δ increases, the right-hand side decreases, making decentralization more likely.

[10] The derivative of the right-hand side with respect to ϕ is:

$$\delta(1 - p_1)/(\delta + \phi)^2$$

which has a positive denominator and a positive numerator, since $p_1 < 1$. This means that, as ϕ increases, the right-hand side increases, making decentralization less likely.

closer to the end of the term. Notice that the actual degree of power decentralized (the value of the q_i) does not play a role in the final inequality. This model determines only whether or not parties face an advantage from some level of decentralization; to determine the equilibrium level of decentralization that a government would like to choose would require a much more sophisticated model and lies outside the scope of this analysis.

What happens when a party with strong support at the national level again comes to office, performs this same calculation, and realizes that it would profit from a centralized system of government? In practice, parties that decentralize will make recentralization costly. The post-decentralization calculation would have to include a measure of these costs. Parties can make recentralization costly by writing decentralization reforms into law; they can write them into the constitution and make it difficult to change. Also, reforms that allow subnational elections may be difficult to change because voters – once enfranchised – may refuse to be denied their voting rights without massive demonstrations or even violence. Once passed, decentralization builds a constituency for itself, as Gustavo Bell Lemus (1998) notes in the Colombian case:

today decentralization has become politically hard to reverse, mainly as a result of the consensus it provokes. It is now the subject of intense local feelings; it raises hopes of change for a large majority of Colombians. (97)

To bolster this argument that recentralization is unlikely once political decentralization has been adopted, I looked at the Polity II data set, which contains a measure of decentralized government that ranges from 1 to 3, with 3 representing the most decentralized end of the spectrum. The data set contains a measure of decentralization for twenty-five countries in Latin America beginning in 1860 and spanning through 1986. The only cases in which countries shifted from a more decentralized rating to a less decentralized rating occurred under authoritarian regimes. Within a democratic context, it is extremely difficult to take away citizens' rights to elect officials once that right has been extended. The country studies and the epilogue discuss recentralizing trends (particularly on the fiscal dimension) in particular cases.

Insights from the Formal Model

The modeling exercise just presented formalizes what seems an obvious intuition: Executives decentralize if their parties benefit from it. Was this modeling exercise so very useful, then? In actuality, this model gives us more insight than may be apparent at first glance. It directs us to the specific factors parties consider when making their decisions.

This formal modeling exercise should not be misconstrued as the search for a definitive answer to this volume's question. Using this set of equations, one cannot derive predictions such as: When party support reaches 53 percent for a party with a 5 percent change in its vote share in each of the previous three elections, decentralization will occur. Instead, this formalization allows for a slightly more rigorous presentation of some intuitive relationships. It also provides a clear basis for extracting general hypotheses. The form of the equation directs the researcher to specific pieces of evidence and clearly states the relationships between those measures. The model predicts the extent to which parties will push for decentralization based on the support their party receives at various levels of voting; it also predicts the party's preference for the timing of decentralization within presidential terms. The remainder of the book will focus on evidence derived from this modeling exercise regarding party support for decentralization based on the party's (1) national level electoral support, (2) subnational level electoral support, and (3) time rate of preference.

The fourth factor singled out by the formal model – the issue of timing – receives less emphasis. Whereas the other factors measure a party's disposition toward decentralization, the timing decision depends on the party's interaction with other actors, particularly legislatures. All other things being equal, parties would like to decentralize at the end of their terms; however, all other things are not equal. The party's desire to push decentralization through the legislature may predispose its members toward an early introduction to capitalize on the honeymoon effect at the beginning of a term. Alternatively, politicians may worry that the public may perceive a last-minute decentralization as a ploy to win support at the start of new elections and may punish the party for that in the next election (thus affecting future presidential electoral chances negatively). While these types of interactions can be modeled in principle, they add a level of complexity that cannot be rigorously analyzed with the few cases examined here. This issue receives some attention in the discussion of individual cases, but it is of secondary importance.

. It is also worth pointing out two subsidiary hypotheses that will be given some, but more limited, attention in the analysis to come: that these same factors will affect the form decentralizing reform takes and that the evolution of decentralization across administrations should respond to electoral factors, as well. If politicians decide the timing of decentralization by consulting their electoral fortunes at different levels of government, those same criteria might also determine the level to which power will be decentralized (regional, provincial, or local, for example). Likewise, as decentralizing administrations are replaced in national government, one might expect subsequent administrations to tinker with decentralization guided by their own electoral considerations.

Simulating the Model's Dynamics

One way to explore the dynamic properties of a model and to see whether they bear out our intuition is to use simulation techniques. Simulation allows the researcher to demonstrate the dynamics of a model by choosing values for the factors anticipated to determine decentralization that do not necessarily occur in reality. For all its richness, real world data do not allow one to change these values one by one to illustrate patterns predicted by the model. The simulations reported here demonstrate the dynamics predicted by the model, but should not be viewed as a test of the model. Empirical tests using data from five countries across several time periods provide the real trial of the model's usefulness (Chapter 3 is devoted to this task).

To build the simulation, it is necessary to address the manner in which votes are converted into office (the p_i from the model). To predict a party's prospects in each electoral district, parties must consider not only the level of support they can expect in that community, but also the uncertainty surrounding that support and the electoral rules that translate votes into positions. In this model, parties are primarily concerned with executive positions: the presidency at the national level, the governorship at the regional level, or the mayoralty at the municipal level. Because these are single positions (not seats in legislatures), voting will generally follow majority or plurality rules. Under such a system, small changes in electoral support near the threshold for winning translate into significant changes in the probability of electoral victory; large changes in the level of support that do not center around the victory threshold affect the results less substantially. In other words, the probability of winning an election is not a linear function of electoral support.

When a party competes against a single competitor for the presidency, the threshold for winning is 50.1 percent of the (valid) votes. As party support changes from 10 percent to 20 percent, this change translates into a minuscule improvement in the party's election prospects (since the probability is near zero); similarly, changes from 60 percent to 70 percent do not greatly affect the probability of winning (which is near one). As party support grows from 49 percent to 50 percent, however, the probability of winning skyrockets. In multi-party systems a similar dynamic holds, although the threshold is lower than 50 percent.

An accurate model requires an appropriate functional form to translate support into the probability of winning. So far in the modeling exercise, p has been taken as given. In a more realistic model, p must be seen as a function of (1) the support for the party in each contest, (2) a measure of the uncertainty surrounding the point estimate of the party's support, and (3) the voting rules that determine the outcome. A logistical expression of the following type performs this task well:[11]

$$p = 1 \big/ \left(1 + e^{(\lambda - s)}\right)$$

The variable s represents the support of the party in a particular district, and λ represents the threshold electoral support needed to win the position and depends on the voting rules and the number of parties contesting the election.

---

[11] The logistic function possesses the intuitively nice properties that it increases sharply near the threshold for victory, it is concave at low values of s (rewarding volatility when the party does not have much support), and it is convex at high values of s (punishing volatility when party support is strong). Different functional forms provide different outcomes. If one assumes that parties are risk-averse (convex preferences over the entire spectrum), for example, then the incentives to decentralize rise at each point. It is interesting to note that the properties of the model hold even without assuming risk aversion and that there may be good theoretical reasons for assuming that a party with low levels of support may be risk taking when party members have good alternatives if support for the party declines.

TABLE 2.1: *Summary of Simulation Results*

Mean	Standard Deviation≈9		Standard Deviation≈12		Standard Deviation≈25	
	Districts	National%	Districts	National%	Districts	National%
25.0	01.1	25.0	03.4	25.0	18.3	25.1
40.0	14.0	40.3	20.3	40.5	35.4	40.0
50.0	50.0	50.0	50.2	50.0	50.0	50.0
60.0	84.3	60.0	80.9	60.6	64.8	60.0
75.0	98.9	74.9	95.3	74.9	81.8	74.9

Using this functional form does not change any of the properties already derived. Conveniently, the functional form set out above can simply be substituted for p in the previous equations. Specifying a functional form allows for some nice comparisons, using simulation to illustrate the consequences of different configurations of the factors that have been isolated as affecting decentralization decisions.

To perform the simulations, I wrote a program that produces a hypothetical political system with 100 election districts where 50 percent of the vote is needed to win the presidency.[12] From a single distribution of national support, the program draws 100 values (constrained between 0 and 100 percent of the vote),[13] representing the percentage of the vote won in each district. Two interesting results can be drawn from this simulation: the national vote for the party and the percentage of the districts in which the party won a majority. The national vote for the party represents its strength at the national level in a presidential vote. The percentage of the districts won by the party provides a good indication of the percentage of subnational elections the party might expect to win in a decentralized system. From these two values, it is possible to predict whether the party will find decentralization attractive.

Table 2.1 summarizes the simulation results after running the experiment outlined above 1,000 times. Row headings indicate the mean of the distribution of support for the party from which the individual district support levels are drawn. Column headings indicate the

---

[12] More complex programs can be written to examine the dynamics of systems with more than two parties. The basic dynamics of the model should hold under multiparty systems, as well.

[13] I used a beta distribution because it has the nice property of being constrained between values of 0 and 1.

standard deviation of the distribution, a measure of its variability. Column subheadings refer to the percentage of the districts in which the party wins a majority (Districts) and the percentage of the national vote won (National%). Not surprisingly, the latter coincides closely with the distribution's mean.

Comparing the party's national level election prospects with its subnational strength determines the attractiveness of decentralization. In the case of all simulations with mean national support less than 50 percent, the probability of winning the presidency is effectively zero, while the probability of winning at least a few subnational elections is positive. This suggests that nationally weak parties should favor decentralization. Similarly, parties with mean national support above 50 percent are assured of winning the presidency and therefore face no incentive to decentralize. As the mean level of national support rises, decentralization becomes less attractive because the chance of winning a monopoly of power (the presidency in a centralized system) begins to outweigh the increased number of districts that could be won under decentralization.

Using this technique, I also examine the effect of changes in variance on outcomes. Although the model predicts that higher variance will be associated with less decentralization, it is notable that increases in variation of support for nationally weak parties *increases* the number of districts won in a decentralized system (making decentralization more attractive). At the same time, increased variation *decreases* the percentage of districts won by nationally strong parties (making decentralization less attractive). In this simulation, the variance across districts within a single election speaks to the geographic concentration of support (the subnational electoral strength of parties). As mentioned in the first chapter, a party with 40 percent national support could correspond to one with 40 percent of the vote in each of 100 districts (low variance) or to a party with 100 percent of the vote in forty districts and none in the other sixty (high variance). The first party would not benefit from decentralization if voting occurs by plurality, but the second party would stand to benefit considerably, winning a sure 40 percent of the subnational contests.

Figure 2.2 illustrates how increased variation in national support helps nationally weak parties and hurts those with strong national level support. The horizontal axis measures the standard deviation of national support, and the vertical axis measures the percentage of

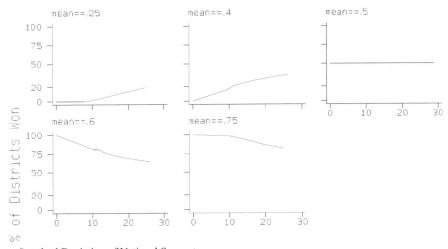

FIGURE 2.2: Dynamics of the percentage of local contests won as mean and variance change.

local districts won by the party. The relationship between variation and local support is clearly illustrated by the case with mean national level support of 40 percent. As variation increases (from a standard deviation of 0 to 25), the percentage of local contests won increases (from 0 to 35 percent). The higher the variation of support, the more concentrated support is in some districts, relative to others. For weak parties, this improves the chances of winning subnational contests. For strong parties, it concentrates support in some districts, leaving the party weaker in others. Concentration of support therefore affects the decentralization decision in different ways for parties with weak or strong national level support.

The statistical test of the electoral model of decentralization operates differently from the simulations described here. In addition to using real empirical evidence, it looks for the relationships just described by testing the incidence of decentralization against data on national level support (the mean discussed above) and data on local level support (the variance discussed above). It will also add data on the change in a party's vote share from one election to another to probe the role played by the uncertainty of national level support. All else being equal, decentralization should become more likely as national level support declines and as local level support increases. The simulation results suggest that the latter is likely when nationally weak parties have geographically concentrated support or when nationally strong parties have geographically dispersed support.

Underlying Assumptions

While this model allows the derivation of logical, testable hypotheses, all models are only as good as the assumptions on which they rest. Before discussing alternative theories, it is crucial to discuss the assumptions on which this theory rests, paying particular attention to their plausibility and the likely consequences of relaxing them. Four key assumptions underpinning this model are: the unity and discipline of political parties, the monopoly of power exercised by the executive, the office-seeking nature of parties, and the restriction that decentralization is not a major campaign issue in elections. I treat each of these in turn.

Latin American parties are notorious for their lack of discipline. Can we really expect parties to act as coherent units, as the model implies? In reality, the threshold of unity required for the model is set rather low. Parties need not act as coherent units in all aspects of their behavior, but need only prefer to see members of their own party (as opposed to members of other parties) in national or subnational offices. Thus, parties that split over which candidate to select for presidential contests need only agree that they would rather see either of their own candidates win office over the opposition's candidate(s). While this level of loyalty may exist for most party members, it also must exist for presidents, given the executive focus of this model. Parties may be able to discipline their legislators, governors, and mayors through their influence over candidate placement on party lists, campaign finance, access to political resources once elected, or influence on future career paths, but these mechanisms would seem to hold less leverage over sitting presidents. In many Latin American cases, presidents are term-limited, which should weaken party leverage over them even more. However, in many cases, presidents are also party leaders who have a great deal of identification with the party; many can run for re-election after sitting out a turn or aspire to positions of influence within the party structure after they have served in the executive. Finally, the worth of any assumption is its ability to predict outcomes consistently (Friedman 1953). If this assumption is weakened, it is easy to predict the consequences: less decentralization.

A second assumption that seems a grave departure from the growing influence of research on government institutions is this model's nearly complete ignorance of the legislature as an actor. This model focuses on the executive for a number of reasons, the most important of which is empirical: In almost every Latin American case of major decentralizing reform, presidents initiated the reform and championed it through the approval process. Latin American presidents possess significant legislative powers relative to the more studied U.S. presidential system (Shugart and Carey 1992).[14] In fact, presidents initiate most legislation in Latin America. In addition to strong legislative powers, presidents in the region also exercise significant powers in making cabinet appointments and through party leadership. Given that many countries in the region use some form of party list to elect legislators, partisan powers can give executives and party leaders quite a bit of influence in systems with closed and blocked lists.

Still, unless the president uses decree power to establish decentralization, assemblies must ultimately approve the reforms. If assemblies were strongly dominated by the president's party and if parties behaved in a highly disciplined fashion, then legislator incentives would mirror the president's, and an in-depth analysis of legislative behavior might seem redundant. However, in the Andean cases, each of the major decentralizing reforms was approved by a legislature in which the president's party held less than a majority of the seats. In most cases, no party held a majority of the legislative seats,[15] allowing for the possibility that several smaller parties also perceived electoral benefits from decentralization and voted with the president's party. Note, however, that Colombia's first major decentralizing laws were passed by a Conservative president facing a Liberal majority in the legislature. It thus seems worth asking not only why particular presidents initiated decentralizing reforms, but also why divided assemblies approved them.

In general, the basic theory linking party electoral prospects to support for decentralization should apply to legislatures to the extent that legislators respond to party pressures. In fact, Escobar-Lemmon and

---

[14] Ranking the legislative powers of executives in a number of presidential systems around the world, the United States scored a low 2 points, while the Latin American average was 3.7.

[15] The coalition of parties supporting the MNR (National Revolutionary Movement) president in Bolivia in 1994 held a majority of legislative seats.

Moreno (2003) find statistical support linking membership in non-majority parties with a legislator's propensity to initiate decentralizing legislation in the Colombian and Venezuelan legislatures. However, analyzing legislative behavior in the wake of executive support for decentralization is complicated by the extremely popular nature of this reform in most cases. Once the president has placed decentralization on the legislative agenda and championed it publicly, parties (and their legislators) whose distribution of electoral support may not predispose them to support it may face strong pressure from their constituents to vote for the measure. Where parties exert weak influence over the electoral prospects of legislators (open-list ballots and/or intra-party competition), individual party members may respond to less partisan interests in determining their support for decentralization. Even where parties enjoy strong influence over legislator incentives (closed and blocked list ballots), if the legislative balance in favor of decentralization is strong, the party itself may decide not to risk losing popular support by voting against the reform.

I try, where possible, to explore legislative behavior during the approval process in the case chapters that follow. Assembly behavior receives particularly careful attention in the exceptional cases of constitutional assemblies that initiate or significantly expand decentralization. Given the strong agenda-setting power of the president in the normal course of governance, the empirical evidence that most reforms are initiated by executives, and the seeming irrationality of their behavior in championing reforms that will decrease their own power, I continue to emphasize their incentives in modeling the initiation of decentralization. Relaxing this assumption, one should find that the more powerful the legislature within a country and the more able a particular party is to win legislative seats, compared with its ability to win subnational government positions, the less that party should support decentralization.

Finally, this model assumes that parties are mainly motivated by the search for election and models them as unconstrained by ideological considerations; it also assumes that decentralization does not become a campaign issue in elections. One might expect political ideology to play an important role in whether or not parties support decentralization. On the one hand, parties of the left might be expected to support decentralization, as it moves power away from central governments and allows for more diverse expressions of political wants. On the other hand, left parties might be interested in a stronger central government, with more capacity for redistribution. In practice, Latin America's parties are notoriously hard to array along any kind of ideological spectrum, as they fit more closely into the category of catch-all parties (Kirchheimer 1966) whose electoral contests revolve more around clientelist networks than they do around ideological appeals (Mainwaring and Scully 1995). In the empirical chapters to come, it is clear that parties loosely affiliated with the right and the left both decentralize and recentralize power in different periods of time, based more on electoral support than on ideology. If we were to relax the assumption that ideology does not play a major role in partisan support for decentralization, we might imagine that electoral concerns matter only up to the point where they conflict with ideology. In this case, ideology might be seen as a bound on how far electoral concerns might affect partisan support for decentralization.

The assumption that decentralization does not become a campaign issue allows the model to maintain the simplicity of using elections purely as measures of electoral support; it eliminates the possibility that decentralization is adopted as an electoral ploy to win current elections. A party that promises decentralization in a bid to win votes may face heavy disincentives to enact decentralization once in office; at the very least, the party may attempt to enact a weaker version of decentralization – one that grants only limited political or fiscal autonomy to subnational governments. While parties may promise decentralization during campaigns, I suggest that only those parties who face the correct constellation of electoral incentives are likely to work hard to enact effective decentralization. Relaxing this assumption, we might expect to see parties in close contests use decentralization as a campaign issue, but many of them may water down the reforms once in office. In fact, more than one of the country studies uncovers instances where this occurred.

An Important Extension

To this point, the model has focused on executive decision making; however, other governing bodies may find themselves in a position to affect decentralizing reforms. In a few instances, constitutional assemblies adopted decentralization reforms, or special commissions, set up to examine problems of governance, popularized them. Can the logic of this argument be extended to these extra-presidential bodies? Two important issues differentiate decision making by assembly from the executive model: calculating support for a collection of parties rather than for an individual party, and the cost of decentralization in the present term.

In the case of executive decision making, parties compare their support at various levels of government with their national-level support. When many parties participate in decision making, the outcome will reflect the national and regional support for each party, commensurate with its representation in the collective. If decisions are made in assemblies dominated by nationally strong parties, decentralization will be less likely than in assemblies dominated by parties with stronger subnational than national-level electoral support.

The more critical difference between executive and committee decision making is the issue of sacrifice. When executives decide whether or not to decentralize power, they must consider the cost of giving up power in the present term. If the executive cannot postpone implementation, he or she will lose some power immediately. Commissions and assemblies do not face the same present-period loss of power. Constitutional assemblies and special commissions do not possess executive power in their terms of service; therefore, their decisions regarding future decentralization require the comparison of only future national versus future subnational electoral support for their parties. Committees with power to affect decentralizing reforms will face the same incentives to compare national with subnational electoral support as executives but, all else equal, will be more likely to decentralize because they face no loss of power in the present period.

Tying this back in to the formal model presented above, each party performs the calculation:

$$\sum_{i=2}^{N} \frac{p_i}{(N-1)} > p_1$$

choosing to support decentralization if the inequality holds. Assigning a 1 to all parties that fulfill this condition and a 0 to those that do not, one can multiply the dichotomous results by the percentage of seats held by each party in the assembly. If the total exceeds 50 percent, then the assembly should produce a pro-decentralization result, if the matter is central to the assembly's agenda.[16]

It is notable that the time rate of preference term, δ, does not appear in this equation, indicating that high discount factors do not necessarily deter parties within these non-executive, deliberative bodies from decentralizing. This reflects the fact that parties in these temporary bodies do not have to consider the possibility of giving up centralized power in the present for future opportunities at subnational levels, as discussed above. As long as parties judge that their subnational electoral prospects outweigh their national prospects, decentralization will be a likely outcome.

The main objection to extending the model to these extra-presidential committees is that their existence and composition may not be wholly exogenous from the president who empowers them (or allows them to be brought into existence). The link between the executive and these extra-presidential bodies must be carefully examined to determine how much autonomy in decision making these units enjoy. Most of the constitutional assemblies examined were popularly elected; even where presidents encourage their formation, they were often unable to control the agenda (or pieces of it) once the body was convened.

ALTERNATIVE THEORIES

The model just presented predicts decentralization using political variables. The main, alternative hypothesis predicts decentralization using fiscal data. Another hypothesis suggests that international pressures impose decentralization from the outside. Finally, others argue that political institutions or regional heterogeneity of preferences may predict decentralization. This section explores alternative theories in more detail, teasing out the testable hypotheses they imply. These competing hypotheses are tested in the remaining chapters.

While the literature on decentralization is less well developed than the literatures on federalism or delegation mentioned in Chapter 1,

---

[16] Decentralization may be only one dimension of the talks occurring within the assembly. If votes hinge on this issue, the above calculation is correct; however, voting may pivot on a completely different set of issues, so votes for and against the final product of the assembly – if it includes several issues – may not fall along party lines in the way suggested here.

political scientists have recently taken an interest in the phenomenon. The electoral theory just derived adds to a growing number of theories to explain the flurry of reform throughout the world, and particularly in Latin America. Alternative theories have sought the impetus for reform in democratization, in the power of the international consensus supporting decentralization, as a response to either political or fiscal crisis, as an attempt to improve government efficiency, as a result of international pressure, as a capitulation to pressures from below, or in political institutions.

The utility of theories that aim to explain decentralization must be measured against their ability to answer two questions: Why this new flurry of decentralization in the 1980s and 1990s? And why is decentralization being adopted unevenly across the Latin American political landscape? That is, theories must be able to account not only for intertemporal variation in the adoption of decentralizing reforms, but also for cross-national variation. My theory attempts to answer both of these questions by looking at political party evolution over time. After briefly summarizing each alternative theory, I address its ability to answer both the where and the when questions. While most of these theories contain at least a partial explanation for some types of devolution, none of them alone seems to explain the variety of Latin America's decentralizing reforms.

Democratization

It is hard to ignore the fact that decentralizing reforms in Latin America have been concentrated in the 1980s and 1990s. This high incidence of reform appears to dovetail with the general shift toward democratic government in the region. It is tempting to think that decentralization is a logical extension of this wave of democratization. While the return to democracy in Argentina, Peru, Chile, and Brazil has also brought a return to previously decentralized systems or the extension of democracy to more local levels than had been the case before authoritarian rule, democratic transition alone cannot explain the adoption of decentralizing reform. In countries such as Bolivia, decentralization (1994) has lagged well behind the return to democracy (1982); in Colombia and Venezuela, decentralization has occurred despite uninterrupted democratic rule since the 1950s. While the broad trend toward decentralization roughly matches the period of Latin America's democratization, a closer look reveals significant inconsistency.

International Consensus

A second broad trend that coincides with the timing of decentralization in the region is the adoption of neoliberal-inspired economic reforms and a growing consensus among international actors that decentralized power structures are preferable to centralized structures. The international consensus promoting decentralization certainly helps to explain increased decentralization in the 1980s and 1990s relative to earlier decades; however, it is not sufficient to explain the variation across cases within this more recent time frame. International opinion has changed over time, but it is available to all countries equally once it has coalesced around a particular issue. If decentralization has become internationally popular and it is this consensus that is motivating governments to adopt decentralizing reforms, we should see all countries in the region decentralizing at roughly the same time. In fact, decentralization has been adopted in some nations in the region and not others. The timing of decentralization's adoption across those that have embraced it varies as well, with reform in several countries (Colombia, 1982–1986; Peru, 1980; and Venezuela, 1989) predating the 1990s consensus.

This is not to say that the flow of ideas or the resurgence of democracy plays no role in the decision to decentralize. The coincidence of reforms in the late 1980s and 1990s across these countries is not incidental. Instead, the relationship among international consensus, democratization, and decentralization is a more nuanced one. The return to democratic forms of government encourages decentralization by allowing parties to compete for power. When elections determine who holds office, and thus who controls political and fiscal resources, parties face incentives to create new avenues to power. Likewise, the prevalence of positive policy discourse provides instant credibility and international support for reformers who propose decentralization. While decentralizing reforms seem concentrated in recent years, the variation in timing across countries suggests that the international consensus on decentralization has its greatest influence when it coincides with the electoral incentives of those in a position to initiate change.

Efficiency

In addition to democracy and neoliberal reform, efficiency is another idea that may promote decentralization. Many proponents of decentralization laud the potential efficiency gains of making subnational governments responsible for local goods provision. These arguments rely heavily on Tiebout's (1956) conclusion that, when populations have heterogeneous preferences over local goods, and localities can provide differentiated bundles of those goods, welfare is improved by allowing consumer-voters to self-sort into communities providing different bundles of local services. Although the rhetoric of efficiency gains pervades the discourse surrounding decentralization, an efficiency explanation for decentralizing reforms requires national politicians to realize a significant improvement in their vote due to the efficiency gains of decentralization. Efficiency gains become manifest only in the long term, and there is little certainty that credit for those gains will accrue to the party responsible for the reform, rather than the party at the local level providing the more efficient local goods. For these reasons, I find the efficiency argument compelling from a normative perspective but weak as a causal mechanism for change.

International Pressure

Closely related to the theory that international networks of ideas have delivered decentralization is the theory that international pressure has forced this wave of reform. Here, ideas alone do not lead to decentralizing innovation, but pressure from the international community to adopt these ideas sparks reform. By this reasoning, international financial institutions and lending countries, convinced that decentralization improves efficiency and perhaps even democracy, pressure client governments to decentralize.[17] The pressure from these organizations rises

---

[17] The international financial institutions do not usually agree on all policies, and decentralization is no exception. Given that the IMF's mission is to deal with short-term crises, decentralization is less attractive, as negotiating with a single government is far preferable to negotiating with several levels of government. The reader may

when the organizations possess greater leverage over client countries; these conditions are met when nations face fiscal crises and must borrow from abroad. Particularly famous are International Monetary Fund conditionality agreements that accompany that institution's loans. If decentralization has been imposed from without, decentralization should occur when countries are most vulnerable to international lenders.

Exposure to pressure from international lenders is difficult to isolate in one measure. Inflows of debt often signal a glut in credit markets and, if interest rates are low, may correspond to a strong bargaining position for the debtor. This possibility is best illustrated by the petro-dollar recycling that occurred in the 1980s as oil wealth filtered through financial institutions, seeking investment opportunities far and wide. Large debt inflows alone do not capture national exposure to international lenders. The World Bank Debt Tables list over a hundred measures that, when combined, provide a fairly good picture of a country's overall exposure to creditor pressure. Chapter 3 looks at several different measures, including total debt as a percentage of GNP, net debt flows as a percentage of GNP, and debt rescheduled as a percentage of GNP. Lagged variables are also used to account for the possibility that international pressure precedes the adoption of reform by a year. Finally, the change in each of these measures from year to year will also be tested as a predictor of decentralization: Often, the amount of pressure alone does not help to explain policy decisions; rather, the relative amount of pressure may cause new policies to be adopted. These measures allow for variation both across countries and over time also, making the investigation of this hypothesis promising. If the international pressure hypothesis holds, the relationship between each of these measures of susceptibility to international pressure and the incidence of decentralization should be positive and significant. While this relationship is tested more rigorously in the next chapter, there is reason to think it will not bear fruit: Colombia decentralized when it had very little debt; Bolivia's greatest vulnerability to international pressure (around 1985)

---

also recall from the Introduction that decentralization generally lies in tension with macroeconomic stabilization, the primary concern of the IMF. The World Bank and Inter-American Development Bank, on the other hand, deal with longer term projects of development and therefore have greater reason to support decentralization if it is believed to improve development outcomes in the longer term.

had long passed when it decentralized (1994); and Peru recentralized power when it was still vulnerable to international pressures (1992). Furthermore, previous studies have found little empirical support for this theory (Campbell 2003).

Pressure from Below

In addition to pressures from the international community, it is easy to imagine how decentralization may be fostered by strong domestic pressures. The literatures on fiscal federalism and economic geography (Alesina, Perotti, and Spolaore 1995; Alesina and Spolaore 1997) and also Stepan's "holding-together" federalism (1999) point to heterogeneity of preferences as the driving force behind territorial division (either decentralization or secession). Widely divergent preferences might be fostered by factors such as ethnic background or economic specialization. Whatever the roots of these differences, where people cannot agree on the general outlines of government policy, they may attempt to form separate governments or to seek greater autonomy from a highly centralized decision-making structure. Two possibilities exist through which this tension may lead to policy changes: Central-level politicians, maximizing social welfare, may respond to this heterogeneity by decentralizing, or regional politicians (and/or their constituents) may actively press for greater decentralization. If the heterogeneity hypothesis holds, decentralization should occur in more heterogeneous nations or when pressure from below compels central governments to distribute more power to subnational levels. While heterogeneity is largely time-invariant, the transformation of that heterogeneity into political demands may differ widely both over time and across nations. This hypothesis is explored further in the next chapter, but note that Bolivia – with the largest indigenous population – and Colombia and Venezuela – with the smallest indigenous populations – all decentralize, while Peru and Ecuador – the two countries in between – end the period rather centralized.

Political Crisis

Perhaps the most common explanation given for decentralization relates this reform's adoption to a crisis of the state; decentralization may be a method of rejuvenating imperiled governments (Rodríguez

1997; Grindle 2000). Where regimes confront crisis, they may use drastic measures to shore up their support, increase their legitimacy, or decrease the central government's financial responsibilities. Barr (2001), in a variation on this theme, suggests that traditional politicians facing a crisis decentralize to shore up legitimacy, while nontraditional politicians facing a crisis capitalize on the crisis in order to centralize power. Many difficulties confront these explanations. Why do some nations – even those presided over by traditional politicians – respond to crisis with decentralization, while others attempt different remedies? Why has decentralization become such a popular response to crisis in the last two decades, when previous periods of crisis saw no such tendency?

Individual country studies seeking reasons for decentralization seem to ascribe particular weight to the concept of crisis as a motivating factor. Even cross-country studies find the crisis hypothesis appealing. One of the major flaws in these studies is that they tend to select on the dependent variable; that is, they look only at instances of decentralization and find that there are crises in each country they examine. What this theory cannot explain is why other countries in crisis – such as Ecuador throughout the 1980s and early 1990s – do not decentralize. It also cannot explain why decentralization occurs when it does in each crisis situation. For example, Colombia has been described as a nation in crisis for most of the twentieth century, so why does it adopt a series of reforms in the 1982–1986 period, in particular? Bolivia experienced its greatest crises (within a democratic context) in the 1980s, yet decentralization occurred when it was relatively crisis-free (1994). Political crisis appears to offer little leverage over either the where or the when question, when examined in comparative perspective.

Fiscal Crisis

Like the so-called abdication hypothesis discussed in the first chapter, the fiscal crisis hypothesis springs from the assumption that politicians seek credit for popular measures and shirk blame for the rest. In the context of an expanding state, all levels of government compete to allocate the fruits of expansion to their supporters. In states facing budget austerity and cutbacks in social programs, central governments may attempt to shirk responsibility for these tough choices. In addition to dividing the political blame, delegating responsibility for public services to local governments (even when accompanied by intergovernmental transfers) may decrease the drain on scarce funds. Decentralization can thus be used to devolve responsibilities for costly local spending to subnational officials when budgets are tight. Based on government initiatives in such nations as the United States and United Kingdom in the 1980s, this argument (Pierson 1996) explains decentralization as the attempt to pass on the responsibility for fiscal austerity to politicians at lower levels of government.

An empirical test (which is applied in the next chapter) should show decentralization episodes following fiscal deficits, downturns in GDP growth, or other instances of fiscal distress. The fiscal crisis hypothesis also would appear more plausible if central governments devolve responsibilities to subnational governments without devolving substantial fiscal resources along with them. In this way, central governments contribute to the vertical imbalance as they attempt to improve the deficit. While this may explain the devolution of responsibilities without resources, it does not seem to explain decentralization as I have defined it. In addition, it appears that recent economic downturns in the region have been accompanied by a call for reconcentrating power in the central government, not for greater decentralization. Anticipating the results of the next chapter's empirical test of this hypothesis, it is notable that Colombia decentralized in times of fiscal balance; Bolivia faced severe fiscal imbalance in the 1980s and did not decentralize then, but decentralized at a time of near fiscal balance, in 1994; Ecuador has faced volatile fiscal outcomes without decentralizing significantly; and Peru has decentralized at times of minor fiscal imbalance and recentralized after years of fiscal difficulty, in 1992. Thus, the timing of decentralization in the Andean region does not appear to coincide with high fiscal deficits.

Institutions

In Chapter 1 I argued that the literature on the origins of federalism offers little insight into understanding decentralizing reforms; however, Riker's (1964) exploration of the institutional features that sustain federalism once adopted may be more useful. In this work, Riker finds that a decentralized party system is a key factor. Building on this insight, Willis, Haggard, and Garman (1999) and Garman et al. (2001) explore the extent of decentralization in Latin America, arguing that decentralization will extend furthest in political systems where subnational interests within the party wield influence over national party leaders:

If party leaders are organized at the subnational level and occupy positions in subnational governments, then national legislators often act as "delegates" representing subnational interests. Alternatively, if party leaders preside within a national party organization or occupy executive and legislative posts at the national level, then legislative interests over decentralization will coincide more with executive or "national interests." (Willis et al. 1999: 18)

Their work looks specifically at party rules of nomination, ballot format (open vs. closed lists), and the timing of national and subnational elections.

While this theory addresses decentralization's extent, one could tease out the logic underlying decentralization's adoption: that subnational interests may use institutional mechanisms to their advantage to press for decentralization. The Colombian case seems a particularly good example of this theory: In Colombia, subnational party members exert strong influence within Colombia's parties, and the proliferation of party lists approximates an open list system; it is also the Andean country that has decentralized the furthest. Even so, both Bolivia's and Venezuela's party systems at the time of decentralization were tightly controlled by national elites who ordered candidates into closed lists for legislative contests. In general, institutional rules do not change much over time, making it difficult for a theory based on these features to explain variation across time in the initial adoption of reform. For example, while Peru's more open ballots may accord with decentralization there in the 1980s, the same ballot structure and electoral timing was in place when Fujimori recentralized power in the 1990s. While I agree with their primary claim that the content of decentralizing reforms is importantly shaped by institutional structures of the governing bodies constructing and implementing decentralization, I find these features less useful in explaining the timing of decentralization.

EVIDENCE

Succeeding chapters will evaluate the theories developed in this chapter against the evidence from five Andean countries: Bolivia, Colombia,

Ecuador, Peru, and Venezuela. These countries were chosen because they share similar cultural and historical backgrounds, allowing many cultural and historical explanations to be ruled out. They also begin the period under investigation with a long history of unitary government (despite the fact that Venezuela calls itself a federal system). This is not the case in countries such as Brazil, Argentina, and Chile, which begin their most recent periods of democratic rule with a long legacy of subnational government autonomy and with the recent memory of authoritarian rule in which (in some cases) the powers of subnational governments were suspended.[18] In cases where decentralization coincides with redemocratization, it is difficult to tease out the separate influences exerted by authoritarian legacies, the return to a previously decentralized system, and the interest of political parties in propelling the decision to decentralize. A focus on the Andean region largely minimizes these concerns, although in Peru in the 1980s, democratization and decentralization do, in fact, coincide.

In addition to a history of unitary government, the Andean countries provide variation along the dependent variable, with two Colombian administrations decentralizing, one Bolivian administration decentralizing, an instance of decentralization and one of recentralization in Peru, some decentralization in Venezuela, and almost no decentralization in Ecuador.

Because the theory assumes an electoral motivation for decentralization, it pertains only to periods in which free, open, and fair elections determine access to executive office. During these periods of democratic contestation, each administration enters office with a new opportunity to decentralize. As a result, the number of cases examined expands from five to more than twenty, as each observation represents not the entire experience of each country but the experience of each presidential administration within each country. All together, twenty-eight cases are analyzed.

The chapters that follow also empirically test competing hypotheses, comparing their performance with the book's main theory of political motivation. Chapter 3 begins this process by combining evidence from all five countries, across all time periods considered, to test

---

[18] For excellent discussions of decentralization in Brazil and Argentina, see Eaton (1998, 2004) and Samuels (2000), respectively.

the theories in comparative perspective. Subsequent chapters provide more detailed examinations of individual country experiences with decentralization.

Chapter 3 is followed by in-depth country discussions. In each of these, the history of regionalism and party competition is explored to seek out earlier patterns of national-subnational power relations and their relationship to party politics. The link between decentralization and electoral considerations is then scrutinized in more detail by bringing a greater range of electoral data to bear on the theory. Primary and secondary sources also contribute to analyzing specific instances of decentralization. While the statistical model of Chapter 3 confirms that decentralization episodes generally follow the logic of the political motivation theory, these in-depth analyses investigate whether the theory improves our understanding of each, individual case. These chapters also provide an opportunity to flesh out the nature of party competition within each country over time, exploring its changes and their impact on decentralization decisions. They also allow secondary implications of the theory to be examined in specific cases. Finally, some of these cases provide excellent opportunities for exploring the consequences of relaxing some of the simplifying assumptions necessary for the formal model.

SUMMARY

This chapter sets the groundwork for a comparison of theories explaining the decision to decentralize. While the theories outlined here appear disparate in their motivations and testable implications, they share one, common thread: Each attempts to rationalize a behavior that challenges the standard assumptions of political science. In general, political science assumes that politicians seek office to control political and fiscal resources – either for their own financial gain or to impose their policy preferences. It is puzzling, then, when leaders of strongly centralized governments relinquish substantial power to subnational levels. Competing parties in a decentralized system can capture portions of the decentralized power at subnational levels and use it in ways inimical to the executive's wishes. In the absence of pressure from below, how can we square the existence of decentralization with our belief that policy makers act rationally?

Decentralizing the State attempts to solve this puzzle by developing and testing a political theory of decentralization. This theory models policy makers as representatives of political parties. As larger political organizations, parties enjoy longer planning horizons than do individual politicians, yet they seek the same goal: access to political and fiscal resources through elective office. From this foundation, this chapter has developed a theory explaining decentralization as the reasoned act of parties who care about future access to political office. When a party's national-level support is weak and its subnational-level support is strong, decentralization may provide long-term access to power for parties doubtful of their re-election prospects. The predictability of future elections plays a key role in this calculation, raising the desirability of decentralization for parties enjoying relatively stable support across elections over time.

Competing theories attempt to make sense of decentralization in different ways. Institutional theories predict decentralization when particular political features coincide to make decentralization both possible and desirable. The fiscal crisis theory explains decentralization as a central government's attempt to avoid responsibility for budget cuts in an economic crisis. The international pressure hypothesis argues that decentralization is the rational act of a country beholden to international creditors pressuring for such a reform. Rather than a response to international pressure, decentralization may be a response to internal pressures – either direct pressures from below to decentralize or pressures to resolve a political crisis or improve the administration's democratic credentials. Decentralization may be motivated by democratization, the drive for efficiency, or the international flow of pro-decentralizing ideas. This chapter ended by extracting the testable implications from each of the competing theories and began to draw conclusions based on the evidence from the five countries examined here. Chapter 3 draws on the experiences of all the countries considered in this book, examining the evidence for the competing theories in comparative perspective. Subsequent chapters examine each country's experience with decentralization in more detail. In all of these chapters, the political motivation theory outperforms competing theories by a wide margin.

Peering ahead to the results of empirical testing, I believe that the evidence linking decentralization to political motivations is provocative.

Decentralization tends to occur in one of two circumstances: when the executive comes from a party that faces uncertain national-level electoral support in the future, but has strong local or regional level support, or when non-traditional political parties (or political parties with weak national-level support and stronger regional- and/or local-level electoral support) find themselves in a position to decentralize power without having to give up power at the central level. Centralization of previously dispersed power occurs in only one case:[19] Fujimori's first term in Peru. Fujimori's party, Cambio 90 (Change 90), enjoyed strong national-level support and uncertain future support at all levels – the reverse constellation of support that is hypothesized to lead to decentralization. In addition, the delegitimation of traditional political parties and the strong charismatic appeal of Fujimori reduced the costs of such a move. While the political motivation theory performs well under empirical scrutiny, explanations relying on fiscal crisis, foreign pressure, and heterogeneity do not strongly predict instances of decentralizing reforms once viewed over time and across the five countries.

APPENDIX TO CHAPTER 2

Decentralize if:

$$(1 - \phi) + \phi \left(q_1 + \sum_{i=2}^{N} p_i q_i \right) + \delta \sum_{i=1}^{N} p_i q_i > 1 + \delta p_1$$

A few important conditions:

(1) $0 \leq p_i \leq 1, \forall_i$
(2) $0 \leq q_i \leq 1, \forall_i$
(3) $\sum_{i=1}^{N} q_i = 1$
(4) $q_i = q_j \forall_{i,j \neq 1}$

Step 1: Subtract 1 from each side:

$$-\phi + \phi \left(q_1 + \sum_{i=2}^{N} p_i q_i \right) + \delta \sum_{i=1}^{N} p_i q_i > \delta p_1$$

---

[19] As I discuss below, decentralization did at least slow down in Bolivia under Banzer and in Venezuela under Caldera and Chávez.

Step 2: Factor out $p_1 q_1$ on the left-hand side:

$$-\phi + \phi \left(q_1 + \sum_{i=2}^{N} p_i q_i \right) + \delta p_1 q_1 + \delta \sum_{i=2}^{N} p_i q_i > \delta p_1$$

Step 3: Rearranging (so that all p_1 and q_1 are on the right-hand side):

$$\phi \sum_{i=2}^{N} p_i q_i + \delta \sum_{i=2}^{N} p_i q_i > \delta p_1 + \phi - \phi q_1 - \delta p_1 q_1$$

Step 4: Using conditions 3 and 4, we know that

$$\sum_{i=2}^{N} p_i q_i = \frac{(1 - q_1)}{N - 1} \sum_{i=2}^{N} p_i$$

Step 5: So the left-hand side becomes:

$$(\phi + \delta) \frac{(1 - q_i)}{N - 1} \sum_{i=2}^{N} p_i$$

Step 6: Factoring the right-hand side leaves:

$$(\delta p_1 + \phi)(1 - q_1)$$

Step 7: The revised inequality after the last two steps is:

$$(\phi + \delta) \frac{(1 - q_1)}{N - 1} \sum_{i=2}^{N} p_i > (\delta p_1 + \phi)(1 - q_1)$$

Step 8: Factoring out $(1 - q_1)$ on both sides leaves:

$$\frac{(\phi + \delta)}{N - 1} \sum_{i=2}^{N} p_i > (\delta p_1 + \phi)$$

Step 9: Divide both sides by $(\phi + \delta)$ yields the final inequality:

$$\frac{\sum_{i=2}^{N} p_i}{N - 1} > \frac{\delta p_1 + \phi}{\delta + \phi}$$

3

Decentralization in Comparative Perspective

INTRODUCTION

The Andean countries present a rich and bewildering variety of experiences with intergovernmental power sharing. Despite their common geographical location, shared history, and roughly similar economic development, Bolivia, Colombia, Ecuador, Peru, and Venezuela behave quite differently during this time period in terms of decentralization. The richest and poorest countries – Venezuela and Bolivia – decentralize. Those with the greatest and least percentages of indigenous population – again, Bolivia and Venezuela – decentralize, while those in the middle – Ecuador and Peru – end the period very centralized. Looking at these countries over time, the experience becomes even richer, with Peru decentralizing in 1980, then recentralizing in 1992. Bolivia, Colombia, and Venezuela all decentralize in the 1980s and 1990s, but at different times, with Colombia decentralizing in two stages, first in 1982 and again in 1991, Venezuela decentralizing in 1989 and Bolivia waiting until 1994 to devolve power to localities. Ecuador and Peru end the period quite centralized, although Ecuador's 1998 constitution and political debates in Peru early in the Toledo presidency reveal some signs of change. How can this variety be explained?

The fact that decentralizing experiences differ across time within countries as well as between countries forces this analysis to look beyond country studies to explore the features of individual executive administrations within each country over time. Chapter 2 developed the argument that decentralization follows an electoral logic, along with several competing hypotheses. This chapter critically assesses the electoral theory and competing hypotheses, using evidence from successive administrations in the five Andean countries. This chapter draws together statistical data and also summarizes some of the information that is more deeply fleshed out in the country discussions to follow.

To recap briefly: The electoral theory assumes that parties maximize their access to political and fiscal resources by pursuing elected office. When parties find themselves in a position to change the distribution of power between national and subnational levels, they compare their long-term electoral prospects under decentralized versus centralized systems. Three considerations influence how parties in power assess the attractiveness of decentralization. First, parties with weak national-level support may prefer a decentralized system if they are unsure of returning to the executive in the longer term. Second, decentralization is particularly attractive to parties with strong electoral support at the subnational level. Subnational support ensures that parties will hold a substantial portion of the subnational positions in a decentralized system. Third, decentralization requires the party in power to give up centralized power today in order to compete under decentralized rules in the future. As a result, parties with longer time horizons and a greater ability to predict their future levels of support – both features captured in the stability in party support across consecutive elections – are more likely to decentralize than others. If power is allocated not according to democratic elections but through the use of military force or elite bargaining, instead, then this theory is not pertinent. Consequently, the appropriate time period for testing this theory is circumscribed by the presence of democratic elections.[1]

This chapter links the theory laid out in Chapter 2 and the detailed case studies comprising the remainder of this book. I examine evidence from democratically elected presidential administrations in all five countries elected before 2000 (yielding twenty-eight observations) to judge the fit between the electoral theory of decentralization developed

---

[1] This is not to say that devolution never occurs under authoritarian governments. Both Argentina (Eaton 1998, 2004) and Chile (Bland 1998) devolved important aspects of government during periods of authoritarian rule; however, those episodes did not fit the definition of decentralization – including the devolution of both political and fiscal power – used here.

here and the empirical evidence. Because this chapter brings together evidence from all five countries, it allows for a comparative perspective both across countries and over time. Its scope also makes this chapter the best place to judge the empirical fit of competing theories and to adjudicate between them and the theory linking decentralization to electoral considerations.

This chapter is divided into two parts. The first examines evidence for the electoral theory of decentralization developed in Chapter 2. The second looks at the competing hypotheses in light of the evidence. The first section presents evidence in two ways: through statistical analysis and then through a series of tables illustrating electoral patterns within each country at national and local levels. Subsequent chapters include detailed studies of the countries and their experiences with decentralization. The statistical exercise and the tables help us to sift through the evidence, searching for the hypothesized pattern linking decentralization with electoral outcomes. Decentralizing reform is expected to correlate with weak national support for the president's party, strong subnational support for the president's party, and a pattern of steady support for that party across previous elections. Before launching into an analysis of the evidence, the next few pages acquaint the reader with the cases to be examined.

EVIDENCE

The electoral theory of decentralization developed in Chapter 2 views the incentives to decentralize from the perspective of an executive administration. As a result, the cases considered are presidential terms within each country.

In addition to directing attention toward presidential terms, the notion that decentralization follows an electoral logic suggests that the relevant period of study will be confined to the period in which elections determine each country's successive administrations.

With the exception of Cuba, the countries of the Western hemisphere had all adopted democratic rules and procedures by the 1990s. This contrasts sharply with historical experience, even if we confine our retrospective to this half-century. One of the most remarkable trends of the 1980s and 1990s has been the turn from authoritarian to democratic rule in Latin America (Huntington 1991; Domínguez

TABLE 3.1: *Cases*

Bolivia	1982–2000
Colombia	1974–2000
Ecuador	1979–1996
Peru	1980–2000
Venezuela	1958–2000

and Lowenthal 1996). Freedom House scores[2] attest to significant improvements in both political rights and civil liberties. Combining the two for a composite average score, South American countries and Mexico averaged a score of 3.9 in 1973; by 1990, this score had improved[3] to 2.6.[4] The five countries examined in this project mirror this trend. Their average score improved from 3.9 in 1973 to 2.7 in 1990.[5] Political rights scores drive much of this improvement, increasing from 4.3 to 2.3 between 1973 and 1990 for the average South American country, including Mexico. Over the same seventeen years, this indicator changed from 4.6 to 2.0, in just the five Andean countries.[6] Although this trend swept the region over a relatively short time period, each country began convening democratic elections at a different moment. As a result, I confine my cases to the time periods listed in Table 3.1.[7] This affords five presidential terms in Bolivia, seven in Colombia, four each in Ecuador and Peru, and eight in Venezuela, for a total of twenty-eight cases. My examination of Ecuador is truncated to 1996 because, since that time, Ecuador averaged roughly a presidential turnover each year until the end of the period, with several interim presidents, whose support cannot be adequately measured by election results. This is not to say that Ecuador from 1996 to 2000 is not worth studying, just that it poses unique challenges, particularly for statistical analysis. This period of Ecuador's experience is treated in Chapter 6.

Table 3.2 provides a short summary of the cases from each country, listing the years of each term, the president's name, and his party

---

[2] These scores can be obtained from the website www.freedomhouse.org.

[3] Higher Freedom House scores indicate more restrictive regimes.

[4] By 2000, that number had risen slightly to 2.8.

[5] However, the average had risen to 3.4 by 2000, driven largely by the decline of traditional parties and the rise of populist president Hugo Chávez in Venezuela.

[6] Between 1990 and 2000, the regional average rose slightly to 2.6 and rose more rapidly in the Andes to 3.2.

[7] The choice of years is discussed more fully in the country chapters that follow.

TABLE 3.2: *Presidencies and Party Affiliations*

Country	Years	President	Party
Bolivia	1982–1985	Hernán Siles Zuazo	UDP (Popular Democratic Union)
Bolivia	1985–1989	Victor Paz Estenssoro	MNR (National Revolutionary Movement)
Bolivia	1989–1993	Jaime Paz Zamora	MIR (Revolutionary Movement of the Left)
Bolivia	1993–1997	Gonzalo Sánchez de Lozada	MNR
Bolivia	1997–2002	Hugo Banzer Suárez	ADN (National Democratic Action)
Colombia	1974–1978	Alfonso López Michelsen	Liberal
Colombia	1978–1982	Julio César Turbay Ayala	Liberal
Colombia	1982–1986	Belisario Betancur	Conservative
Colombia	1986–1990	Virgilio Barco Vargas	Liberal
Colombia	1990–1994	César Gaviria Trujillo	Liberal
Colombia	1994–1998	Ernesto Samper Pisano	Liberal
Colombia	1998–2002	Andres Pastrana Arango	Conservative
Ecuador	1979–1984	Jaime Roldós Aguilera[a]	CFP (Concentration of Popular Forces)
Ecuador	1984–1988	León Febres Cordero	PSC (Social Christian Party)
Ecuador	1988–1992	Rodrigo Borja	ID (Democratic Left)
Ecuador	1992–1996	Sixto Duran Ballén	PUR (Republican Union Party)
Peru	1980–1985	Fernando Belaúnde Terry	AP (Popular Action)
Peru	1985–1990	Alan García Pérez	APRA (American Popular Revolutionary Alliance)
Peru	1990–1995	Alberto Fujimori	Cambio 90 (Change 90)
Peru	1995–2000	Alberto Fujimori	Cambio 90
Venezuela	1958–1964	Rómulo Betancourt	AD (Democratic Action)
Venezuela	1964–1969	Raúl Leoni	AD
Venezuela	1969–1974	Rafael Caldera López	COPEI (Social Christian Party)
Venezuela	1974–1979	Carlos Andrés Pérez	AD
Venezuela	1979–1984	Luis Herrera Campins	COPEI
Venezuela	1984–1989	Jaime Lusinchi	AD
Venezuela	1989–1994	Carlos Andrés Pérez	AD
Venezuela	1994–1998	Rafael Caldera	CN (National Convergence)
Venezuela	1998–2005	Hugo Chávez	PP (Patriotic Coalition)

[a] His vice president, Osvaldo Hurtado Larrea, replaced him after his death in 1981.

TABLE 3.3: *Decentralization Episodes*

Country	Year	Summary
Bolivia	1994	Popular Participation Law decentralized power to the local level by allowing for the popular election of mayors, dividing the country into municipalities, and crafting a system of automatic fiscal transfers to the new municipalities.
	1994	Administrative Decentralization Law increased transfers to regional governments.
Colombia[a]	1983	Law 14 increased fiscal resources available to municipal governments.
	1986	Popular election of mayors first enacted (first election 1988); Law 12 allowed for distribution of the value added tax to municipalities
	1991	Constitution reformed to include the popular election of regional governments plus reform of fiscal transfers to both local and regional governments.
Ecuador	1997	Law of 15% stipulates that 15 percent of the national budget should be transferred to subnational levels (not implemented).
	1998	New constitution extends the scope of local elections, reforms fiscal transfer mechanisms, and requires that fiscal transfers proceed only with corresponding increases in subnational responsibilities.
Peru	1980	New constitution allowing popular election of mayors and fiscal transfers to local governments.
	1989	Election of regional governors approved (first election 1990).
	1992	End of mayoral elections; followed by reform of laws regarding local elections (more centralized).
	1993	Local government reinstated but Decree Law 776 takes away local taxation power and increases the central government's discretion over fiscal transfers to local governments
Venezuela	1989	LORM (Ley Orgánica de Régimen Municipal) enacted the popular election of mayors.
	1989	LERGE (Ley de Elección y Remoción de Gobernadores de Estado) enacted the popular election of governors.
	1990	LOD (Ley Orgánica de Descentralización, Delimitación y Transferencia de Competencias del Poder Público a los Estados) governing the devolution of administrative responsibilities and fiscal transfers.

[a] The most important reforms are listed in the table. For a more complete list of laws affecting municipal governments, see the appendix to Gaitán Pavía and Moreno Ospina 1992, compiled by Fernando Guzmán Rodríguez.

affiliation. Decentralization episodes occurred in several of these administrations. Major shifts in the balance of power between central and subnational governments are catalogued in Table 3.3.

LINKING DECENTRALIZATION TO ELECTORAL CONSIDERATIONS

This section subjects the theory linking decentralization to electoral forces to two rigorous tests. First, logistic regression is employed to examine whether the hypothesized relationships hold between the incidence of decentralization and the pattern of each administration's electoral support. This regression includes data from twenty-six[8] cases for which comparable data were available. Next, evidence from each country is presented in tabular form so that the reader can inspect the election results for the proposed relationships.

Logistic Regression

The logit model is a convenient statistical tool when the object of interest takes on a dichotomous value (e.g., either an event occurs or it does not). In this case, I examine whether or not decentralizing reforms are adopted in twenty-six separate cases.

Since the vast majority of the decentralization episodes centered on extending local power (not regional power), I include measures of each governing party's national-level strength, local-level strength, and the change in its national support across consecutive elections.

I use two alternative specifications to illustrate the statistical relationships between decentralization and the factors hypothesized to influence it. Based on the formal model derived in Chapter 2, the measure of national level support (p_1) and vote change between elections (δ) should enter the equation together, while local support $(\Sigma p_i/(N-1)$, where $I = 2 \ldots N)$ enters independently. The first column of results

---

[8] You may recall that the sample suggested by the limits of democratic contestation yielded twenty-eight cases. Election results at subnational levels were not available for all of these cases; however, at least one instance is included for each country. Disaggregated data at the local level were available only for Bolivia in 1993 and 1997. I have also run the regression using Bolivian data for 1985 and 1989 elections, using the percentage of the vote received by the president's party at the local level instead of the percentage of local-level contests that were won by each party. Using this measure of local strength, the coefficients of the regression change little; both the coefficient for local and for vote change become more significant and the R^2 increases slightly.

TABLE 3.4: *Logit Results*

Variable	LOGIT #1 coefficient (*P* value)	90% confidence interval	LOGIT #2 coefficient (*P* value)	90% confidence interval
NATL			−0.112 (0.241)	−0.270 to −0.045
LOCAL	0.140 (0.054)	0.020 to 0.252	0.141 (0.047)	0.024 to 0.259
VOTECHG			−0.515 (0.059)	−0.963 to −0.067
INTER	−0.011 (0.053)	−0.020 to −0.002		
CONSTANT	−4.723 (0.090)		0.272 (0.935)	
	$N = 26$, Pseudo-$R^2 =$ 0.54		$N = 26$, Pseudo-$R^2 =$ 0.54	

in Table 3.4 stays true to this formulation by regressing decentralization against LOCAL (the percentage of contests won by the president's party at local levels) and the interactive term INTER,[9] the product of NATL (the percentage of the vote won by the president's party at the national level in the most recent presidential election) and VOTECHG (the absolute value of the difference between NATL and the party's percentage of the vote in the previous presidential election). The second specification allows each of the key variables – LOCAL, NATL, and VOTECHG – to enter the equation independently. Both specifications support the theory's prediction: Decentralization is more likely where support for the president's party is strong locally, weak nationally, and where the change in the party's vote share across consecutive elections is low. These hypotheses are confirmed by the negative coefficients on INTER in the first specification and on NATL and VOTECHG in the second specification, and the positive coefficient for LOCAL. The significance of each effect is not uniform, however: In the first statistical

---

[9] The interactive term captures the combined effect of national support and vote change in this way: When vote change and national support are both high (both bad for decentralization), the chances of decentralizing should be at their lowest. When both are low, the chances of decentralizing should be highest; when one is high and the other is low, the results should be mixed. This suggests that a negative coefficient would support the theory.

model, both variables are statistically significant at just under the 95 percent level, and the 90 percent confidence intervals around the estimated coefficients do not include zero (suggesting that the direction of the effects of each is correct). In the second model, large changes in the party's national vote across elections decreases the chance of decentralization at just over the 95 percent level; local support increases decentralization prospects at just under the 95 percent level and the effect of national level support, though negative, is not statistically significant.

Regardless of the exact specification, these results suggest that the factors hypothesized to influence decentralization do affect outcomes – and in the direction anticipated by the model. The coefficients do not have very intuitive interpretations, however, due to the form of the logistic function. The following comparative statics, based on the first statistical model,[10] provide a more substantive interpretation.

With the vote-change held constant at five percentage points and local support held constant at its mean (45%), an increase in national support from its mean, 49 percent, to 59 percent decreases the probability of decentralizing by 28 percent (from 26.4% to 18.9%). Just as increases in national support decrease the probability a party will decentralize, increases in local support increase that probability. Holding vote change constant at five percentage points, keeping national support constant at its mean (49%), and increasing the percentage of local contests won from 45 percent (its mean) to 55 percent, the probability of decentralizing rises by over 100 percent, from 25.7 percent to 53 percent.

Holding all other variables constant at their means, a decrease in vote change from ten to five percentage points in consecutive presidential elections increases the probability of decentralizing by over 300 percent, from 6.7 percent to 26.4 percent. Parties with more stable bases of support can afford to plan long-term electoral strategies and can expect to reap the benefits of decentralization in future elections. When the percentage of the vote won by a party changes by twenty percentage points from election to election, the probability of decentralizing is minuscule, registering only 2.7 percent. Ecuador, Peru, and Venezuela each provide several instances in which parties have won the presidency with a vote swing of at least twenty percentage points over their previous showing in presidential elections.

---

[10] The results do not differ sharply if one uses the second statistical model.

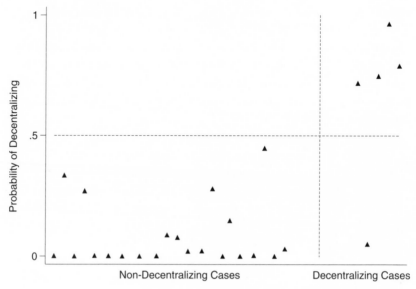

FIGURE 3.1: Fit of the model.

One test of the model's fit can be seen in the Pseudo-R^2 statistic displayed in the table of results. This figure signifies that roughly 54 percent of the variation in the dependent variable (decentralization) is explained by the variation in the explanatory variables. The fit of the model can be judged in more visually appealing ways, however.

In the absence of more independent observations against which to test the model, I use simulation to illustrate the contribution of this model and its limitations. Utilizing the data available, I employ the CLARIFY software package[11] to simulate a pool of 1,000 observations based on the parameters of the existing data. First, I test the logit model, using these observations to determine its ability to sort properly the decentralizing from the non-decentralizing cases. Next, I compare actual decentralization outcomes with the predictions derived from the model, generating a picture of how well the model fits the cases.[12] To illustrate this comparison, Figure 3.1 plots the predicted values derived from the model (on the vertical axis) against the actual cases of

[11] King, Tomz, and Wittenberg 1998; Tomz, Wittenberg, and King 1999.

[12] A better test would apply the model to predict decentralization episodes out of the sample (in countries or time periods not included here), but the small amount of data available restricts this possibility.

TABLE 3.5: *Fit of the Model to the Data*

	No decentralization	Decentralization
Model predicts $Y > 0.5$	0	4
Model predicts $Y < 0.5$	21	1

decentralization (on the horizontal axis). The horizontal axis neatly splits the sample between those cases where decentralization occurred and those where it did not; the horizontal distribution appears more continuous since the values predicted are the probabilities that decentralization occurred in each case.[13] The fact that most of the cases are clustered in the upper right-hand corner and the lower left-hand corner provides strong evidence that the model has correctly sorted the majority of the cases. If we take $Y = 0.5$ as the cutoff between those that will decentralize ($Y > 0.5$) and those that will not ($Y < 0.5$) – that is, those in which the model predicts a probability of decentralizing as greater than or less than 50 percent – the model correctly categorizes all but one case: Colombia in 1990–1994 (in the lower left-hand corner).

The dashed lines divide the figure into four quadrants. The lower left-hand corner contains those observations with a low predicted probability of decentralizing (probability < 0.5) where decentralization did not, in fact, occur. The upper right-hand corner contains those with a high predicted probability of decentralizing (probability > 0.5) where decentralization did occur. The upper left-hand corner, which is empty, delimits cases with a high predicted probability of decentralizing that did not decentralize. Finally, the lower right-hand corner contains a single observation in which the predicted probability of decentralizing was low and yet decentralization occurred. Table 3.5 creates a tally of the observations in each quadrant.

With only twenty-six cases, the logit model correctly sorted more than 95 percent of them into the correct categories.[14] Still, the levels of significance in the regression results are not overwhelming. In fact, we can use the same data to illustrate not only point estimates based

[13] Using the second logit model yields similar results; the second model correctly sorts the same percentage of cases.

[14] When the regression is run including Bolivia in 1985 and 1989, the resulting model also correctly sorts these two cases. See note 8.

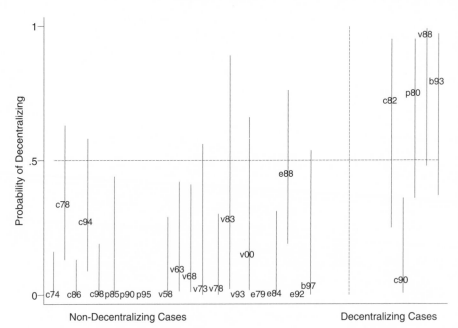

FIGURE 3.2: Fit of the model with 90 percent confidence intervals.

on the simulations, but also confidence intervals around those point estimates. Figure 3.2 labels each point estimate with the first letter of the name of the country it represents, followed by the two-digit year in which that administration's presidential contest was held. A line connects the two ends of the ninety-degree confidence interval around the point estimate.

This exercise shows that, while several cases are correctly sorted when we rely on point estimates, there is a great deal of uncertainty surrounding those estimates in many cases. If we change our criterion to demand that the entire ninety-degree confidence interval lie within the correct quadrant of the figure, then the model correctly sorts just over 50 percent – a less than stellar result. This often high degree of uncertainty and the fact that even one case remains incorrectly classified reveals that an analysis based purely on statistical tests remains incomplete, particularly where more information is available, if not in statistical form.

Subjecting the electoral data of several countries over many time periods to statistical analysis is tricky. The percentage of the national vote won by the president's party means slightly different things in comparison. A low value may signify weak national support in one case, or it may result from a multi-party system: 23 percent of the vote in a two-party system means something different from 23 percent of the vote in a five-party system (perhaps the difference between winning and losing!).

Due to differences between political systems and the availability of data, the measure of local support is not uniform across cases. In all cases this measure captures support for parties at the local level; however, important differences remain. In countries where elections were held at the local level, their results appear in the data set as the measure of local strength. Where no local elections took place but presidential or congressional voting results were available disaggregated to the local level, the data set uses these as its measure of local strength.

Even where local level contests occurred, they did not always coincide with presidential elections – the source of data for national-level support – so the results from the closest local contest were used.

Where non-concurrent or midterm elections occurred, parties could track their rising or waning support at the national and/or local level during their tenure (as they contemplated decentralizing), while in systems without midterm elections, this was not possible. These nuances are also absent from the statistical model. Just as midterm election results inform each party's changing perceptions of its ability to win the next national election, so do polling results and other types of information that may be available for individual cases, but not in a form that is comparable across cases. Obviously, parties examine evidence both retrospectively (previous voting results) and prospectively (polling results and midterm election results, where available). Prospective evaluations are most likely to diverge from past results where parties have a history of volatile support. In such cases it is particularly important to examine the available, prospective information to determine the party's sense of its future national (and subnational) electoral prospects. To run the statistical test, many data that were not comparable were not used; that is not to say that these pieces of information are irrelevant, however. Analysis of these data is taken up in the in-depth country studies that follow this chapter.

Finally, this model does not capture the dynamics behind decision making outside the executive. Because the statistical test relies on support for the president and the president's party at various levels, it cannot provide insight into the electoral incentives of different groups participating in extra-presidential assemblies or in legislatures. Including a dummy variable for the presence or absence of special assemblies is meaningless in this sample because there is simply not enough joint variation in a dummy variable for decentralization and a dummy variable for extra-presidential assemblies to determine the relationship between the two. In nearly every case (except Peru in 1992 and Venezuela in 1998) where a constitutional assembly has been convened, decentralization has occurred within the same administration.

This last point helps to explain why the statistical test presented above failed to explain the outcome of Colombia in 1990–1994. In 1991, Colombia deepened the decentralized governing scheme established between 1982 and 1986 through an elected constitutional assembly. Although the statistical test does not capture the nuances of this case, the logic of the model still proves useful in explaining it. The regression considers data on national- and local-level support for parties in the presidency, leaving it unable to predict the outcomes of extra-presidential policy-making institutions. A look at the national and local support for the parties composing these institutions provides an equally valid test of the theory. This technique is applied in the sections to come.

While the statistical exercise represents one useful tool for teasing out the pattern suggested by the model – and it does an excellent job given the limitations just described – it is but one of many available tools. The next subsection provides election results from each country to allow the reader to discern patterns of support that correlate with decentralization experiences in each. In addition, the country studies in the following chapters provide the most detailed evidence of each country's experiences with decentralizing reform. Combining the insights of the statistical analysis with these more detailed analyses allows for the benefits of each approach to be combined in what Tarrow (1995) terms "triangulation." He states that "a single-minded adherence to *either* quantitative or qualitative approaches straightjackets scientific progress" (474). To avoid this pitfall, this book combines both into a strong test of the theory that electoral concerns play an important role in driving decentralization.

Statistics, by Country

This section presents each country's electoral results in tabular form, so the reader can peruse them, noting the trends within each country over time and the correspondence between the electoral data and the prediction that governments with weak national support, strong local support, and stable support over time decentralize. These short sections are meant to whet the reader's appetite for the more detailed analysis of country experiences contained in Part II of this book.

Bolivia. Bolivia's 1994 Popular Participation Law created hundreds of new municipalities where no formal local government recognized by the state had previously existed. These new governing institutions gained real power through automatic transfers of substantial fiscal resources allocated solely on the basis of population. Representing such a sharp break from previously centralized development policies, this reform gained strong popular support and captured imaginations well beyond Bolivia's borders.

Table 3.6 presents the available information, showing the pattern of support for various parties in Bolivia's system as they evolved over the democratic period. Bold typeface distinguishes the support of the party in the presidency. Only those parties with 10 percent or more of the national vote in presidential votes are shown in most cases.

In Bolivia's first, post-transition election, the MNR (National Revolutionary Movement) captured the presidency with weak national support but local support that significantly outweighed that of its rival, the ADN (Nationalist Democratic Action). In 1989, the MIR (Movement of the Revolutionary Left) gained the presidency by combining its strength with the ADN to keep the MNR – the party winning a plurality of the national votes – from taking the executive.[15] The MIR took office despite weak national support and ambiguous local support, given its alliance with the ADN in that year's municipal elections. Midway through its term, in the 1991 municipal elections, support for this MIR-ADN alliance had waned to 28.5 percent, while support for the MNR had grown to 24.8 percent. Finally, in 1993, the MNR won the

---

[15] Under Bolivian law at the time, if no party won a majority of the votes, the president was chosen by the legislature from among the top three vote-getting parties.

TABLE 3.6: *Bolivian Election Results, 1980–1999[a]*

Year	National (% of vote)	Local (% of vote 1980–1989; % of contests 1993–1999)
1980	38.7 UDP 20.2 A-MNR 16.8 A.D.N.	
1985	32.8 A.D.N. 30.4 MNR 10.2 MIR	25.1 A.D.N. 31.4 MNR 10.1 MIR
1989	25.8 MNR 25.4 A.D.N. 22.0 MIR	19.3 MNR 33.6 AP[b] 18.8 CONDEPA
1993	35.6 MNR 21.1 AP[b] 14.3 CONDEPA 13.8 UCS	71.9 MNR 8.6 CONDEPA 6.8 UCS
1995		40.0 MNR 12.3 UCS 11.5 ADN
1997[c]	22.3 ADN 18.2 MNR 17.2 CONDEPA 16.8 MIR 16.1 UCS	
1999[d]		25.6 MNR 24.9 ADN 19.2 MIR 9.9 UCS

[a] UDP: Unidad Democrática y Popular (Popular Democratic Unity); A-MNR: Alianza de Movimiento Nacional Revolucionario (Alliance of the National Revolutionary Movement); MNR: Movimiento Nacional Revolucionario (National Revolutionary Movement); ADN: Acción Democrática Nacionalista (Nationalist Democratic Action); MIR: Movimiento de Izquierda Revolucionario (Movement of the Revolutionary Left); CONDEPA: Conciencia de Patria (Conscience of the Fatherland); UCS: Unión Cívica Solidaridad (Civic Solidarity Union).

[b] AP is a combination of MIR and ADN.

[c] In the 1997 elections, new voting rules took effect. Whereas the legislative elections had previously occurred using a single, closed-list PR ballot, now voters cast two ballots. These results reflect the voting results in the multi-member districts, which elect the larger number of legislators. The single-member district results closely parallel the multi-member votes: 22.2 ADN, 17.9 MNR, 17.3 MIR, 14.1 CONDEPA, 14.0 UCS. Results were obtained from http://www.bolivian.com/cne, accessed December 16, 1998. The author retains a printed copy of the results.

[d] Local results from 1999 come from the Web-based resource http://www.vppfm.gov.bo, accessed October 3, 2000. The author retains a printed copy of these results.

presidency with strong support; subnational elections held that year underlined the MNR's dominance over its traditional rivals – the ADN and the MIR – who won less than 10 percent of the local contests. By contrast, the MNR won a plurality of the vote in over 70 percent of the provincial sections that would later become municipalities. The MNR, a party without overwhelming support at the national level, but with strong support at the local level and the most stable support over time of any Bolivian party, decentralized power during its term. This government made the election of local mayors and the distribution of more central government funds to municipalities the centerpiece of its administration.

Colombia. Colombia displays a different pattern of party support. Two parties, the Liberals and Conservatives, dominate elections at all levels in this case, with the Liberals generally beating the Conservatives at all levels and in all years. From 1958 to 1974 Liberals and Conservatives operated within a political pact known as the National Front, which bound the two parties to alternate terms in the presidency and divided national and subnational appointments equally between them.

When the National Front terminated in 1974, electoral support for the Liberals overwhelmed that of the Conservatives at all levels. In fact, between 1974 and 1994, the Liberals won the presidency in all elections but that of 1982. Moreover, in each of these victories, the Liberals displayed electoral strength at both national and local levels. Colombia held both regional and local elections for departmental and municipal assemblies before either subnational level of government gained much access to central government funds or could levy local taxes. While assemblies at these levels were elected, governors and mayors continued to be appointed by the national executive. The figures in Table 3.7 correspond to election results for these subnational assemblies until mayors faced popular election in 1988. The party occupying the presidency is highlighted in boldface type.

In the 1982 presidential election, the Liberals split their votes between two candidates, allowing a Conservative to win the national race. A quick look at the 1982 legislative voting results reveals that support for the Liberal party remained stronger than support for the Conservative party, notwithstanding the presidential victory. In fact, comparing the 1982 legislative results to the 1978 results suggests that

TABLE 3.7: *Colombian Election Results, 1972–2000*

Year	National (% of vote)	Local (% of contests)
1972		54.8 Liberals 37.2 Conservatives
1974	56.2 Liberals 31.4 Conservatives	57.6 Liberals 41.5 Conservatives
1978	49.5 Liberals 46.6 Conservatives	56.4 Liberals 44.0 Conservatives
1980		57.6 Liberals 41.1 Conservatives
1982	41.0 Liberals 46.8 Conservatives 10.9 New Liberalism	57.4 Liberals 42.4 Conservatives
1984		56.1 Liberals 43.4 Conservatives
1986	58.4 Liberals 35.8 Conservatives	53.9 Liberals 44.6 Conservatives
1988		44.7 Liberals 41.9 Conservatives
1990	49.9 Liberals 24.7 Conservatives	52.9 Liberals 36.9 Conservatives
1991		48.7 Liberals 40.7 Conservatives
1994	50.6 Liberals 48.7 Conservatives	48.5 Liberals 40.7 Conservatives
1997[a]		38.4 Liberals 29.3 Conservatives
1998	46.5 Liberals 50.4 Conservatives	
2000[b]		37.9 Liberals 24.9 Conservatives

Note: Local elections after 1988 are mayors elected after decentralization measures. Where not otherwise noted, all election results come from publications of Colombia's Registraduría Nacional del Estado Civil.

[a] Figures based on the article "Colombia: Local Elections Carried Out amid Violence" 1997.

[b] These figures based on results posted at http://www.registraduria.gov.co, accessed January 1, 2001, with results from 954 municipalities reported (out of approximately 1,075).

levels of support for the two parties had scarcely changed. This 1982 split in the Liberal party allowed the Conservatives – a nationally weak party with weak regional support, but strong and steady local level support – to control the executive and introduce decentralizing reforms at the municipal level. Conservative support in 1982 precisely fits the profile of a decentralizing administration derived from the theory that parties decentralize based on their perceived electoral prospects.

In 1991 Colombia adopted a new constitution, which strengthened and extended decentralization. It strengthened decentralization by writing the earlier reforms into the constitution, making them harder to alter than mere legislation; it extended decentralization by allowing the popular election of departmental governors. To understand this process in light of the theory, it is useful to examine the composition of the convention and the support for parties shown in its election.

If presidential parties calculate their electoral chances under decentralized and centralized systems when deciding whether or not to decentralize, extra-presidential assemblies with the power to alter these relations should perform a similar calculus. Extending the theory requires only a sense of whether each party's electoral base encourages decentralization, weighted by each party's representation within the assembly. When commissions and assemblies stand to gain from decentralization and they have the power to effect such changes, decentralizing reforms are a likely outcome.

Colombia's seventy-member constitutional assembly was composed of 24 Liberals, 19 members of the M-19 (Democratic Alliance, a formerly violent guerrilla force that became a legal party just prior to these elections), 11 members of the Movement for National Salvation (one wing of the Conservative Party), nine Social Conservatives (the other wing of the Conservative Party), and seven members who eschewed all party labels. Although they had won the presidency in 1990, the Liberals did not win a majority in the constitutional assembly. Regional and local-level support for the traditional parties declined in the wake of a new choice: the M-19. Neither the Liberals nor the Conservatives won a majority of votes in any department or in any of thirty-eight major cities (except in Barrancabermeja) for which vote totals were available. In Colombia in 1991, a collection of parties that perceived their subnational electoral chances as better than their national election prospects and that had no need to sacrifice short-term power (due to the nature of the constitutional assembly in comparison to the presidency) saw an advantage in further decentralizing the system – just as the theory predicts.

Ecuador. In sharp contrast to the steady pattern of support for the Liberals in Colombia, the Ecuadorian experience is characterized by sharp shifts in support between parties and by the constant generation and disappearance of parties from the electoral arena. In the period under study, 1978–1996, no party won more than one national election, illustrating the mercurial nature of support for political parties (see Table 3.8).

TABLE 3.8: *Ecuadorian Election Results, 1978–1995[a]*

Year	National (% of vote)	Local (% of contests)
1978: Round 1	27.7 CFP	30.0 CFP
	23.9 PSC	40.0 PSC
	22.7 PLRE	5.0 PLRE
1979: Round 2	68.5 CFP	
	31.5 PSC	
1984: Round 1	27.2 PSC	55.9 ID
	28.7 ID	6.3 PSC
	13.5 CFP	
1984: Round 2	51.5 PSC	
	48.5 ID	
1988: Round 1	24.5 ID	51.5 ID
	17.6 PRE	11.8 PRE
	14.7 PSC	
1988: Round 2	54.9 ID	
	46.7 PRE	
1992: Round 1	31.4 PUR	3.7 PUR
	25.0 PSC	18.5 PSC
	22.0 PRE	
1992: Round 2	57.3 PUR	
	42.7 PSC	

[a] CFP: Concentración de Fuerzas Populares (Concentration of Popular Forces); PSC: Partido Social Cristiano (Social Christian Party); PLRE: Partido Liberal Radical Ecuatoriano (Radical Liberal Party of Ecuador); ID: Izquierda Democrática (Democratic Left); PRE: Partido Roldosista Ecuatoriano (Ecuadorian Party in support of Roldos); PUR: Partido Unión Republicana (Republican Union Party).

National-level results reflect votes for presidential and legislative offices. Local-level results in the earliest election are for members of an assembly at the level of cantons; in 1984 the local contest displayed is the result of voting for municipal councils (in 127 municipalities); in 1988 it is the result of contests for 136 municipal council presidents; and in 1992 it is the result of elections for municipal mayors.

In the first election considered, the PSC (Social Christian Party) won the presidency with strong national-level support but weak local support. In the subsequent national election, the PSC, despite lagging behind the ID (Democratic Left) in the first round, went on to win the national election with the same combination of strong national support and weak local support. When the ID won the presidency in 1988, its support at all levels had grown strong. The winner in 1992, the newly created PUR, won the presidency with a strong national showing but weak local support.

Of the four administrations covered here, only one approximates the pattern of electoral support hypothesized to encourage decentralization: the ID in 1988. Since the ID was the only party with a strong local base of support, one might suppose that the party leadership would be sympathetic to decentralization after being denied the presidency in the second round of the previous national election. A closer look at the administration reveals that its economic program caused it to lose precious support at all levels of government from the beginning of its term. This hemorrhage of support quickly diminished its future electoral expectations at all levels for the next elections. It is telling that ID did not even place in the top three vote-getters in the 1992 contest.

Although not covered in the statistical analysis, Ecuador has made cautious strides toward decentralization since 1996. Most notably, Ecuador's constitutional assembly in 1998 fiercely debated the issue of decentralization. Despite much debate both in this assembly and in subsequent legislatures, actual reform has been limited. The constitution contains decentralizing language, but little enabling legislation has yet been passed, owing mainly to the primacy of the economic crisis that has gripped the country in recent years and the political unrest that led to the ouster of its elected president in January, 2000.

Peru. Peru provides a set of interesting cases that help to illustrate the theory developed here. Unlike any other country considered thus far,

TABLE 3.9: *Peruvian Election Results, 1962–1999[a]*

Year	National (% of vote)	Local (% of contests)
1962	33.0 APRA 32.1 AP	
1963	34.4 APRA 39.1 AP	50.0 APRA 50.0 AP
1966		52.8 AP 37.8 APRA
1978	**35.3 APRA** 29.3 IU	**65.1 APRA** 24.3 IU
1980	**45.4 AP** 27.4 APRA	**65.4 AP** 15.6 APRA
1983		47.7 APRA **23.2 AP**
1985	**53.1 APRA** 7.3 AP	
1986		**91.8 APRA** 0.0 AP
1989		46.0 Fredemo 16.0 APRA
1990: Round 1	32.6 Fredemo **29.1 Cambio 90** 22.6 APRA	
1990: Round 2	**62.4 Cambio 90** 37.6 Fredemo	
1993		59 OTHERS 16 INDEPENDENTS
1995	**64.4 Cambio 90** 4.1 APRA 1.6 AP	

[a] APRA: Alianza Popular Revolucionaria Americana (American Popular Revolutionary Alliance); AP: Acción Popular (Popular Action); IU: Izquierda Unida (United Left); FREDEMO: Frente Democrático (Democratic Front); Cambio 90: Cambio 90 (Change 90).

the Peruvian experience includes an instance of recentralization after a prior period of decentralization.

After a period of democratic governance in the 1960s, Peru succumbed to military control in 1968. In 1978, the military government signaled its retreat by allowing the convening of a constitutional assembly to craft new rules for an eventual return to civilian rule. The 1978 elections mark the democratic opening. Table 3.9 includes election results from before the military period to show the continuity of party identity and strength between the two periods of democratic elections, despite the military interruption. Such strong continuity makes it possible to imagine that parties returning to democratic institutions may have taken clues about their election prospects from previous elections. The stability of the parties over this period may have focused political attention on the long-term rewards of decentralization for parties such as the AP (Popular Action) and APRA (American Popular Revolutionary Alliance) that had previously enjoyed strong support throughout the country without having been able to dominate national power.

The 1980s witnessed growing changes in party support as each of the traditional parties – AP and the APRA – was discredited by futile attempts to brake the economy's sharp downward spiral. Thus, the end of the decade witnessed the rise of more personalist parties and a turn toward a more authoritarian model under Alberto Fujimori.

Steps to decentralize power in Peru were taken in 1980 within the constitutional assembly dominated by APRA and parties of the left. APRA had experienced strong local-level support and consistently strong but not overwhelming national-level support in the previous democratic period. The 1978 constitutional assembly elections reinforced this pattern: relatively strong national-level support with much stronger local-level support – a pattern hypothesized to create a favorable disposition toward decentralization.

The electoral victory of the AP in 1980, with strong support at all levels of government – particularly regional and local levels – provided few incentives to quash what had begun in the constitutional assembly immediately preceding its term. In addition, AP support appeared relatively stable from its previous electoral showing in 1963, where it received roughly 40 percent of the vote (having boycotted the constitutional assembly).

In 1985, the APRA won in the face of the AP's failed orthodox economic program. APRA introduced a heterodox alternative, winning the party massive support at all levels. Midterm elections at the local level show a sharp decline in that support when the heterodox policies also failed. In addition, the APRA had proven itself unable to deter the escalating guerrilla insurgency led by Sendero Luminoso (Shining Path). After hastily passing a law to elect regional governors, the APRA lost national elections by an overwhelming margin in 1990 (but they managed to win the vast majority of the governorships). At this point, Peruvian politics deteriorated into extreme volatility.

The 1990 presidential race led to a second-round run-off between two candidates from hastily assembled parties – parties with no political history, reliant on the personalities of their leaders. With a strong national showing in the second round (after narrowly losing the first round), Alberto Fujimori of Cambio 90 acceded to the presidency, where he remained until a scandal forced his resignation after the controversial national election of 2000. Fujimori instigated an *autogolpe* in 1992, dissolving Congress in order to remake the rules of the state through a handpicked constitutional convention. Despite this autocratic approach, Fujimori remained extremely popular at the national level in successive elections. Fujimori continued to win presidential votes, but the succession of parties he formed to channel his support was unable to win contests at subnational levels. As a result, Fujimori's popularity and strength lay purely at the national level; it is not surprising that his presidency marks the first case of recentralization in this discussion of Andean cases. During Fujimori's first administration, he abolished popularly elected regional governorships; he delayed local elections, reinstating them under rules that disadvantaged the already weak traditional parties; and he made fiscal transfers to subnational levels less automatic and more discretionary. This president, with strong national support, weak subnational support, and no sign of a successor to pass power to in the longer term, capitalized on opportunities to recentralize power. In 2002, Peru again held elections for regional governors; however, the fiscal resources and responsibilities for these officers have yet to be defined.

Venezuela. As in Colombia, two parties have dominated Venezuelan politics through most of its democratic history. In this case, Democratic Action (AD) and the Social Christian Party (COPEI) monopolized the presidency since the beginning of democratic contestation in 1958, until the 1990s. Between 1958 and 1992, five presidencies were won by AD, with only two going to COPEI, in 1968 and 1978 (see Table 3.10).

TABLE 3.10: *Venezuelan Election Results, 1958–2000*

Year	National (% of vote)	Local (% of contests)
1958	**49.2 AD**	80 AD
	34.6 URD	10 COPEI
	15.2 COPEI	
1963	**32.8 AD**	60 AD
	20.2 COPEI	26 COPEI
	18.9 URD	
	16.1 IPFN	
	9.4 FDP	
1968	**28.7 COPEI**	37 COPEI
	27.5 AD	54 AD
	22.3 URD	
	19.4 MEP	
1973	**48.6 AD**	85 AD
	35.3 COPEI	14 COPEI
	5.1 MEP	
1978	**45.2 COPEI**	42 COPEI
	43.3 AD	58 AD
	5.2 MAS	
1983	**55.3 AD**	94 AD
	32.6 COPEI	5.5 COPEI
1988	**52.9 AD**	81 AD
	40.3 COPEI	19 COPEI
1993	**30.5 CN**	
	23.6 AD	
	22.7 COPEI	
	22.0 Causa R	
1998	**56.2 MVR**	
	40.0 PRVZL	
2000[a]	**56.9 MVR**	25.5 AD
	19.0 Causa R	**25.3 MVR + MAS**
	2.7 Encuentro	10.4 COPEI

[a] National and local results for 2000 come from a web-based resource at http://www.cne.cantv.net/Inicial.html, accessed September 26, 2000. Author retains a printed copy of election results.

Strong national, regional, and local support have characterized AD presidencies. With such strong support at all levels, it is not surprising that the AD did not decentralize until practically forced to do so by the extra-presidential Presidential Commission to Reform the

State (Comisión Presidencial para la Reforma del Estado, or COPRE). COPRE, a body created by AD president Jaime Lusinchi but without an AD majority, pushed the issue of decentralization into the spotlight, causing all parties in the 1988 elections to adopt some type of decentralization plan. Despite the pressure from COPRE, the AD in 1989 did not stray far from the decentralizing party profile derived from the model. The AD in 1989 had recently won the presidency with a strong but declining share of the national vote and enjoyed strong local support in a fairly stable party system.

A more intriguing question raised by Table 3.10 is: Why did the COPEI not decentralize in 1968 or 1978? Both COPEI victories were closely contested, with a victory margin smaller than two percentage points in both cases. With this tight differential at the national level, one might expect decentralization by COPEI during its short terms in the executive. A closer look into each administration sheds light on these apparent anomalies. COPEI's first victory (1968) represented a sharp upturn in the party's support. Party leaders expected this growth to continue. One account notes that the party leadership was stunned by its 1973 defeat: "None had seriously entertained the possibility of defeat, given the brilliance of the government record, the size and magnitude of the Fernández [COPEI's presidential candidate] crowds, the support of influential independents, and the technical brilliance of the electoral organization."[16] With expectations of national dominance, COPEI had few incentives to decentralize. COPEI's second victory did not yield such high expectations; on the contrary, it appears the party began losing support at all levels shortly after gaining office. With local prospects falling along with national prospects, COPEI mustered little enthusiasm for decentralizing.

Venezuela's traditional party system steadily deteriorated in the 1990s. First, Rafael Caldera – a member of the traditional political class – formed a new party coalition to win the presidency in 1993. This coalition proved unwieldy, showed no strong support in subnational contests, and did not return as a major electoral force in 1998. Instead, 1998 saw the election of Hugo Chávez, a former military leader who had gained countrywide recognition by leading a coup attempt in 1992. Like Fujimori, Chávez sailed into office on a wave of national support,

[16] Martz and Baloyra 1976: 235.

with much more uncertain subnational support. While Chávez and his supporters won the presidency by a large margin, many congressional seats and several key governorships and mayorships remained in the hands of the traditional parties. Under Chávez, Venezuela has embarked on an ambitious political restructuring, with a new constitution. Although approved by a wide majority, arguments against the reformed charter focused on the damage it would do to the decentralization process. This should not be surprising, given that Chávez and his movement have neither a reliable, long-term record of support on which to base calculations of future access to power nor dependable measures of the movement's ability to place its candidates in local and regional offices. In electoral terms, Chávez in 2000 looks much like Fujimori in 1993.

Summary. Taken together, the evidence supporting the theory is significant. Colombia begins to decentralize when the Conservative party – an established party with strong pockets of reliable support in particular regions – wins power for the first time in decades, due to a temporary split in the Liberal party that had dominated the presidency. Bolivia decentralizes under the presidency of its most stable party and the party with the broadest territorial support base. Dominant parties fail to decentralize after strong presidential showings in Colombia in the 1970s, Venezuela up until 1988 and under Chávez, and Peru in the 1990s. In addition, Bolivia's less stable parties did not further decentralization, and Ecuador, with the most chaotic party system in the region, ends the period having made the least progress toward decentralization.

ALTERNATIVE THEORIES

Chapter 2 described several alternative explanations for decentralizing reforms. Because this inquiry looks both at cross-national and intertemporal variation, strong alternative theories must be able to explain both the variation in decentralizing experiences across countries (the *where* question) and the variation in decentralizing experiences over time within countries (the *when* question). Several of the alternatives described in the previous chapter fail to explain both. Two theories that are well positioned to explain both where and when and that appear most susceptible to statistical testing link decentralization to fiscal crisis and international pressure. Other alternative theories are considered more carefully in the chapters that delve more deeply into country experiences.

Fiscal Crisis

The fiscal crisis hypothesis explains the devolution of responsibilities to subnational governments as a form of central government shirking. In times of fiscal difficulties, national politicians seek to escape the blame for unpopular budget cuts by transferring responsibilities for several spending areas to subnational levels. According to the logic of this argument, central governments transfer responsibility for some services to subnational governments, giving them a fixed proportion of the central budget. This allows the central government the twin benefits of placing a hard constraint on how much of the budget will be spent on such programs and of transferring responsibility for the quality and quantity of services in these spending areas to subnational officials. This argument implies a coincidence between the adoption of decentralization and high budget deficits.

Is the fiscal crisis explanation useful in predicting decentralization in the Andes? Figure 3.3 presents the deficit as a percentage of GDP for the five countries studied here between 1970 and the early 1990s. In the five countries, decentralization episodes do not appear to coincide with major dips in the fiscal balance. Presenting these graphs together adds another dimension to the comparison. In the case of Colombia, for example, the 1986 reform does seem to coincide with a period of rising fiscal imbalances relative to Colombia's recent history; however, other countries in the region suffer much greater fiscal deficit problems and yet do not decentralize.

A second way to judge the relationship between fiscal crises and decentralization is to include a fiscal variable in the statistical analysis. The logistic regression presented earlier in this chapter displayed results from regressing decentralization episodes against three features of the governing party: its national support, local support, and the stability of its support across elections. It is possible to add a variable reflecting the fiscal health of each economy during each term. If the fiscal crisis theory holds, a high deficit to GDP ratio should be

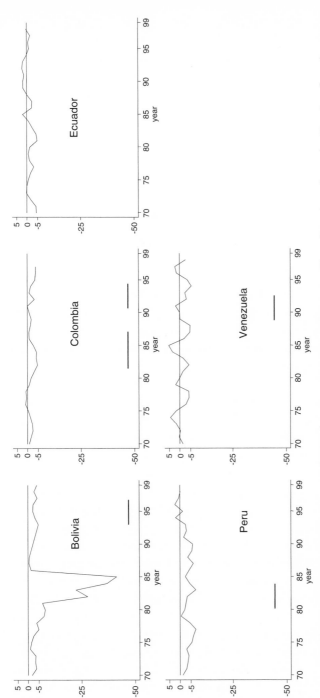

FIGURE 3.3: Budget surplus as a percentage of GDP, by country, 1970–1999. *Note:* Short lines just above the X-axis reflect the years of decentralizing administrations. *Source:* Data from IMF, *International Financial Statistics Yearbook.*

TABLE 3.11: *Logit Results with Deficit/GDP Included*

Variable	Coefficient	Standard error	P value
LOCAL	0.098	0.067	0.145
INTER	−0.008	0.005	0.074
DEF/GDP	0.540	0.536	0.313
Constant	−4.037	3.373	0.231
$N = 21$	Pseudo-$R^2 = 0.574$		

positively related to decentralization and the effect should be significant. Table 3.11 presents the results of adding a measure of the average fiscal deficit/GDP ratio over the course of each administration to the regression using LOCAL and INTER (as in Table 3.4). Again, the coefficients on LOCAL and INTER fit the theory's hypotheses, although their level of statistical significance is somewhat lower here. The fiscal crisis variable appears positively related to decentralization, just as the fiscal hypothesis predicts; however, the statistical significance of this variable is quite low – in fact, it is the least significant variable in the equation – indicating a high level of uncertainty in specifying the relationship between fiscal crises and decentralization. Including fiscal data averaged over the years of each presidential term may not seem the optimal test of this theory since the averaging may lessen the effects of deep, one-year crises. Since fiscal data can be examined more frequently than the political data on which the electoral motivation theory depends, it is also possible to run a regression looking only at the fit between annual fiscal data and the incidence of decentralizing reforms. This approach increases the number of episodes that can be examined, as it uses annual data for each of the five countries beginning in 1970. Because there may be a lag between the onset of a fiscal crisis and the decision to decentralize, this theory is also tested lagging the deficit/GDP variable one year. The results of regressions using annual budget deficits as a percent of GDP as the single explanatory variable and of using a lagged version of this variable are shown in Table 3.12.

In both cases, the coefficient linking fiscal balance to decentralization is extremely small. The Pseudo-R^2 is also negligibly small. In both the lagged and unlagged cases, the signs of the coefficients indicate that smaller deficits lead to more decentralization; this contradicts the theoretical prediction that deficits lead to more decentralization. The

TABLE 3.12: *Logit Decentralization against Deficit/GDP*

Variable	Using Deficit/GDP			Using lagged deficit/GDP		
	Coefficient (P value)	First difference	Effect	Coefficient (P value)	First difference	Effect
Deficit/GDP	−0.034 (0.766)	3.0%, 4.0%	3.89%, 3.83%			
Lagged deficit/GDP				−0.0008 (0.992)	3.0%, 4.0%	4.03%, 3.97%
Constant	3.207 (0.000)			3.271 (0.000)		
N = 139		Pseudo-R^2 = 0.003		N = 137	Pseudo-R^2 = 0.000	

significance levels are extremely low for both lagged and contemporaneous measures of the deficit/GDP ratio, however. Finally, in addition to being weak statistically, the size of the effects in both cases is also small. A 1 percent increase in the deficit to GDP ratio from 3 percent to 4 percent (2.8 percent is the sample mean) leads to a less than 1 percent change in the probability of decentralizing, lowering it from 3.89 percent to 3.83 percent in the case of contemporaneous deficit to GDP, and lowering it from 4.03 percent to 3.97 percent in the case of lagged deficit to GDP. Overall, evidence for the fiscal crisis theory of decentralization is weak, particularly when compared with the electoral theory.

International Pressure

Closely related to the fiscal crisis theory is a theory linking decentralization to international pressure from creditors. If international creditors make loans conditional on certain political and economic reforms, including decentralization, then decentralization should be related to the exposure of each country to creditor pressure. This exposure can be examined by exploring each country's debt history. Measuring the exposure of debtors to their creditors is not a simple task. The World Bank's *World Debt Tables* (1996) provide over a hundred different pieces of information bearing on this relationship, and a complete picture of exposure can be constructed only by using several of them in combination.

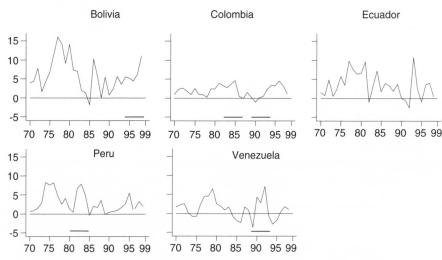

FIGURE 3.4: Net debt flows as a percentage of GNP, 1970–1999. *Note:* Short lines just above the X-axis reflect the years of decentralizing administrations.

Countries are more open to international pressure not when they already have a large portfolio of debt but when they are attempting to increase their debt. Figure 3.4 shows the net debt flows to each country between 1970 and 1995. If decentralization occurs when international lenders place conditions on borrowers, decentralization should occur when this value is high.

No country decentralized at the peak of its debt flows: Bolivia decentralizes long after its debt inflows peak in the 1980s, Colombia decentralizes between 1982 and 1986 at times of relatively high net inflows compared with its own past, but at low levels compared across cases. Peru decentralizes during a period of debt repayment (1978–1980) and recentralizes when debt inflows are positive but not remarkable. Venezuela decentralizes at the deepest nadir in its debt inflows and Ecuador does not decentralize, despite periods of high debt inflows.

One can imagine cases in which large debt inflows signal a borrower's strength; if interest rates are low, for example. In the early 1980s, petro-dollar recycling drove down interest rates as money sought good investment opportunities. As a result, countries could take on huge debt loads with very little conditionality as lenders competed for market opportunities, turning world capital markets into venues of borrower strength. Debtors are most vulnerable to lenders when they must repay loans and do not have the cash to do so. This suggests looking at debt flows over time, instead of looking at the overall stock of debt.

Ideally, I would like to disaggregate debt into its long- and short-term components. High short-term debt flows – because they typically carry higher interest rates and less flexible payback schedules – indicate greater exposure to lender pressure. One of the best measures of exposure to lender pressure, then, would be information on short-term debt schedules; this information was not available for a sufficiently long time period for the cases studied here but data beginning in 1985 were available. Inflows of short-term debt should be associated with decentralization if this theory holds.

Figure 3.5 shows short-term debt as a percentage of GDP for the years 1985–1994. While Bolivia decentralizes with a positive short-term debt inflow, the 1991 decentralization reform in Colombia occurs in the absence of short-term debt. Venezuela decentralizes while paying back short-term debts and Ecuador fails to decentralize despite increasing its short-term debt more dramatically than any other country in the region during the early 1990s. There does not appear to be a strong relationship between short-term debt incursion and decentralization.

Finally, debtors who cannot pay their debt may opt to reschedule them with creditors. During rescheduling, creditors may exert

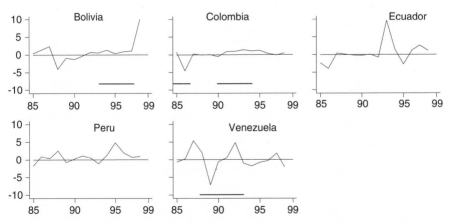

FIGURE 3.5: Short-term debt flows as a percentage of GNP, 1985–1999. *Note:* Short lines just above the X-axis reflect the years of decentralizing administrations.

TABLE 3.13: *Logit of Decentralization versus Measures of International Pressure*

Variable	Coefficient (P value)	First difference	Effect	Observations
Net flows % GNP	−0.219	2.26%	3.83%	145
	(0.227)	3.26%	3.23%	
Debt rescheduled % GNP[a]	−0.437	3.15%	3.72%	144
	(0.471)	4.15%	3.69%	

[a] This variable is lagged one time period.

considerable influence over debtors because they set the terms of the new repayment schedule. As the debt rescheduled rises, creditors are in a stronger position relative to debtors.

Based on the theoretical issues raised above and the availability of data, the international pressure theory will be tested using:

(1) net debt flows as a percentage of GNP[17] (is new debt coming in faster than old debt is being repaid?)

and

(2) debt rescheduled as a percent of GNP (is debt being rescheduled and is it a large amount relative to the economy?)

Each of these measures can be used to help assess the international pressure hypothesis. As in the previous section testing the fiscal crisis hypothesis, two tests can be run: One regresses decentralization on annual data using each of the measures outlined above, and the other adds each of them (averaged over each presidential administration) to the original regression reported in Table 3.4.

If the international pressure theory holds, decentralization should be positively related to debt inflows and debt rescheduling. Table 3.13 provides partial results from regressing decentralization against each measure of exposure to international pressure, using annual data for each country from 1970 to 1994.

[17] GNP is used instead of GDP because the *World Debt Tables* list the former instead of the latter. Since both are contained in the same database, this improves the quality of the ratios and their comparison over time.

Two conclusions can be drawn from a cursory look at the table. First, the relationship between these measures of exposure to international lending pressure and decentralization is generally negative. Second, the significance of these effects is both statistically and substantively weak. The negative relationship between debt flows and decentralization implies that decentralization occurs not when debt flows into these economies but when it is being repaid. This contradicts the theory, since lenders should have more power over policy when they are giving money rather than when the country is strong enough to repay. In each year that decentralization occurred, the amount of debt rescheduled for the decentralizing country was zero. Due to this perfect coincidence between zero debt rescheduling and decentralization, the lagged rescheduled debt was used for the logit regressions reported in the table.[18]

Significance levels for all three measures are remarkably low, as reflected in their P values (listed in parentheses just under the coefficient). Columns 3 and 4 also provide a sense of the magnitude of the expected effects. As each variable is increased 1 percent from its mean (values listed in column 3), the probability of decentralizing is recorded in column 4. In all cases, the effects appear unremarkable. A 1 percent increase in the ratio of debt rescheduled causes only a 0.03 percentage point decrease in the probability of decentralizing (from 3.72% to 3.69%), for example.

The results of including measures of exposure to international pressure from lenders in the original regression appear in Table 3.14. A net increase in debt flows increases the probability that a presidential administration decentralizes. Increases in debt rescheduled actually decrease that probability – a finding counter to the theory. In both cases, however, the coefficients linking decentralization to the measure of exposure to international pressure are statistically insignificant in the regressions. Overall, the case for international pressure as the primary cause of decentralization remains weak.

---

[18] Lagged values were also calculated for each of the other measures of international pressure, and because no significant differences were found, they are not reported. One might also think that the absolute level of each measure is not the correct measure of international pressure, but rather one should examine the relationship between changes in these variables and the incidence of decentralization. These regressions were also run, but their results were similarly unimpressive and are therefore also excluded from this tabular report.

TABLE 3.14: *Logit Results of Decentralization Including Measures of International Pressure*

Variable	Variation 1 coefficient (*P* value)	Variation 2 coefficient (*P* value)
LOCAL	0.108 (0.142)	0.176 (0.102)
INTER	−0.009 (0.145)	−0.011 (0.005)
NET/GNP	0.044 (0.937)	
DSCH/GNP		−0.380 (0.344)
Constant	−3.491 (3.207)	
Observations	20	21

CONCLUSION

This chapter has tested the electoral theory of decentralization using evidence from five countries across twenty-eight presidential terms. A variety of methods was used, since the theory was subjected to both quantitative and qualitative analysis. Information on each administration was pared down to a few essential numbers to test the applicability of the theory to all the cases, then individual cases were examined in more detail to determine whether the theory could explain each one. The first method ensured that the theory could explain the broad pattern of decentralization over time and across administrations, while the second method checked that the broad generalization of the theory fit the individual complexities of each case. This second method is amplified in the chapters below.

After subjecting the electoral theory of decentralization to several empirical tests, alternative theories were examined with equal tenacity. Under empirical scrutiny, neither fiscal crisis nor international pressure provided a better fit for the evidence assembled here. In fact, the competing theories that decentralization responds to fiscal stimuli or international pressure both performed rather poorly in predicting the adoption of decentralizing reforms.

Decentralizing reforms seem deeply connected to electoral concerns. Parties in power attempt to maximize their continued access to office, trading off the loss of centralized power in the present term for an opportunity to compete for subnational offices under a decentralized system in the future. They are most likely to support decentralization when their national support is weak, their subnational support is strong, and the change in the party's vote share across elections is low. According to the interactive model, decentralization is most likely when national support is weak and relatively stable and least likely when national support is strong and volatile. Simple logistic regressions using only these three pieces of information correctly sort twenty-five of the twenty-six cases available for testing. While this evidence provides a strong case for the electoral theory of decentralization, a more detailed look at each case can provide an even greater test of the theory's ability to explain each particular decentralization episode.

The chapters that follow delve into the wealth of evidence surrounding decentralization reforms in each of the five countries considered. The next chapter focuses on the experience of Colombia, a country that has experienced successive decentralization reforms that have left it one of the most effectively decentralized states in the region. The fact that decentralization has proceeded in stages there and the overall depth of decentralization that has resulted from these reforms make Colombia a rich source for clues to the causes of decentralization. In addition, the Colombian experience includes the one case not correctly sorted by the statistical model utilized in this chapter (Colombia, 1990–1994); it therefore provides an intriguing starting point for more in-depth analysis.

PART II

IN-DEPTH COUNTRY STUDIES

4

The Colombian Experience

[I]t was evident, if you looked at the political map, that the Liberal party was a definite majority in the country so it seemed logical that the Conservatives in highly conservative regions gave a lot of support to the idea of decentralizing power. It is interesting to note that even in large cities with Liberal majorities, there are Conservative mayors due to the factioning of the Liberal party there.

Interview with Humberto de la Calle, Ministro de Gobierno,[1] to César Gaviria (1990–1994)[2]

INTRODUCTION

Comparative studies of Latin American political economy often treat Colombia as an enigma or ignore it completely. In a region marked by political upheaval, Colombia plods quietly along without major military coups in the twentieth century, boasting a rather stable two-party system and the region's longest enduring constitution (1886–1991). In a region known for economic booms and busts, sharp fluctuations and hyperinflation, Colombia has generally enjoyed slow but steady growth and has long commanded an excellent credit rating for its debt repayment record. The country has been most often associated with its role in the illegal narcotics trade and the longest and largest guerrilla

---

[1] The government minister is a key position in government. This minister is the highest-ranking cabinet member and advises the president on all domestic matters.

[2] The interview was conducted in August 1997.

war on the continent, so studies of Colombia have often focused on the negative. Colombia's, major political problems are tempered with profound achievements, however. The fact that Colombia was one of the earliest countries in the region to adopt decentralization and one of the most diligent in extending it stands out as a true accomplishment. Decentralization was brought about through fundamental changes in Colombia's governing system in 1982 and 1991. Why would the nation with the region's most stable political system and most stable economy suddenly adopt profound changes in its structure?

This chapter demonstrates that decentralization in Colombia cannot be counted as yet another enigmatic aspect of Colombian political life. Instead, the adoption of decentralizing reform follows a political logic. In fact, the very stability of Colombia's major parties plays a key role in explaining the move toward greater decentralization there. As hypothesized in Chapter 2, decentralization should occur when the party in power believes it will control more resources under a decentralized system rather than under a centralized system. Colombia's experiences during its most recent period of electoral contestation supports this hypothesis, even though Colombia's 1990–1994 regime did not fit the predictions of the statistical model showcased in Chapter 3.

The main argument of this chapter is that decentralization occurred in Colombia when the party in a position to reorganize intragovernmental power saw its probability of gaining or retaining the presidency as weak. The first reform, which included the popular election of mayors and a substantial increase in central revenues to subnational levels, occurred when a Conservative president was elected due to a temporary split in the Liberal party. This represented the first Conservative victory in open elections in which both parties had fielded candidates since 1922. The second reform, which introduced the direct election of governors and increased fiscal transfers to regional and local governments, occurred when several small parties – most notably the M-19[3] (Democratic Alliance) – gained a strong voice in a constitutional assembly empowered to change the constitution without restriction. The goal of this chapter is twofold: to place these two episodes into the context of party competition and to explain the lack of similar

---

[3] The M-19 (or AD M-19) became a political party in 1990 when it laid down its weapons after years of guerrilla warfare against the state.

decentralizing reforms during the rest of this period. Applying the theory that support for decentralization follows an electoral logic is rather straightforward in the majority of the presidential administrations examined during this period. To examine the Constitutional Assembly in 1991, I apply the extension of the theory spelled out in Chapter 2 that looks at extra-presidential bodies invested with the power to alter power-sharing relations between levels of government.

This chapter opens with a brief history of party competition in Colombia, paying particular attention to historical shifts toward and away from federalism initiated by the parties. The chapter then turns to a focused examination of the variables outlined in Chapter 2 as good indicators of decentralization: the governing party's electoral strength at the national level and at subnational levels and factors that influence its rate for discounting future time periods. The chapter concludes with a more in-depth discussion of critical periods in Colombia's decentralizing reforms, exploring the debates that defined these periods.

A BRIEF HISTORY OF PARTY COMPETITION IN COLOMBIA

This discussion does more than just provide necessary context for the analysis that follows, it also illustrates that decentralization is not ideologically linked to either of Colombia's major parties. Furthermore, this discussion serves to justify the focus on parties – rather than on factions – in the electoral analysis to come.

Like most Latin American countries, Colombia's most recent experience with democracy is not its first; in fact, Colombia's two major parties – the Liberals and the Conservatives – can be traced back to the aftermath of the War of the Supremes, waged from 1839 to 1842. In fact, national versus regional power was at the center of this episode: It began when the region of Pasto rebelled against a congressional decision to repress its small monasteries. This regional skirmish escalated when José María Obando – an individual associated with Liberal factions in the government – gave his support to the regional movement, which sought a reorganization of the state along federal lines,

illustrating once again the particular appeal of federalism for factions out of power. Santander and his friends had dabbled in federalism in 1828, in opposition to Bolívar's dictatorship, but were quite content with the centralist Constitution of 1832 as long as they were in control of the government at

Bogotá. Now, following a change of administration, more and more of the Progresistas rediscovered the theoretical advantages of federalism. (Bushnell 1993: 91–92)

This quotation accentuates the fact that federalism was variously adopted and rejected by parties who were in and out of power throughout Colombian history. The "Progresistas" mentioned in the quotation were the forerunners to the Liberal party.

The Liberals and Conservatives were founded in a period of Conservative strength. After a series of Conservative presidencies, the Liberal José Hilario López came to power when the Conservatives split their votes between two candidates in 1849. During his term, the Liberals decentralized some power to local government; the constitution adopted in 1853 allowed for the popular election of provincial governors.[4]

This constitution was replaced just five years later by Conservative president Mariano Ospina Rodríguez. The new Constitution increased federalism:

[M]any of the leading Conservatives had now come to the support of federalism as a form of political organization – whether moved by theoretical arguments, by the successful example of federalism in the United States, or by the tactical consideration that under a federal system they could always expect to enjoy a solid control of at least those regions where they were strongest. If Liberal ideologues should regain power in Bogotá, Conservatives could still do in Antioquia, say, whatever they wanted. (Bushnell 1993: 115)

Five years later (1863), still another constitution under Liberal Tomás Cipriano de Mosquera pushed federalism to the extreme, changing the country's very name to the "United States of Colombia" (Estados Unidos de Colombia). This constitution cut the presidential term from four to two years and gave regional governments enormous powers.

The year 1880 saw the election of Doctor Rafael Nuñez and a return to centralism. Although officially a Liberal, he was a member of the non-traditional wing of the party: the Independents.[5] Conservative support figured importantly in his election and in his re-election in 1884

---

[4] Although it was a move toward decentralization, few authorities (and few resources) were actually devolved.

[5] In the 1850s Nuñez had been a staunch Liberal, but he was later accused of betrayal. Although he depended greatly on Conservative support in 1880, 1884, and 1885, he never joined the Conservative Party. Instead, he founded the National party, which he hoped would replace the Liberal-Conservative split. In 1894 the National party was subsumed into the Conservative party.

(he was legally barred from re-election in 1882). In 1885, the Radicals (the traditional core of the Liberal party) revolted against Nuñez, perhaps fearing his reformist agenda. This revolt was put down quickly, but not before Nuñez took the opportunity to suspend the old constitution. Nuñez took a giant step toward recentralizing power in the constitution of 1886. Written by a Conservative colleague, Miguel Antonio Caro, the new constitution gave the executive a near monopoly on power, investing this office with the power to appoint and remove departmental governors; these governors, in turn, could name local mayors. This centralist constitution remained in effect until 1991, making it the oldest constitution in the region when it was replaced.

As a quick summary, this section has noted four specific changes that shifted the balance of power between central and subnational levels. Federalism was increased in 1849 under a Liberal president; it was furthered under a Conservative president in 1858 and taken to an extreme under a Liberal president in 1863. Finally, Rafael Nuñez – elected a Liberal but accused of "turning Conservative" – recentralized power in 1886. It can be seen that instead of following strictly partisan lines, both Liberals and Conservatives took part in increasing federalism and centralism at different times. Identifying support for federalism with one party is too simple.

A second pattern worth noting is that the first change in 1849 followed an election won by the Liberal candidate due to a split in the Conservative Party. The subsequent 1858 reform occurred when Conservatives regained power after two Liberal presidencies and a period of interim presidents. The next change, in 1863, occurred during a period of non-elected rule by a Liberal after two Conservative victories. Finally, the last episode occurred during the presidency of a Liberal who had been challenged by his own party and whose retention of the presidency depended on Conservative support. Clearly, party dominance has followed a pendular pattern; internal splits in the ruling party mark the peak of each arc, shifting power back toward the opposition. As the next section illustrates, this pattern continues in more contemporary Colombian politics.

Unfortunately, shifts in power between parties were historically accompanied by violence;[6] fresh access to power was often abused to

---

[6] For an analysis linking Colombia's current violence to this early, interparty conflict, see Bergquist (2001).

settle the score with old rivals. The War of a Thousand Days (1899–1902) and the period know as "La Violencia" (1946–1958) are the most dramatic examples. These repeated violent encounters defined party distinctions in blood, not programmatic appeals. Commitment to party identity has been described by one scholar as the result of "hereditary hatred" (Dix 1987: 211).

To put an end to the carnage of La Violencia, the military intervened in 1953. General Rojas Pinilla orchestrated a coup supported by most Liberals and Conservatives alike. Despite this auspicious beginning, Rojas Pinilla's lack of a coherent political and economic strategy, his increasing turn to repression to staunch continuing violence in the countryside, and his evident hunger for a second term galvanized leaders of both traditional political parties to negotiate a pact. This "National Front" agreement simultaneously removed Rojas Pinilla from government and ended partisan rivalry for the foreseeable future. In brief, Liberals and Conservatives agreed to share power by rotating in the presidency and splitting legislative and subnational positions equally from 1958 to 1974.

The National Front period succeeded in establishing some order after La Violencia, and despite splits within each of the two parties, the majority of voters continued to support the arrangement throughout its tenure. With interparty competition highly constrained, competition between the well-established factions within parties flourished. As the National Front agreement approached its end, the two traditional parties began to coalesce, each around a single presidential candidate. The Conservative party, despite its extreme division in the 1970 election,

[i]n September of 1973 . . . held one of their most united conventions since 1949. . . . 635 delegates on 4 September unanimously proclaimed [Alvaro] Gómez [Hurtado] the party candidate. This had been preceded by the withdrawals of Betancur, Jaramillo Ocampo, and J. Emilio Valderrama in the face of domination by party traditionalists. (Martz 1997: 154)

Similarly, the Liberals sought to unite behind a single candidate but found the process more rocky. Three different individuals sought the candidacy: López Michelsen, Julio César Turbay Ayala, and Carlos Lleras Restrepo. In the end,

a tacit understanding between López and Turbay led to the nomination of the former. The son of former president Alfonso López Pumarejo received 162 votes to 88 for Lleras Restrepo. With López Michelsen the candidate, Turbay was named the new Liberal *jefe único*. (Martz 1997: 55)

In elections that represented a remarkable increase in voter turnout, López Michelsen won the 1974 presidential elections with 56.2 percent of the vote, against 31.4 percent for Alvaro Gómez.

The party system in Colombia is made complex by intra-party rivalry, but the competition between party lists has not obliterated the usefulness of the larger party identity. This is particularly true in presidential contests. While party factions compete vigorously for legislative seats, only in the most extreme cases do they put forth more than one presidential candidate.[7] Because the factions within both parties have more in common with one another than with the opposing party, splitting their votes between two or more candidates provides the opposition (if it remains unified) a chance to gain power:

While occasionally driven to the point of violent conflict, neither of the parties could afford to remain sectarian. Faced with the need to win elections, partisans grudgingly put aside extremist positions and yielded to the necessity of seeking votes from those less passionately committed to the same cause. Each party contained a militant core, violently opposed to the suzerainty of the other; but, driven by the necessity of seeking electoral majorities, each also accommodated more moderate factions. (Dix 1987: 182)

My argument that parties are the primary actors in this model should not be interpreted as a claim that they are the only important actors; factions also play a role. The evidence that factions and party identities coexist, with unified party support for presidential candidates and separate lists for factions, suggests a ranking of party identity above faction identity. Within parties, the effects of decentralization continue to vary across factions, with some gaining (or losing) more than others do. When Conservatives are weak nationally (but strong at subnational levels), their party stands to gain more from decentralization than the nationally strong Liberals do. Within the Liberal party, factions that exercise less control over naming the Liberal presidential candidate (and heads of subnational governments) stand to lose less from decentralization than other factions.

---

[7] For an excellent summary of party divisions and their electoral effects, see Delgado (1986).

Throughout its political history, Colombia has been divided by strong partisan divisions that have often been expressed through violence. The National Front period attempted to ease some of these tensions by greatly restricting the arena of political competition for a set period of time; while partisan violence declined during this period, intra-party competition between factions increased apace. With the end of the agreement in 1974, parties began to coalesce around single candidates in executive elections, while party lists continued to proliferate in legislative contests. In what follows, I explore the electoral fortunes of Colombia's major parties, linking patterns of national and subnational electoral support to partisan support for decentralizing reform.

ELECTORAL FACTORS AND DECENTRALIZATION IN COLOMBIA

Unlike the other countries considered in this volume, the appropriate starting point for analyzing the Colombian case is not obvious. In Ecuador, Peru, Venezuela, and Bolivia, dictatorships transfer power to democratically elected governments at particular times. In Colombia, elections begin to determine who holds office in 1958, but institutionalized restrictions keep the system from being fully competitive. I use 1974, the end of the National Front period, as the starting point for this study.[8]

Since the end of the formal National Front agreement, the Liberal party has dominated the presidency. The first national elections of this era, the 1974 presidential elections, were won decisively by Alfonso López Michelsen; in 1978 Julio César Turbay Ayala clinched the second Liberal victory. In 1982, the pattern changed when Belisario Betancur won the presidency for the Conservative party. This victory owed primarily to a split within the Liberal party, which divided its votes between two candidates: Alfonso López Michelsen and Luis Carlos Galán. Having recuperated from the earlier division, the Liberals fielded a single candidate in 1986 and Virgilio Barco won with

---

[8] Those familiar with the Colombian case will point out that, although both parties openly contested elections after this date, vestiges of the National Front arrangement continued. It was not until the Barco presidency (1986–1990), for example, that the ruling party ceased to share the division of most appointed government positions with a significant number from the opposition party (Cepeda Ulloa 1996).

a comfortable margin. The Liberals succeeded again in 1990 with the total Liberal vote twice that of the Conservative total; Daniel Samper Pisano clinched another Liberal victory in 1994. A Conservative president, Andres Pastrana, came to office in the 1998 elections, although the Liberals won the plurality of votes in the first round.[9]

This section carefully explores the incentives each of these administrations faced to decentralize. The discussion of these incentives must explain not only why decentralization occurred during the Betancur and Gaviria presidencies, but also why it did not occur during the presidencies of López Michelsen, Turbay, Barco, or Samper. This section is divided into subsections focused on each of the variables expected to determine a party's support for decentralization: its national strength, subnational strength, and the change in its support over time.

National Strength and Vote Change

Presidential and legislative election results are the obvious place to begin an assessment of party strength at the national level (see Table 4.1). Looking at party support over time for obvious trends, the Liberals appear stronger than Conservatives do at the national level, whether including or excluding National Popular Alliance (Alianza Nacional Popular, ANAPO) lists.[10] During the National Front period, only Liberal and Conservative parties could field candidates, so candidates of the fledgling ANAPO party (supporters of former president General Rojas Pinilla) ran lists of candidates on traditional party lists. Support for the Liberal party in the presidency seems consistently strong from 1974 to 1998, despite the split candidacy in 1982. Legislative votes corroborate this tendency.

Another way to measure the relative support for each party at the national level is to look at the margin of victory between the two parties in each legislative election. Table 4.2 presents this evidence. In all cases but one (the Senate election in 1970), Liberals beat the Conservatives by a healthy margin. If ANAPO votes are not

---

[9] Colombia moved to a two-round balloting process for the presidency in the 1994 presidential elections.

[10] ANAPO was founded in 1971 by supporters of General Rojas Pinilla, who had been overthrown as part of the National Front agreement.

TABLE 4.1: *National-Level Voting Data for the Liberals and Conservatives, 1962–1998 (figures are percentage of the vote for each party)*

Year	Presidency Liberals	Conservatives	Senate Liberals	Conservatives	Chamber Liberals	Conservatives
1962	National Front		54.5	45.4	54.5	45.5
				(41.7)		(41.7)
1964	National Front		51.2	48.4	52.4	47.2
			(50.5)	(35.5)	(50.5)	(35.6)
1966	National Front		52.4	47.2	55.5	44.2
			(52.1)	(31.0)	(52.0)	(29.8)
1968	National Front		53.2	46.5	52.9	46.8
			(49.9)	(33.7)	(50.0)	(33.0)
1970	National Front		46.6	53.0	51.1	48.5
			(37.0)	(27.0)	(37.0)	(27.2)
1974	56.2	31.4	55.6	31.9	55.6	32.0
1978	49.5	46.6	55.2	39.7	55.2	39.5
1982	41.0	46.8	56.6	40.5	56.4	40.3
	10.9[a]					
1986	58.4	35.8	49.3	37.1	47.7	37.0
1990	47.8	23.7	58.5	31.2	59.1	31.3
		12.1[a]				
1994–1	45.3	45.0	52.8	27.4	52.8	26.4
1994–2	50.6	48.5				
1998–1	34.6	34.3	47.3	22.5	49.4	23.6
1998–2	46.5	50.4				

Note: Parentheses enclose the vote totals for Liberal and Conservative candidates, excluding ANAPO lists running under Liberal and Conservative labels. Beginning in 1974, ANAPO candidates were no longer forced to run on these lists. Data compiled from RNE 1970, 1975, 1989; Base de Datos Políticos de las Américas 1999a, 1999b, 1999c, 1999d, 1999e.
[a] The vote was split for the party between two candidates.

included, the margins of victory for the Liberal party are even larger and always positive. Judged by this measure, the Liberal party appears generally stronger than the Conservative party at the national level.

National electoral results can also be used to shed light on the parties' expectations of future electoral viability. Here I explore changes in national vote shares over time to get a sense of how parties viewed the stability of their support bases, as this influences the length of their time horizons. Table 4.3 summarizes the change in the percentage of the vote captured by each party from election to

TABLE 4.2: *Margin of Victory in the Legislature (Liberal vote (%) − Conservative vote (%))*

Year	Senate	Chamber
1962	9.1 (12.8)	9.1 (12.8)
1964	2.8 (15.0)	5.2 (14.9)
1966	5.2 (21.1)	11.3 (22.2)
1968	6.7 (16.2)	6.1 (17.0)
1970	−6.4 (10.0)	2.6 (9.8)
1974	23.7	23.6
1978	15.5	15.7
1982	16.1	16.1
1986	12.3	10.7
1990	27.3	27.8
1994	25.4	26.4
1998	24.8	25.8

Note: The margin not including ANAPO votes is in parentheses until the end of the National Front agreement.

TABLE 4.3: *Changes in Parties' Vote Share from one Election to the Next, 1962–1998 (figures represent percentage points; + or − indicates direction)*

	Senate		Chamber	
Time Period	Liberals	Conservatives	Liberals	Conservatives
1962–1964	−3.3	+3.0	−2.1	+1.8
	(−4.0)	(−6.2)	(−4.0)	(−6.1)
1964–1966	+1.2	−1.2	+3.1	−3.0
	(+1.6)	(−4.5)	(+1.5)	(−5.8)
1966–1968	+0.8	−0.7	−2.6	+2.6
	(−2.2)	(+2.7)	(−2.0)	(+3.2)
1968–1970	−6.6	+6.5	−1.8	+1.7
	(−12.9)	(−6.7)	(−13.0)	(−5.8)
1970–1974	+9.0	−21.1	+4.5	−16.5
	(+18.6)	(+4.9)	(+18.6)	(+4.8)
1974–1978	−0.4	+7.8	−0.4	+7.5
1978–1982	+1.4	+0.8	+1.2	+0.8
1982–1986	−7.3	−3.5	−8.7	−3.3
1986–1990	+9.2	−5.8	+11.4	−5.7
1990–1994	−5.7	−3.8	−6.3	−4.9
1994–1998	−5.5	−4.9	−3.4	−2.8

Note: ANAPO exclusive numbers are shown in parentheses. After 1974, ANAPO could run its own lists, eliminating the need for parentheses.

election for both chambers of the legislature from 1962–1964 through 1994–1998.[11] This table reinforces the fairly stable pattern of support for the two parties. The two elections that signaled the end of the National Front, 1968–1970 and 1970–1974, are exceptions to this generally stable pattern. In this period, the increased variation reflects the departure of ANAPO first from the lists of the two main parties and then from the political scene. Between 1978 and 1982 vote totals remain remarkably stable. This may seem surprising since the 1982 election produced the change from a Liberal to a Conservative president. Since two Liberals ran for president, thus splitting the presidential vote, the legislative data provide a means of measuring the change in support for the two parties more generally. It appears that support for Liberals and Conservatives remained very steady, despite the division in the presidential race. Although Conservatives enjoyed a presidential victory, support for the Conservative party does not appear to have changed.

In their analysis of party system stability, Mainwaring and Scully (1995) focus on stability across elections over time. To imitate this broader measure, I summed the absolute value of the vote change between each legislative election and divided by the total number of elections. This yields an average vote change of 4.9 percentage points for the Liberals in the Senate in the six elections from 1974 to 1998; 4.4 for the Conservatives in the Senate; 5.2 for the Liberals in the Chamber; and 4.2 for the Conservatives in the Chamber. These figures indicate a fairly low level of vote change for each party across time. In the Mainwaring and Scully treatment of party system volatility, Colombia ranked as the system with the lowest average party volatility (compared with eleven other Latin American countries), with approximately eight percentage points of change over the five elections occurring between 1970 and 1990. Given the high degree of national vote predictability,

---

[11] This measure demonstrates not only the level of the change, but also its direction. A vote change level of 4 percent over three consecutive elections could mean that a party lost, gained, and then lost again 4 percent of the electorate, leaving it with 4 percent less of the vote in the final election considered relative to the first election; alternatively, the party could have lost 4 percent of the vote over three consecutive elections, leaving it with a total loss of twelve percentage points relative to the first election considered.

parties can make fairly good predictions of their future vote shares at the national level.

The national level electoral data describe a system in which party support is fairly stable across elections for each party and in which the Liberals are consistently stronger than the Conservatives. Given their strong and steady domination of presidential elections, Colombia's Liberal administrations faced no real electoral incentive to decentralize in the post–National Front period. No evidence suggests waning support for the Liberals, giving them few reasons to doubt the continuation of their support between elections. Similarly, the Conservatives in 1982 had little reason to expect a great swell of support in future elections; their victory had not been caused by Liberals switching parties, and no sign of such a mass defection arose during Betancur's presidency. The next section briefly discusses the relative strength of the two parties at the regional level.

Regional Strength

The purpose of measuring the regional-level strength of parties is to predict how they would fare if power were decentralized to regional governments. The ideal measure should approximate actual voting for a regional executive. If parties were attempting to judge their regional electoral strength before governors were freely elected (which did not occur until after the adoption of the 1991 constitution), they could look either at national-level election results by region (i.e., percentage vote for the Conservative presidential candidate versus percentage vote for the Liberal presidential candidate in Antioquia) or at regional-level elections for departmental assemblies. I use the latter.

Even though regional governors were appointed by the executive prior to the 1990s, elections for regional assemblies took place at two-year intervals. Table 4.4 simplifies the results of regional assembly elections by state from 1962 to 1990. This table results from comparing the vote totals in each department for each party. Where Liberal votes outnumber Conservative votes, an "L" appears in the appropriate box; a "C" denotes a Conservative majority. The final row tabulates the number of regions each party might expect to win in departmental elections for governors.

In-Depth Country Studies

TABLE 4.4: *Regional Assembly Results, by Majority Party*

Region	1970	1972	1974	1978	1980	1982	1984	1986	1988	1990
Antioquia	C	L	L	L	L	L	L	C	L	L
Atlántico	L	L	L	L	L	L	L	L	L	L
Bolívar	L	L	L	L	L	L	L	L	L	L
Boyaca	C	L	C	C	C	C	C	C	C	L
Caldas	C	C	C	C	C	C	C	C	C	L
Caqueta						L	L	L	L	L
Cauca	L	L	L	L	L	L	L	L	L	L
César	L	L	L	L	L	L	L	L	L	L
Córdoba	C	L	L	L	L	L	L	L	L	L
Cundinamarca	L	L	L	L	L	L	L	L	L	L
Chocó	L	L	L	L	L	L	L	L	L	L
Huila	C	L	L	C	L	L	C	C	C	L
La Guajira	L	C	L	C	L	L	L	L	L	L
Magdalena	L	L	L	L	L	L	L	L	L	L
Meta	C	L	L	L	L	L	L	L	L	L
Nariño	C	L	C	L	L	C	L	L	L	L
N. de Santander	C	C	C	C	C	C	C	L	L	L
Quindió	L	L	L	L	L	L	L	L	L	L
Risaralda	C	L	L	L	L	L	L	L	L	L
Santander	L	L	L	L	L	L	L	L	L	L
Sucre	L	L	L	L	L	L	L	L	L	L
Tolima	L	L	L	L	L	L	L	L	L	L
Valle de Cauca	C	L	L	L	L	L	L	L	L	L
Totals	22	22	22	22	22	23	23	23	23	23
Liberals	12	19	18	17	19	19	19	19	20	23
Conservatives	10	3	4	5	3	4	4	4	3	0

Table 4.4 makes two points very clearly. First, the majority party in each region is fairly stable across elections. Second, the Liberal party enjoys a majority in nearly all regions. This Liberal hegemony at the regional level actually becomes stronger over time. Liberal support at the regional level mirrors its strength and stability at the national level. Since the popular election of governors began in 1990, Liberals have won 67 percent of the gubernatorial positions in 1991, 69 percent in 1994, and 61 percent in 1997; Conservatives have won 11 percent in 1991, 22 percent in 1994, and 9.7 percent in 1997.[12]

[12] These figures come from Dávila and Corredor 1998: 113.

TABLE 4.5: *Percentage of Municipalities Won by Each Party in Municipal Council Elections*

Election Year	Liberals (%)	Conservatives (%)
1972	54.75	37.16
1974	57.64	41.48
1978	56.42	43.69
1980	57.60	41.11
1982	57.42	42.37
1984	56.06	43.43
1986	53.85	44.62

Local Strength

As with the regional-level measure, the ideal measure of local electoral strength should approximate the preferences of voters for local officials. Although mayors were appointed, not elected, before 1988, data on municipal council elections are available for the period 1972–1986 (mayors were directly elected beginning in 1988). Table 4.5 presents the percentage of municipalities in which each party won a plurality of the municipal council votes in each local election.

These data reinforce the conclusion reached by Patricia Pinzón in her remarkable work on the stability of local level elections (see Pinzón de Lewin 1989). Liberals win a majority of the votes in more than half of the municipal council elections in the country, but Conservatives win a majority in a respectable percentage of the municipalities. Looking at individual municipalities over time, she also concludes that party loyalty within municipal districts is strong over time – for the most part the municipalities that elect Conservatives in one election are likely to continue to elect Conservative candidates. Osterling (1989) concurs on this point:

The majority of Colombia's municipalities, regardless of such issues as political campaigns, ideological statements, the performance of the incumbent President or congressmen, or historical events, traditionally have cast their votes to the same political party. Therefore, it can be said that Colombia has a large number of clearly defined Liberal and Social Conservative municipalities. (Osterling 1989: 159)

If mayoral elections followed the trajectory of municipal council elections, Conservatives appear poised to win at least 40 percent of local mayor positions. In reality, Conservatives won mayoral contests in 32 percent of municipalities in the 1988 elections, 29 percent in 1990, and 26 percent in 1992, compared with the Liberals, who won 46 percent, 57 percent, and 39 percent, respectively (Gaitán Pavía and Moreno Ospina 1992: 144). Using data from the official electoral institutions of Colombia (Registraduría Nacional del Estado Civil, RNE), which grouped candidates from "movements associated with the Liberals" and "movements associated with the Conservatives" due to the proliferation of splinter parties from these main parties (Gaitán Pavía and Moreno Ospina count only candidates who claim the Liberal and Conservative labels, thus undercounting these splinter groups), Conservatives won approximately 41 percent of the mayoral positions in 1994 and 29 percent in 1997, while Liberals won 49 percent and 38 percent, respectively. Using official numbers from the RNE for those running on Liberal and Conservative labels only for 2000, Liberal mayors prevailed in 38 percent of municipal elections, while Conservatives prevailed in 25 percent.[13]

Summary

Table 4.6 summarizes party strength at each level of government – national, regional, and local – from the information discussed in more detail above. This table underlines two important aspects of party support in Colombia during this period: its stability over time and the differences in party support by level of government. While consistently receiving strong representation in the legislature, the Conservative party rarely captures the presidency. In 1982, when a Conservative candidate does win the presidency, the Conservatives fail to win a legislative majority. The Conservative presidential victory cannot be tied to an upsurge in support for the party; rather, it depended critically on the split within the Liberal party. In addition, there is no evidence of growing support for the Conservatives during the Betancur administration

---

[13] Slightly different numbers are reported in Dávila and Corredor 1998: 114: Liberals won 45.4% in 1988, 56.1% in 1990, 40.5% in 1992, 51.1% in 1994, and 44.8% in 1997; Conservatives won 41.3% in 1988, 38.8% in 1990, 27.2% in 1992, 36.8% in 1994, and 27.9% in 1997.

TABLE 4.6: *Summary of Elections at all Levels*

	National		Regional		Local	
Year	Liberals	Conservatives	Liberals	Conservatives	Liberals	Conservatives
1972			86.4	13.6	54.8	37.2
1974	56.2	31.4	81.8	18.2	57.6	41.5
1978	49.5	46.6	77.3	22.7	56.4	44.0
1980			86.4	13.6	57.6	41.1
1982	41.0	46.8	82.6	17.4	57.4	42.4
1984			82.6	17.4	56.1	43.4
1986	58.4	35.8	82.6	17.4	53.9	44.6
1988			87.0	13.0	44.7^a	41.9^a
1990	49.9	24.7	100.0	0.0	52.9^a	36.9^a
1992			66.7^b	11.1^b	39.0^a	26.0^a
1994	50.6^c	48.5^c	68.8	21.9	48.7^a	40.7^a
1998	46.5^c	50.4^c	61.3^d	9.7^d	38.4^{a,d}	29.3^{a,d}
2000					37.9^a	24.9^a

Note: Figures in the National column are percentage of vote for each party. Figures in the regional and local columns are percentage of total regions or localities in which each party won a plurality of the vote.
^{a} Local elections in 1988 and later are percentages of municipalities in which each party won a majority of local voting.
^{b} Regional results for 1992 represent results from 1991 gubernatorial elections.
^{c} These are presidential election results from the second round of balloting.
^{d} Local and regional results for 1998 represent results from 1997 municipal and regional elections.

that might raise the party's expectations for a second term. Regional and local victories at midterm appear almost frozen at 1982 levels. In the final period of his presidency, Betancur encountered serious criticism for his handling of several domestic policies, which dampened any optimistic predictions for Conservative votes in 1986.

A note about interpreting the results is in order: Taking the year 1982, it appears that national-level support (in terms of percentage of the vote in the legislature) for the Conservative party is roughly equal to the percentage of municipalities that it could win if mayors were popularly elected – so why the desire to decentralize? Be sure to keep in mind that the percentage vote for national offices does not translate directly into the probability of winning the presidency. If, for example, the Conservatives were assured of receiving 40 percent of the national-level votes in a presidential election, this would not translate into a 40 percent chance of winning the election; instead, the probability of winning the presidency increases at an increasing rate as national-level support approaches 50 percent (as long as two parties continue to dominate national elections).[14] In the case of local elections, the 40 percent figure corresponds to winning a majority in 40 percent of the actual local elections. A party expecting 40 percent of the presidential votes in a national election with only two major parties knows that it has *no* probability of winning the presidency, regardless of the 40 percent of the vote it captures.

This section has examined Colombian election data, exploring their fit with the theory that decentralization occurs when parties with weak national-level support and strong subnational support gain the executive, view their tenure there as short, and expect their levels of support at each level of government to be fairly stable into the future. In the case of Colombia, Liberal presidents after the National Front period do not decentralize, and the first Conservative president to be popularly elected (in a contest in which both Liberal and Conservative parties fielded candidates) in sixty-four years decentralizes both fiscal and electoral power to the local level. This decentralizing measure – legislating the popular election of mayors – was the first constitutional reform in eighteen years to survive Supreme Court review (Van Cott 2000: 50). Liberals do not decentralize in this period because they have a strong chance of retaining power at the national level and therefore no electoral incentive to allow their rivals to compete for positions at regional and local levels. The Conservatives, coming to power during a temporary split in the Liberal party and with strong support at the municipal level (but not at the departmental level) decentralize to the local level. Given the fact that Liberals also enjoyed strong pockets of support at the municipal level, they had only weak incentives to block the change. What is more, strong public support for the change made opposition to decentralization politically difficult. In fact, some sections of the Liberal party actively supported this change – a theme that is elaborated below in this chapter.

---

[14] In the 1998 national elections, Colombia adopted a two-round voting system. If no candidate wins a majority of the votes in the first round, the top two candidates compete in a second round of voting. This new institutional configuration changes party incentives.

CONSTITUTIONAL ASSEMBLY

The next episode of decentralization occurred under a Liberal president, in 1991. Among the many innovations affecting decentralization, governors were to be popularly elected and given new resources and responsibilities; the term of office for mayors was extended from two to three years; and the formula governing the automatic transfers of fiscal resources to regional and local governments was re-engineered.[15] These changes occurred not due to presidential initiative but within the working of a constitutional assembly elected in 1990.

While the events of 1991 cannot be analyzed under the exact model of executive initiative outlined in the first chapter, a simple extension of the formal model outlined in Chapter 2 provides a framework for understanding the assembly. Extending the electoral logic beyond the incentives of the president's party, it is possible to consider the incentives faced by each party represented in the assembly, keeping in mind the relative weight of each party's delegation. If the assembly is largely composed of parties with strong electoral incentives to decentralize, then decentralization appears a likely policy outcome. The statistical model in Chapter 3, because it requires comparable data across cases, did not take advantage of this extension. Using data that reflected only on the president's support, the statistical model failed to classify correctly the Colombian administration of 1990–1994 as pro-decentralization. This in-depth analysis is able to use the rich data at hand to understand better the political dynamics that led to increased decentralization in Colombia in 1991.

The initial call for a constitutional assembly[16] received hearty support from the newly elected Liberal president, César Gaviria. At the beginning, the administration wished to confine the assembly's purview to a restricted set of topics – allowing only a selective revision of the

---

[15] See Angell et al. 2001 and Dugas 1993 for a more thorough discussion of decentralizing reforms resulting from the 1991 Constitutional Assembly.

[16] The initiative behind the Constitutional Assembly began with a student movement that encouraged voters to take part in an unofficial plebiscite to call for such a body. When more than one million voters included a note voicing their support of this measure in the ballot envelopes in the legislative elections of March 1990, momentum began to turn in favor of constitutional revision. In an official plebiscite on convoking a constitutional assembly that coincided with the 1990 presidential elections, more than 88 percent of the vote was counted in favor of the measure. For more information, see Buenahora Febres-Cordero 1991 and Nielson and Shugart 1999.

constitution. It was the decision of the Supreme Court – and not of the executive – that any constitutional assembly must have full freedom to decide what to amend and how to amend it.[17] A Conservative member of the Supreme Court, Dr. Hernando Gómez Otálora, cast the decisive vote in favor of the assembly, on the condition that its mandate remained unrestricted.[18]

The assembly itself was composed of many non-traditional political actors: representatives of indigenous groups, feminists, and independents, along with the traditional parties. This diversity owes quite a bit to the electoral rules under which representatives were chosen – with candidate lists competing in a national district instead of the more common district-by-district voting that tends to favor the largest parties. The most surprising result is that the M-19, a formerly violent guerrilla group that had recently negotiated its entry into the political system, gained nineteen seats in the assembly, making it the body's second largest bloc. It is striking that the same movement that attacked the Supreme Court and held its magistrates hostage just six years earlier (provoking an extremely harsh reaction from the Colombian military that left most of the insurgents and Justices dead) was now in a position to rewrite the country's constitution. Of the Constitutional Assembly's 70 members, 24 were Liberals, 19 were from the M-19, 11 were members of the Movement for National Salvation (one wing of the Conservative party), and nine identified themselves as Social Conservatives (the other wing of the Conservative party). The remaining members eschewed traditional party labels.

The traditionally dominant Liberals clearly lacked a majority in the assembly. A look at disaggregated vote totals (Registraduría Nacional del Estado Civil 1991) demonstrates their weak showing at the subnational level as well as at the national level. In none of the twenty-three departments did the Liberals (or the Conservatives) win a plurality of the votes. This also held true in the four *intendencias* and five *comisarias*.[19] Results were not available at the municipal level, but vote totals

---

[17] For a good discussion of the Court's role in establishing the Constitutional Assembly and also for a good discussion of party strategies in the assembly elections, see Buenahora Febres-Cordero 1991.

[18] Interview with Dr. José Gregorio Hernández, the assistant to the Conservative Justice in question.

[19] These are subnational designations of territories without the status of departments.

were reported for thirty-eight major cities. Of these, Liberals won a plurality of votes only in Barrancabermeja. In no other municipality listed did either of the major, traditional parties surpass the votes for "other parties."[20]

The individual lists of candidates that won the largest percentages of votes were headed by (in descending order): Antonio Navarro Wolff of the M-19 with 27 percent, Alvaro Gómez Hurtado of the Movement for National Salvation (MSN) with 15 percent, Misael Pastrana Borrero of the Social Conservative party (PSC) with 6.4 percent, and Horacio Serpa Uribe – the top Liberal list – with 3.7 percent (RNE 1991). The strong showing of non-Liberal lists at both the national and subnational level augured well for greater decentralization.

Not only was the Constitutional Assembly composed of several non-traditional political actors, but the specific committee charged with debating territorial issues such as decentralization was led by independents and influenced by the participation of formerly armed groups seeking new footholds of power within the state. Within the assembly, several committees were established to concentrate on specific issues. The second of these, focused on territorial issues including regional and local autonomy, was headed by an Independent Conservative president and a vice president elected as an indigenous representative. In addition to several Liberals, the committee also included two members representing the AD M-19, one member of the MSN, and a partisan of the Quintín Lame (a former terrorist group focused on indigenous issues).[21] The composition of the assembly, heavily weighted toward

---

[20] While this clearly reflects the electorate's strong support for nontraditional parties in the rewriting of the constitution, Buenahora Febres-Cordero 1991 also argues that the poor showing of the Liberals had less to do with disenchantment than with their lack of a strong, central leadership during the campaign. While other parties gained strength from party lists with a strong, nationally recognized leader, at the front of the party (Antonio Navarro Wolf for the AD-M19, Alvaro Gómez Hurtado for the MSN, and ex-president Misael Pastrana Borrero for the PSC) several of the most prominent Liberals chose not to run, leaving a leadership gap in the national voting for the Constituent Assembly seats. Three Liberal ex-presidents – Turbay Ayala, López Michelsen, and Lleras Restrepo – declined to run, as did such nationally recognized figures as Ernesto Samper Pisano (who later became president in 1994) and Hernando Durán Dussán.

[21] See Dugas 1993: 60 for a complete listing of the committee members for each of the five committees within the Constitutional Assembly and their political affiliations.

parties with little hope of unseating Liberal dominance at the national level, seemed well suited to create a more decentralized governmental structure.

These last few sections have provided a rough skeleton of inter-party competition during the post–National Front period but a more detailed discussion is necessary to flesh out the debates surrounding decentralization during these years. In particular, the focus purely on electoral contests obscures evidence that the Liberal party fought for greater decentralization during this period. Does this fly in the face of the evidence so far provided? I focus on three issues in the remainder of this section: decentralization efforts of Liberals before Betancur's presidency, a brief look at the debate over decentralization during the Betancur presidency, and a more detailed treatment of the 1991 Constitutional Assembly.

The Liberal party has long been associated with the idea of decentralization. Within the Liberal party, the modern figure most responsible for this association is Alfonso López Michelsen. López Michelsen founded the Revolutionary Liberal Movement (Movimiento Revolucionario Liberal, MRL) within the Liberal party during the National Front period. His outspoken opposition to the National Front agreement rested on the grounds that it denied Liberals their right to the majority of legislative seats and presidential power justified by their numerical superiority in the population.[22] The MRL contested elections throughout the National Front and finally coalesced with the traditional wing of the party toward the end of that period.

The historical instance most often offered as evidence that the Liberals did indeed champion decentralization in the 1970s and 1980s is López Michelsen's attempt to create a constitutional assembly to push through decentralizing reforms during his presidency (1974–1978). This same example, however, illustrates the limited nature of the Liberal plan for decentralization. During López Michelsen's presidency, the legislature passed the Legislative Act Number 2 of 1977. This act would have created a constitutional assembly to consider decentralization, but the Supreme Court declared it unconstitutional

---

[22] See his comments on the National Front agreement written in August 1958, collected in Ardila Duarte, and Suárez de la Cruz 1985.

in May of 1978. In the meantime, much work had been done toward the constitutional project. Looking through a copy of the report from the special commission established to study the structure and administration of subnational governments,[23] one clearly sees that this decentralization project did not include the popular election of mayors and governors. Instead, the plan sought to increase the responsibilities, discretion, and resources of regional decision makers. Mayors and governors would still be appointed under this plan, but they would be given more responsibilities and resources.

In essence, the López proposal sought the strengthening of national planning and control as far as the reorganization of territory was concerned. For this, it proposed more discretion for the central government in the management of public spending, liberating the state from the pressures of mobilized civil society and civic strikes that obligated it to direct resources to immediate objectives that had not been budgeted. In addition, the proposal did not contemplate any kind of mechanism to distribute state resources or for the participation of communities in the management of the state, as one might have expected from a reform that was explicitly presented as an escape from the growth of popular protests. (Gaitán Pavía and Moreno Ospina 1992: 190)

This fits well with López Michelsen's own thoughts about the balance of national and subnational power during this period. On this issue, López Michelsen addressed the town of Líbano, Tolima, in 1975, saying:

I have never been a partisan of returning to a system that proposes democratization of the political class, such as subjecting all governors and mayors to a popular vote. We have already tried this experiment and it brought us to anarchy. (Ardila Duarte and Suárez de la Cruz 1985: 484)

Although the Liberals favored some forms of devolution, it was the Conservatives who pushed for the popular election of subnational officials. Conservative Alvaro Gómez Hurtado first introduced to the legislature a constitutional amendment to effect the popular election of mayors in 1980.[24] Explaining the motivation for the law, its co-sponsors stated:

It is not good for Colombia, neither for its presidential regime, nor for a modern conception of a free society, that the fate of the country is decided by the choice of one single man during the usual, fleeting electoral season. The popular

---

[23] Also in ibid.
[24] Project for Legislative Act no. 7, 1980.

election of mayors permits a moderated distribution of political power and establishes inviolable links of administrative solidarity between the elected and the conglomeration that he should serve. (Isaza Henao and Marín Vanegas 1980: 235)

Ronald Archer notes, "This reform fell apart... in the following year and was shelved due, principally, to the opposition of the Liberal Party" (Archer 1987: 161). It was not until the Conservatives gained power in 1982 that a real move toward political decentralization succeeded.

Once Betancur came to power, his proposed plan for political and economic reform sparked intense debate throughout society, but especially in the legislature. During his campaign, Betancur placed decentralization high on his list of priorities. In a speech accepting the endorsement of the Conservative members of the legislature on October 28, 1981, Betancur focused on four issues: regenerating morality and the family, the popular election of mayors and governors, "work, work, work," and peace (Betancur 1981). Explaining his motivations for supporting greater decentralization in the book *Sí Se Puede* ("Yes, You Can"), Betancur wrote:

The truth is that the citizenry of each town or city can choose better than anybody people who are knowledgeable of their problems and can solve them: this democratic possibility will not be conceded, at least not while the status quo, which has nearly a century of existence, remains. What is the reason for the existence of this status quo? It is the inheritance of fear. In the previous century, the governors of the federal states challenged the central government, sometimes with weapons; and there is fear that this will occur again. Because of this, they accede to the system of naming governors and mayors from the far distant central government, in a repeated act of paternalism, of overprotection, that, in the end, signifies a lack of confidence in the capacity of the people to decide. (Betancur 1982: 108–109)

Once in office, Betancur pushed for decentralizing measures in the legislature. According to one source, the parties divided over the popular election of mayors, with each current supporting it to a greater or lesser degree:

In the most turbulent part of the legislative debate over this proposal, political forces have divided into many currents and these are maintained today. The New Liberalism, sympathetic to the project, would like to see it complemented by a reform of departmental and municipal administration. Conservatives have divided into three strands: followers of Pastrana [Pastranismo], partial to the project but insistent that it be put into practice in 1986, followers of Alvaro Gómez Hurtado [Alvaristas] who want an immediate introduction of the measure, and followers of Ospina [Ospinistas] who oppose the measure. The official Liberal line, although fraught with dissidents, also seems to support the measure and the sectors of the Left that are represented in the legislature also appear to be supportive. (Santamaria Salamanca 1985: 23)

The most traditional factions of both parties were the most reticent to accept a change in the ability of winning parties to control appointments at regional and local levels. This is because, even after the National Front's official end, the practice of including politicians from the opposition in key appointments continued until the Barco presidency in 1986 (by which time the direct election of mayors had been passed into law). Due to this custom, traditional sectors of both parties faced a loss of influence under political decentralization, while factions of both parties that held less control over appointments were more amenable to the change. Thus it took a Conservative president to place this issue on the bargaining table, but it clearly engendered a coalition of support among the less traditionally powerful wings of both parties. Colombian scholars and the recollections of policy makers who took part in the reform process bear this out:

The municipal reform of 1986 was considered one of the most important reforms – if not the most important reform – since the promulgation of the 1886 Constitution.... For this reason, it encountered an atmosphere of resistance within the country's most traditional political sectors. If you look, for example, at the results of the Senate vote over the first legislative act of 1986 (which codified the popular election of mayors), it is clear that the ten votes against the law can be attributed to the most traditional representatives of the Liberals and Conservatives who were notable for being regional bosses dependent upon clientelism and with great influence over their respective departments. (Velásquez 1995: 260)

This observation was further reinforced by my interview with Horacio Serpa, who served as one of Betancur's *ministros de gobierno*. His recollection confirms that voting on this issue roughly followed a generation line, with young members of both parties supporting a reform that would give the newer wings of each party a larger stake in subnational power. The most traditional factions – those that would exercise the most power over appointments – were least supportive of the measure.

> Within the traditional parties, there were many politicians who believed we had to break the monopoly on power of the traditional parties. I am Liberal, but I have been a very unorthodox Liberal. . . . We had to break the centralism that existed in which the president named the *ministro de gobierno* who then named the governors of the departments and these then named the mayors of the municipalities. (Serpa Uribe[25] interview, 1997)

What motivated the members of the constitutional convention as they furthered decentralization in 1991? To understand the motivations of the policy makers, it is important to situate the convention within its context: an extremely turbulent year of Colombia's history. Although violence has always surrounded Colombian politics, the year 1989 produced an uncharacteristically high rate of violence, with drug-related violence concentrated particularly in Medellín. The 1990 election witnessed the assassination of three presidential candidates. Finally, the Constitutional Assembly was approved at a time when terrorists associated with the narcotics trade had kidnapped members of politically powerful families and several journalists.[26] This chaotic atmosphere helped to fuel support for a major political change, but the actual substance of that change had not been clearly articulated when the Constitutional Assembly was inaugurated. As a result, members of the assembly brought many issues to the bargaining table.

Decentralization was by no means the central issue of debate. After the assembly members had been selected but before they began their duties, *Semana* magazine asked the seventy participants to comment on what they most hoped to achieve during the assembly; the replies covered a variety of issues, including issues of public order and peace, increasing respect for human rights and property, and revamping the justice system. Along with these answers, a very significant number mentioned the necessity of enlarging political space. This reason headed the lists of many constituents, particularly those representing opposition parties; for example, Antonio Navarro Wolff (the leader of the M-19) responded that he would like to concentrate on opening

---

[25] One of three co-presidents of the Constitutional Assembly, 1991, vice president to Ernesto Samper, and Liberal presidential candidate, 1998 and 2002.

[26] This was the subject of Gabriel García Márquez's eloquent novel, *News of a Kidnapping*.

political spaces and breaking the president's monopoly on power. Members of the many factions of the Conservative party mentioned similar motivations: Misael Pastrana Borrero listed enlarging the political space; Rodrigo Lloredo Caicedo cited increasing participation. Of course, several Liberals also cited participation and increased decentralization as their primary goals (*Semana*, no. 443, October 30–6 November, 1990). Also, the first month of the assembly "was devoted to oral presentations of general proposals and philosophies.... The most common topics were congress, peace, and extradition" (Van Cott 2000: 65). Extending participation was an important result of the Constitutional Assembly's labor, but it was not the central topic motivating the body.

César Gaviria – the (Liberal) president of Colombia at the time – emphasized somewhat different goals. In a November 1990 interview, Gaviria underlined the importance of controlling violence and increasing local level fiscal accountability. In response to the question "What is the relation between the Constitutional Assembly and peace?" Gaviria responded:

It is enormous. Not only for the possibility that, through this process, new guerrilla groups will disarm themselves and integrate themselves into civil society, but also for the fact that those who continue the armed struggle who do not take advantage of this historical opportunity will find themselves isolated and will have to confront renovated institutions that are stronger and much more legitimate and representative.

Regarding the economy, Gaviria stated:

Finally, an improved development of local power at the administrative, fiscal and political level that will make it so that the regions no longer continue to wait for a check from Bogotá for every public work, for every necessity; instead the regional entities and municipalities will be able to count on their own sources of income and eliminate the centers of dissatisfaction and conflict. (*Semana*, no. 446, November 20–27, 1990).

While Gaviria pushed for a constitutional reform, his ideas about the priorities and possibilities for the convention differed from those of many of its participants. According to one of the three co-presidents of the Constitutional Assembly, Horacio Serpa, the fiscal issues emphasized in Gaviria's comments did not become the focus of the convention. In fact, much more time was spent on political issues than was allocated to economic issues.[27] Though President Gaviria played an important role in ushering in the new assembly, he could not control its workings once it was established. In his wonderfully insightful look into the workings of the Constitutional Assembly, John Dugas notes that "the first attempts of the Government to exert leadership over the Assembly fell apart" (Dugas 1993, p. 54).[28]

Once convened, the Constitutional Assembly was divided into five working committees[29] in which most of the details of the Constitutional Assembly were hammered out. Within the second committee (responsible for issues of territorial organization and regional and local autonomy) the most contentious issues revolved around the degree of autonomy that should be accorded to various territorial divisions, including the departments, municipalities, and indigenous territories that already enjoyed some autonomy; the debate also extended to the role of provinces, districts, and metropolitan areas. The committee divided sharply over the relative importance of regions versus departments and, somewhat less sharply, over the extent to which departments should be strengthened within the overall territorial framework. This debate divided the committee into "regionalists" and "departmentalists" (Orjuela E. 1993: 141). Three Liberals from the Atlantic Coast, the committee's two AD M-19 representatives, and the committee's indigenous vice president supported a regionalist approach that would place greater power in regional governments at the expense of departmental governments. Those favoring departments over regions included the two most prominent Liberals on the committee: Jaime Castro and Gustavo Zafra, as well as Juan Gómez Martínez, an independent Conservative from Antioquia, a traditional Conservative stronghold electorally.

---

[27] Interview with Horacio Serpa in Bogotá, Colombia, July 31, 1997.

[28] He goes on to acknowledge that the government was able to win back some influence over the Constitutional Assembly by "presenting a lower profile, [through] the diligent work of [Gaviria's] *ministro de gobierno* and [through] interventions at opportune moments by President Gaviria" (Dugas 1993: 55).

[29] Committee 1 worked on rights, principles, guarantees, fundamental liberties, the electoral system, political parties, and procedures regarding constitutional reform; Committee 2 focused on the territorial organization of the state and regional and local autonomy; Committee 3 focused on government institutions, the legislature, public force, international relations, and states of emergency; Committee 4 worked on the justice system; Committee 5 worked on economic, social, and ecological issues.

In the background of this highly contentious debate, issues such as increasing the autonomy of municipalities and elevating the election of mayors and other advances legislated in the 1980s to constitutional status found virtually no opposition. In fact, a look at the committee's voting record on each level of territorial entity provides some idea of the tension surrounding the debates over each issue. In seventeen votes regarding municipalities, only one no vote and one abstention were recorded. This contrasts sharply with the nine no votes and fifteen abstentions recorded in thirteen votes pertaining to departments, the twelve no votes and twenty-two abstentions recorded in ten votes regarding regions, and the six no votes received in the single vote over metropolitan districts.[30]

As one might guess from this accounting, expanding the power and autonomy of departmental governments was somewhat more difficult than expanding municipal autonomy, but the measure to elect governors popularly and to increase funding to departments passed in the first debate with a great deal of support from the full assembly.[31] Despite this wide support, debate over the issue of electing departmental governors grew prominent due to the high profile of one of its opponents: Jaime Castro. In a document submitted to the official proceedings of the assembly, Castro spelled out five reasons for his opposition: It would reduce the power of the presidency; the election of governors alone would not solve the crisis of the departments; it would take emphasis away from municipal decentralization; it would centralize power in the regional capitals because the votes of the inhabitants of the largest cities within each department would overwhelm the preferences of the more rural constituents; and it would add politics to the purely administrative nature of the department. He also cited the chaos that had come from adopting a federal government structure under the 1858 constitution (Castro 1991).

---

[30] Actual votes within the full assembly were not available nor was information that would link the votes displayed here to individual members; however, Orjuela (1993) provides a good resource for separating out the partisans and opponents of broad issues regarding territorial autonomy within the assembly's Second Committee.

[31] Van Cott (2000: 66) notes: "Of all articles approved in the first debate, 94 percent passed with 80 percent of the votes, and 43 percent (192/449) were approved unanimously."

Supporters of the popular election of governors were no less strident in their efforts to be heard. On June 18, 1981, three days after Jaime Castro's position appeared in the proceedings, Eduardo Verano de la Rosa (Castro's colleague on the assembly's second committee) published his own document, entitled "Response to the Centralists and Opponents of the Region," arguing:

> It is the fear of those whose minds have been colonized by the past and of indecisive victims who would prolong this document so that they could continue living in the past. (Verano de la Rosa 1991: 7)

Despite strong resistance from such prominent Liberals as Jaime Castro, the popular election of governors passed in the general assembly with forty-seven votes in favor. Although the second committee's proposal to the assembly would have further decentralized the state by giving territorial status to regions and provinces, the assembly did not pass this measure.

Consideration of the details surrounding debates over decentralization in the post–National Front period leads to three conclusions. First, the Liberal party, while championing the devolution of responsibilities and resources to local and regional levels of government, did not attempt the kind of effective decentralization – the election of subnational officials invested with autonomous financial resources – examined in this book. The Liberal party's reputation for supporting decentralization should be construed as support not for effective decentralization as understood here but for fiscal federalism and administrative decentralization. Second, while it required a Conservative victory to place decentralization on the agenda, the parties divided internally in their support for the popular election of mayors. Those sectors of each party that would have the most influence over selecting mayors through an appointment process, should their party be elected, were the most resistant to change, while sectors of each party that stood to gain the most from local elections supported the proposal.[32] Finally, the assembly was

---

[32] It is important to note that there were several Conservatives who stood to lose influence over appointments, even if Liberals continued to win the presidency. Even though Liberal presidents enjoyed exclusive appointment power over mayors, they often appointed Conservative mayors in highly Conservative areas and consulted Conservatives in making these appointments. This "habit" may have been a holdover from the National Front period when the two parties divided subnational appointments equally between them.

not convened for the purpose of furthering decentralization. Liberals in the government sought a restricted agenda for the assembly – a strategy halted by the Supreme Court:

[T]here is a saying here that if you do not want a cup of coffee, you will get two. This is a bit what happened to the government. The government wanted to allow changes to the Constitution, but they wanted to limit the subject matter treated in the Assembly.... The Court said: wait a minute. If we are going to let the people decide to change the Constitution, then we will not set limits on it. This scared the government. The reality is that I was a constituent and initially the government wanted to convene this assembly for a partial reform... but we ended up... changing the entire Constitution. (Zafra interview 1997)

In addition, individual members approached the assembly with different priorities. These priorities seem to follow a party logic with members of the opposition and non-traditional parties focused on broader participation and accountability while traditional Liberals concentrated on issues of fiscal decentralization, judicial reform, and the peace process. Within the committee charged with deliberating territorial issues, the two strongest opponents of further decentralizing measures – such as the popular election of governors and the greater empowerment of regions, provinces, and districts – were the two most prominent Liberals on the committee. Support for greater decentralization came from the members of the committee representing the AD-M19, Liberals from the Atlantic Coast, and the committee's indigenous vice president.

Since the Constitutional Assembly expanded subnational electoral opportunities and solidified the access of elected subnational officials to fiscal resources, decentralization has remained largely unchanged, despite some efforts to curtail it. Gaviria's term ended a period of expanded decentralization. His presidency was followed by the Liberal presidency of Ernesto Samper, whose term was beset by credibility problems after it became clear that his campaign benefited greatly from drug money. Although Samper was himself acquitted of wrongdoing, several of his campaign advisers were convicted and sentenced, and several of his staff, including his vice president, Humberto de la Calle, resigned and encouraged Samper to resign as well. Political survival, not decentralizing policies, was at the heart of Samper's presidency; however, he did attempt to reverse some of decentralization's consequences for the traditional parties. In particular, his 1996 constitutional reform project proposed that national, regional, and local elections should occur simultaneously. This change would have advantaged the traditional parties by increasing their "ability to influence all three levels of elections through clientelist incentives and to improve congressional representation through linkages to popular local candidates. . . . [T]he counterreform demonstrated a clear tendency to reverse the process of decentralization" (Van Cott 2000: 108). This is not surprising, given that Samper won the 1994 presidential race by a significant margin over the Conservative challenger, Andres Pastrana (who would win the 1998 election), and his party won important victories at the regional and local levels. In the end, Samper's efforts came to naught: The reform project was withdrawn in 1997 based mainly on opposition both from minority parties in the legislature and also from the constitutional court.

The presidency of Andres Pastrana, a rare Conservative in a string of Liberals, focused primarily on hammering out a peace agreement between the government and the two large guerrilla groups[33] that have gained ground in the last several years. In the spring of 2000, Pastrana introduced a legal project to reform the congress after another in a string of scandals became public at that time. The project's main thrust was to shrink and reorganize the legislature, but it also had provisions that affected decentralization; in particular, it proposed that elected officials at the local and regional levels should not receive a government salary. This would have clearly favored the more wealthy candidates, countrywide, giving the traditional party candidates – and the Conservatives in particular – an edge over independents. The legal project created the predictable opposition within the legislature, and Pastrana eventually retracted it during the summer of 2000.

Just as those who crafted decentralizing laws in the 1980s and early 1990s consulted their political fortunes in designing the specific features of those laws, so have subsequent administrations sought to tailor the law to benefit their own political strengths. Liberals before Betancur saw no reason to change a highly centralized system that repeatedly placed its candidates in the presidency. Betancur saw opportunities for his partisans and political allies once his presidency ended and sought

---

[33] These are the FARC (Fuerzas Armadas Revolucionarias de Colombia, the Revolutionary Armed Forces of Colombia) and the ELN (Ejército de Liberación Nacional, Army of National Liberation).

to decentralize power where it would do those groups the most good. Non-traditional politicians acted to broaden the space for participation in subnational governments still further during the 1991 Constitutional Assembly. Finally, Samper and Pastrana have attempted to tweak decentralization slightly in ways that would advantage their parties relative to their political rivals, even though neither was ultimately successful.

CONCLUSION

As one of the earliest decentralizers in the region, Colombia now has a substantial experience with decentralizing reform. A growing literature seeks to explore the costs and benefits that Colombia has derived from this experience. The results appear to be mixed, however; even authors who find a multitude of faults seem to agree that decentralization has generally been good for the country and that many of its shortcomings result not from decentralization per se but from inadequate local capacity or poor design or implementation of the reforms. Those focused on the political dividends of decentralization tend to paint the rosiest picture, while examinations of decentralization's economic impact have found less to praise. In particular, many economists charge decentralization with weakening Colombia's economy. Alesina, Carasquilla, and Echavarría (2002) – among others – argue that Colombia's transfer system stifles incentives for subnational governments to raise their own sources of income and raises their incentives to run budget deficits in the hopes of being bailed out by the center – both of these forces serving to weaken the national economy.

On a more positive note, decentralization's popularity among the population has been documented in a number of ways. First, turnout in local and regional elections has been high by Colombian standards. After an abstention rate of 55 percent in presidential elections in 1986, participation in the first local elections of mayors in 1988 rose to 67 percent. In 1990, a participation rate of 43 percent in presidential elections contrasts with participation of 58 percent in local contests. This continues in later years with participation rates of 44 percent (1992), 46 percent (1994), and 45 percent (1997–1998) in local elections and 43 percent (1994) and 59 percent (1998) in national elections (Bejarano and Dávila 1998; Angell, Lowden and Thorp 2001). Public opinion surveys also suggest strong support for elected local and regional leaders (Dugas, Ocampo, Orjuela, and Ruiz 1992). In addition, Castro (1998) suggests that the popular election of subnational officials contributed to governmental stability during the impeachment proceedings against President Samper: Had Samper appointed subnational officials, the taint of his misdeeds might have filtered down throughout the political system. Instead, popularly elected regional and local governments retained their legitimacy, providing a strong bulwark against the crisis of confidence unleashed by the investigation into Samper's campaign financing at the national level. Finally, some investigators find evidence that subnational elections have created new spaces for nontraditional politicians and nascent parties to contest traditional party dominance (Dugas et al. 1992). Furthermore, it seems that Liberal-Conservative dominance in winning mayoral races varies quite a bit by region and also by the size of the constituency. Querubín, Sánchez, and Kure (1998) found that in the 1997 local elections, smaller municipalities were much more likely to elect a Liberal or Conservative mayor than were larger municipalities: 79 percent of municipalities with fewer than 5,000 people elected a mayor from a traditional party, while only 29 percent of municipalities with more than 500,000 residents did so.

Whether the balance of Colombia's experience with decentralization belongs in the positive or negative column remains the basis of a vigorous debate. This chapter does not contribute directly to this debate; however, it does shed quite a bit of light on an overlooked motive for why decentralizing reforms were adopted in the first place. It has explored whether the timing of reforms decentralizing political and fiscal resources fits an electoral logic. Does decentralization occur when far-sighted parties with weak presidential prospects but strong potential to win elected subnational positions find themselves in a position to reform the balance of power between the national and subnational levels in Colombia? The evidence suggests that it does.

This chapter opened with a brief review of Colombian history showing that neither major party has consistently pushed for decentralizing or recentralizing reforms; instead, decentralizing reforms have occurred under both parties, as their electoral fortunes shifted. Since the return to competitive democratic elections at the end of the National Front period, Liberals have enjoyed a significant margin of electoral strength at the national level relative to Conservatives. Even the election of Betancur did not signal a shift in society's support for the Liberal Party; instead, his victory occurred due to the failure of the Liberals to coalesce behind a single candidate. Legislative results support this view: Between 1978 and 1982, legislative vote tallies for the two parties barely budged. The consistent pattern across elections in this period showed Liberals with a comfortable margin of support relative to their rivals and with the votes for each party fairly stable over time. With this information, Conservatives in 1982 had reason to view their stay in the presidency as temporary. The resulting push for decentralization makes perfect sense in this context, given the party's strength at the local level.

The Constitutional Assembly marks the second post–National Front opportunity when non-traditional parties were in a strong position to shape the relationship between national and subnational governments. While all parties generally agreed on the need to reform the constitution, not all parties agreed on which reforms were necessary. Liberals focused on reforms of the judiciary, subnational finances, and the pursuit of peace; non-traditional politicians focused on greater decentralization and participation at subnational levels.

It is somewhat easy to imagine that parties within Colombia's stable political system could reasonably calculate how decentralization would affect their electoral prospects at all levels of government. The level of stability in each party's share of the vote across elections is extremely rare within the region, yet decentralization has become widespread. The next chapter takes up the adoption of decentralizing reforms within one of Latin America's most frequently changing political systems: Bolivia. In this and many other ways, Bolivia's political system provides a foil to the qualities of Colombia's political system, yet both countries decentralize. The next chapter also takes on the challenge of reconciling the very different features of Bolivia's political landscape with the ultimate convergence of both Bolivia's and Colombia's political systems toward decentralizing reform.

5

The Bolivian Experience

We began to look at municipalization and when we began looking into this we discovered something strange which is that more than 40% of Bolivia's population did not have a close public institution of representation. They didn't have mayors. They had corregidores who came by every now and then and who were considered by the people to be like chiefs of police, and not as representatives. They did not give them any sense of being a part of the Bolivian state or that they had a public say in matters of health, or public services, or development, or anything.

Interview with Federico Martínez, member of the technical team
that crafted Bolivia's decentralization law, January 1997

The state gives up its power, takes the money away from the bureaucrats in the capital, and gives it to the ignorant Indian so that he can do with it as he pleases. If this is not revolution, what is?

Luis Ramiro Beltrán in Molina Monasterios 1997: 235

INTRODUCTION

When Bolivia returned to democratic rule in 1982, its executive inherited a highly centralized government following decades of shifting dictatorships punctuated by an occasional, failing civilian regime. This political structure had been built to control political and economic resources from the top down. Financially, 97 percent of Bolivia's budget allocation for regional development remained locked in the three regional capitals of La Paz, Cochabamba, and Santa Cruz (Urioste

Fernández de Córdova 2002: 144). Politically, only forty-one of Bolivia's provincial sections had achieved municipal status, leaving vast swaths of the country without officially recognized representatives of the state at the local level.[1] In addition to centralized decision making, the new democracy inherited a severe financial crisis as Bolivia succumbed to the same economic shocks that were affecting the rest of the region: high rates of inflation, low growth, large public sector deficits, and restricted access to credit occasioned by large unpaid debts. The economic downturn was intensified in Bolivia by its legacy of profligate spending; each new ruler during the late 1970s and 1980s had attempted either to buy popular support or to fund its repression.

Bolivia's experience belies the typical association of authoritarian rule and stability. Between 1978 and 1982, the presidential palace had hosted seven military governments and two civilian regimes. However, between 1982 and 2003, Bolivia experienced remarkable democratic stability. In 1994, the fourth consecutive president elected under democratic rules drastically changed the system by introducing Law 1551, the Popular Participation Law (Ley de Participación Popular, LPP). This law municipalized the entire country, bringing participatory democratic structures to its tiniest hamlets and allowing for the popular election of mayors and municipal councils.[2] In addition, the law granted municipal governments authority to raise certain categories of taxes and guaranteed them 20 percent of the federal budget. Many viewed this reform as a revolution in Bolivian politics second only to the National Revolution of 1952:

This led some analysts to state that the "First Republic" (homogenization, mythical unity in service to the state, the market, money, language, etc.) was destroyed and that because of the Popular Participation Law (respecting

---

[1] This is not to say that local citizens had no formal mechanisms of self-governance. In indigenous areas, long-established forms of self-government exemplified by the *ayllus* performed local government functions. In other areas, neighborhood associations (in urban areas) and peasant unions (in more rural areas) played important roles in the absence of an official state presence. These associations were incorporated officially into the local government structure adopted with the Popular Participation Law that municipalized the country in 1994.

[2] The mechanism for selecting mayors is this: If one party wins a majority of the votes for its list of municipal council candidates, the top candidate on that list automatically becomes the mayor. If an absolute majority is not achieved by any party, then the municipal council chooses the mayor from among its members.

difference, recognizing other cultures and modes of organization, etc.) a Second Republic had begun which offered greater hope of survival and improvement of the quality of life of Bolivians. (Molina and Arias 1996: 10–11)

How can such a drastic change in power sharing between levels of government be explained?

This chapter argues that decentralization under the MNR (National Revolutionary Movement) presidency of Gonzalo Sánchez de Lozada is not nearly as surprising when viewed through the lens of electoral advantage. At the moment of reform, the MNR gripped national power weakly, it had widespread support throughout the country at the local level – particularly in rural areas – and it enjoyed the most stable support across elections of any party in the system. Previous democratic administrations, including the MNR between 1985 and 1989, had a more tenuous hold on subnational support and more volatile support overall, making decentralization less attractive to them.

The Bolivian case, in addition to supporting an electoral motivation for decentralization, also allows the exploration of one of the theory's secondary implications: how leaders choose the level to which power will be decentralized. Based on the insights of the electoral theory, it is no surprise that decentralization conferred power on municipalities in Bolivia despite the growing popularity of a movement aimed at decentralizing power to regional governments. The team of policy makers that was convened to draft the LPP decided to municipalize rather than to federalize in a political context in which the ruling MNR party enjoyed strong electoral support at the local level but weak support in the regional capitals that would have dominated regional electoral results.

When Gonzalo Sánchez de Lozada gained the presidency in 1993, regional and local development was undertaken by centrally administered development corporations (*corporaciónes de desarrollo*) in each of Bolivia's nine regions. These development corporations were centrally directed, located, and funded. In addition, regional civic committees – made up of each regional capital's top business interests – were granted formal representation within them. Invested with 10 percent of the national budget, positions within these units were an attractive source of pork. Despite their titular development focus, the development corporations spent the overwhelming majority of their funds in the three most developed departments (La Paz, Cochabamba, and Santa Cruz), with a remarkable 92 percent of spending concentrated in departmental capital cities (Barbery Anaya 1997: 46). This left only 8 percent for investment in the countryside, where 42 percent of the population lived in rural poverty (Molina Saucedo 1997: 42). It also appears that much of the money funneled through the development corporations was spent on personnel, rather than real development projects. When I interviewed a former head of Bení's development corporation, he admitted:

These development corporations were huge and so the amount for salaries was not sufficient. For example, my secretary had the title of tractor operator because this meant a much higher salary than a secretary did. This person had never gone to the countryside, was not involved in a project there, and did not know how to operate a tractor. (interview 1997)

In addition to the development corporations, regional prefects were appointed directly by the president, and only a few of the country's 311 provincial sections had attained municipal status. Municipal status was enjoyed only in the most urbanized areas of the country, and while local officials were elected in 1963, 1968, and continuously after 1985, these officials were severely limited by their lack of sufficient funds. Carlos Hugo Molina Saucedo, the author of an influential book on municipalization and a leader in drafting and implementing Bolivia's decentralization reform, testified to the legislature in 1994:

Formally our country has 112 provinces, 294 provincial sections and 1408 cantons. As far as administrative divisions are concerned, we should remember that the Executive only reaches to the departmental capitals; the assistant prefects and administrators of the cantons are all but decorative, not only because of the limited capacities that they can perform, but also because of the impossibility of actually completing them due to their lack of economic resources. (Molina Saucedo 1994: 50)

The LPP shattered this framework by introducing effective decentralization: It provided formulaic transfers of funds from the central to subnational governments, increased the ability of subnational governments to raise their own resources, and allowed for the popular election of subnational officials.

The LPP drastically changed the previous system of development funding. It allowed municipal governments to collect resources directly and dissolved the development corporations, redistributing the funds they had controlled – 10 percent of the national budget – to the municipalities. This redistribution occurred on the basis of population (so that the three main cities now get 32 percent of the resources).[3] Politically, the LPP revolutionized the very map of Bolivia by municipalizing the entire country, introducing participatory democracy to these areas through the popular election of municipal councils and mayors.

Newly elected local officials were shocked by this change and, not understanding its origins, were wary of it. When the first transfusion of resources to municipalities arrived in bank accounts set up for each one, several leaders went directly to the banks and withdrew the funds. Fernando Medina, one of the law's architects recalls:

> There were mayors who did not believe it. For example, one mayor and his municipal councilors, they were from Cochabamba, visited the bank, consulted to see if it were true that they had resources there and confirmed that they had 18,000 dollars. They cashed a check within the day, withdrew all of the money and took it back to the town, thinking: "We must be careful or they will take it back." (in Molina Monasterios 1997: 234)

Understanding the motivations behind the adoption of the LPP may seem perplexing at first glance, but electoral advantage provides a useful perspective through which to view the actions of the five presidential periods studied here, spanning 1982–2001. In the remainder of the chapter, I argue that the MNR's decision to decentralize during its 1993–1997 term accords with the electoral theory of decentralization: that governments facing weak national-level support, strong subnational level support, and stable support over time decentralize. Previous democratic governments did not enjoy this constellation of support. I also demonstrate how alternative explanations based on ideological positions, economic factors, and pressure from below fall short of explaining these events.

The chapter begins by exploring each administration's electoral support at the national and subnational levels, paying attention also to the change in the administration's support across consecutive elections.

---

[3] You may recall that these three cities had previously enjoyed just over 90 percent of funds, so why did they not strongly oppose a program that drastically cut their resources? In fact, the amount of funding these cities received did not decline as precipitously as the percentages suggest. Only La Paz suffered a modest cut in the amount of its resources, indicating that the overall amount spent on subnational development shot up from the previous period (Escalante Carrasco 1997).

This is followed by a more in-depth discussion of the LPP's adoption – its historical precedents and the debates that accompanied its drafting and approval. Unlike the Colombian case, an in-depth exploration of Bolivia's decentralizing experience does not allow us to learn much about legislative maneuvering over this issue: The LPP was crafted by an appointed team of specialists who worked behind closed doors; when the LPP was brought to a congressional decision, it passed unanimously after heavy lobbying from the president. Legislative debate did play a key role in obstructing a decentralizing plan during the Siles Zuazo presidency (1989–1993); these themes are more deeply explored in the pages to come. Next, the chapter explores competing theories that arise from the Bolivian context; in particular, I examine whether or not decentralization resulted from the ideological programs of the main parties or from grassroots pressure for reform. Finally, I discuss how electoral motivations help us to understand why the MNR chose to decentralize to local governments rather than to regional governments, and I look at how the first post-decentralizing administration influenced decentralization policies during its term.

EVIDENCE

This portion of the chapter explains the MNR's decision to decentralize during its term from 1993 to 1997 by looking at the party's national support, subnational support, and changes in its support over time. It uses the same factors to explain why decentralization did not occur in the three presidencies preceding that of Gonzalo Sánchez de Lozada.

National Strength and Vote Change

Bolivia's multi-party system and its rather unique rules governing presidential election make it extremely difficult for any particular party to confidently project its political fortunes. According to the rules translating presidential votes into the executive office, only parties with a majority of the vote – 51 percent or more – win the presidency outright. Since Bolivia's democratic regeneration in 1982, this has not occurred. Instead, parties form coalitions to choose the president from the top vote-getting parties.[4] This electoral rule has spawned a party system

---

[4] Prior to 1994, a president could be chosen from the top three vote-getting parties; after 1994, the choice was constrained to the top two vote-getting parties.

TABLE 5.1: *National Level Presidential Results (Percent of Vote),*
1980–2002[a]

Party	1980	1985	1989	1993	1997[b]	2002
UDP	38.7					
MNR	20.2	**30.4**	25.8	**35.6**	18.2	**22.5**
ADN	16.8	32.8	25.4	21.1	**22.3**	3.4
PS1	8.7					
MIR		10.2	**22.0**		16.8	16.3
MNRI		5.5				
CONDEPA			12.3	14.3	17.2	
IU			8.1			
UCS				13.8	16.1	5.5
MBL				5.4		
NFR						21.0
MAS						21.0
MIP						6.1

Note: All parties winning more than 5 percent of the vote are shown. Parties winning the presidency are shown in boldface type.

[a] UDP: Unidad Democrática y Popular (Popular Democratic Unity); MNR: Movimiento Nacionalista Revolucionario (National Revolutionary Movement); ADN: Acción Democrática Nacionalista (Nationalist Democratic Action); PS1: Partido Socialista Uno (Socialist Party One); MIR: Movimiento de Izquierda Revolucionario (Movement of the Revolutionary Left); MNRI: Movimiento Nacionalista Revolucionario de Izquierda (National Revolutionary Movement of the Left); CONDEPA: Conciencia de Patria (Conscience of the Fatherland); IU: Izquierda Unida (United Left); UCS: Unión Cívica Solidaridad (Civic Solidarity Union); MBL: Movimiento Bolivia Libre (Movement for a Free Bolivia); NFR: Nueva Fuerza Republicana; MAS: Movimiento al Socialismo; MIP: Movimiento Indígena Pachacuti.

[b] Electoral rules that were changed in 1994 divide the national votes into single-member and multi-member districts. I use the multi-member district results here as they are more comparable with the earlier results, which all come from multi-member districts.

with a few large parties that contend for the presidency and several smaller parties that play an important role in coalition formation after the initial voting occurs. A second consequence of this electoral rule is that parties with relatively strong national support (those among the top vote-getters) but that lack a majority of the vote cannot be assured of winning the presidency. Table 5.1 breaks down the presidential vote by party, with boldface type indicating the party from which the president was chosen in each election.

A glance at Table 5.1 confirms two characteristics of national support for Bolivian parties: No party can count on winning the presidency outright by capturing a majority of the national vote, and few parties

TABLE 5.2: *Margins of Victory (percentage point differences between the top two vote-getters)*

Election	Percentage points	Party no. 1	Party no. 2
1980	18.5	**UDP**	MNR
1985	2.4	ADN	**MNR**
1989	0.4	MNR	ADN
1993	14.5	**MNR**	ADN
1997	4.1	**ADN**	MNR
2002	1.5	**MNR**	MAS

Note: Boldface type indicates the party winning the presidency.

maintain a strong and stable level of support across elections. No party wins as much as 40 percent of the vote in any election, making all parties weak at the national level compared with the percentage of the vote required to secure the presidency without the coalition-building process. The 1985 and 1989 results confirm that garnering a plurality of the vote does not guarantee a party's access to the executive.

The information in Table 5.2 reinforces the fact that national strength alone assures no party the presidency under Bolivia's complicated electoral system. In 1985 the party that placed second in overall vote share won the presidency (MNR) and ruled in a coalition with the ADN (Nationalist Democratic Action), while in 1989 the executive went to the third place party (MIR, Movement of the Revolutionary Left), which also ruled in a coalition with the ADN. The UDP (Democratic Popular Union) won with the largest margin of victory in 1980; however, this party did not last beyond the first election of this new period. The MNR displays the other, relatively large margin of victory, placing fifteen percentage points above its nearest challenger in the 1993 voting, affording it a strong position from which to pass new reforms.

It is also notable that only one party consistently receives more than 5 percent of the vote across all six elections in Table 5.1: the MNR. In general, support for parties fluctuates both quickly and significantly, suggesting that parties discount future time periods heavily, focusing on the short term. The UDP, despite overwhelming support in the 1980 elections, was not even able to field a candidate in the subsequent elections. Its support evaporated due to its disastrous handling of the economy. The MIR, although fairly strong in 1985 and 1989, combines its prospects with the ADN for the 1993 national race, disappearing temporarily from the political map as an independent force. The MIR's absence and its inability to maintain its leftist support after its alliance with the rightist ADN and its leader, former dictator Hugo Banzer Suárez, opened political space to new contenders. Political space was also forced open by the rising salience of indigenous identity as a force for political organizing. Three new parties eagerly emerged in the 1993 race to take advantage of these factors: CONDEPA, UCS, and the MBL. The first two are regarded largely as populist vehicles for particular leaders, but the MBL showed the makings of an alternative political force. Nevertheless, while support for CONDEPA and UCS grew slightly in the 1997 elections,[5] the MBL did not poll more than 5 percent of the vote; support for all three parties had dropped off sharply in the 2002 elections. Two new parties inserted themselves into this space: the NFR (led by the charismatic mayor of Cochabamba, Manfred Reyes Villa) and the MAS (led by the head of the union of coca growers, Evo Morales). A small indigenous party, MIP, managed to just cross the threshold, winning 6.1 percent of the vote in 2002.

These two characteristics of parties – weak national support and high change in support across elections – work in opposite directions as far as decentralization is concerned. Lack of strong national support makes decentralization more attractive to all parties; a high level of change in vote shares across elections diminishes its appeal.

Looking purely at the national-level electoral support for each party, all Bolivian parties should seek decentralization. This is even more marked if one takes into consideration that all parties during this time period have lost popularity over the course of their terms.[6] A more relevant question, based purely on national-level support, may be, Which party should *not* support decentralization? The unpredictability of partisan support over time undermines the incentive created by weak

---

[5] By 1997 Bolivia's electoral law had shifted to one in which half of the legislature was elected through multi-member districts and half through single-member districts. In these contests, the UCS won 16 percent of the vote in multi-member districts and 14 percent in single-member districts, while CONDEPA won 17 percent and 14 percent, respectively.

[6] This is evident not only from the fact that no governing party won a second term, but also from the significant decline in the vote for each incumbent party in the subsequent presidential election.

TABLE 5.3: *Change in Electoral Support over Time (absolute value of the percentage change in the vote between elections)*

Party	1980–1985	1985–1989	1989–1993	1993–1997	1997–2002
UDP	100				
MNR	50.5	15.1	38.0	48.9	19.1
ADN	95.2	22.6	16.9	5.7	555.9
PS-1	100				
MIR	100	115.7	100	100	3.1
MNRI	100	100			
CONDEPA		100	16.3	20.3	4548.7
IU		100	100		
UCS			100	16.7	192.7
MBL			100	42.6	100
NFR					100
MAS					100
MIP					100

national-level support. Because support for parties changes so dramatically from election to election, time horizons for the typical party are quite short. In fact, most parties disappear altogether after two elections. With electoral support changing so drastically across consecutive elections, parties' time horizons shrink, future support becomes difficult to judge, and decentralization becomes less likely. The next few paragraphs examine change in electoral support more carefully.

Table 5.3 presents the percentage change in vote shares over consecutive elections for all parties winning more than 5 percent of the vote in elections between 1980 and 2002. Two items to note about the table: Numbers are generally high, suggesting that all parties face uncertain electoral outcomes, and the most popular number in the table is 100 percent, signifying the appearance and disappearance of parties from one election to the next. Mainwaring and Scully (1995) rank Bolivia as the fourth most volatile party system out of twelve Latin American countries, reckoning that the mean volatility of the average party in the system between presidential elections is 39.2 percent in the period 1979–1993. Of the parties displayed in Table 5.3, only the MNR and ADN consistently win votes in all presidential elections with vote-change numbers that do not rise above 100 percent. The average vote change of each party over the 1980–1993 period is 34.5 percent for the MNR and 44.9 percent for the ADN. These figures suggest that the MNR had a slightly more stable base of support than the ADN at the time of decentralization; their survival through the time period attests that these are the two most stable parties within the Bolivian system. Including the results from the 1997 elections, the MNR's average vote change for the period edges upward, to 38.1 percent, while the ADN's declines to 35.1 percent. If any party will have a sufficiently long time horizon to consider decentralization, the MNR and ADN are the best candidates.

Table 5.3 presents the percentage change in support at the national level from election to election, but does not express the direction of change or the percentage point amount. These additional factors help to discern short-term trends in national-level support and its volatility. Table 5.4 displays these.

Election results not only provide a snapshot of national-level support every election year, but they also allow the party to check the growth or decline of its support relative to previous periods. While large changes in vote shares across elections depress the desire to decentralize by shortening time horizons, increases in the national vote also increase the party's likelihood of attaining the presidency. Although national support may be weak today, if it is growing at a high rate, the party should anticipate future strength and begin to act as a hegemonic party. On the other hand, waning support may cause a nationally weak party to either worry about its future (making decentralization

TABLE 5.4: *Percentage Point Change in Votes between Elections*

Party	1980–1985	1985–1989	1989–1993	1993–1997	1997–2002
UDP	−38.7				
MNR	+10.2	−4.6	+9.8	−17.4	+4.3
ADN	+16.0	−7.4	−4.3	+1.2	−18.9
PS-1	−8.7				
MIR	+10.2	+11.8	−22.0	+16.8	−0.5
MNRI	+5.5	−5.5			
CONDEPA		+12.3	+2.0	+2.9	−16.8
IU		+8.1	−8.1	+3.7	−3.7
UCS			+13.8	+2.3	−10.6
MBL			+5.4	−2.3	−3.1
NFR					+21.0
MAS					+21.0
MIP					+6.1

less likely) or to plan for its continued but weakened existence in the future by decentralizing if its support at the subnational level is strong.

Table 5.4 illuminates some interesting election-to-election trends. The MNR's 1985 election victory, with 30.4 percent of the vote, indicated a significant increase in its support at the national level. Another trend, which may have raised the MNR's confidence, was the collapse of the UDP, a party originating from the dissident left wing of the MNR. With the ADN – the MNR's biggest rival for power – lying to the right, the MNR stood to gain from this development. The ADN, in fact, loses votes throughout most of the period studied, after an initial increase in votes between 1980 and 1985; it rebounds somewhat with its 1997 electoral victory, before reaching an all-time low in 2002.[7] The MNR loses and then gains points, making it slightly stronger heading into its 1993 presidency. Still, the president who was eventually chosen in 1993 had won a plurality of the vote in 1989 only to be denied the presidency through an ADN-MIR coalition. This experience probably checked any overconfidence inspired by the MNR's large margin of victory in 1993.

Examining national support and changes in national support across elections highlights two main points. First, no party dominates national political support during this period, so all parties face some uncertainty about their ability to hold the executive in the long term. This uncertainty is reinforced by the electoral rules that allocate the presidency not to the party gaining a plurality of the vote but to the winner of complex negotiations involving coalition formation around the top vote-getting parties. At the same time, support for parties at the national level changes dramatically across elections, with few parties enjoying strong and stable bases of national support across the election periods. Based on the theory's predictions, this gives all parties some incentive to decentralize but focuses attention on the MNR as the most likely decentralizing party in the system. Finally, it is notable that all

---

[7] Since its founding, Hugo Banzer had run as the ADN presidential candidate until his death partway through his 1997–2002 term in office. The 2002 elections were thus the first contest in which Banzer did not head the list. It would be too strong a point to say that the party has disintegrated without Banzer's leadership; Banzer's vice president governed well during the remainder of Banzer's term but was constitutionally barred from seeking election in 2002.

incumbent parties lose national support over the course of their terms. This suggests that each of these parties, looking prospectively at their chances in the next election, might have anticipated a loss and perhaps decentralized as a way of ensuring their power at other levels of government. In the context of diminishing national support, the main issue that will determine these parties' attitudes toward decentralization is the strength of their subnational support.

Regional Strength

Bolivia held no regional-level elections during the period under study because the president appoints its regional executives, called *prefectos* (prefects). In lieu of presenting results of regional contests, this section focuses on regional-level results from national elections, recognizing that this is an imperfect measure of preferences for regional officials. Attempting to tease out regional party preferences yields insight into which parties can be predicted to perform well if popular elections were extended to the regional level. An examination of regional support for parties deserves attention because most of the decentralization debate that preceded the LPP's passage focused on empowering regional, not municipal, governments.

Table 5.5 indicates which party won a plurality in each of Bolivia's nine departments in the elections spanning 1985–2002. As seen in the table, party support does not appear to divide firmly (or consistently) along regional lines. Only three regions supplied consistently strong support to the same party through three consecutive elections: Santa

TABLE 5.5: *Regional Party Strength*

Region	1985	1989	1993	1997	2002
Chuquisaca	MNR	MIR	MNR	MIR	MNR
La Paz	ADN	CONDEPA	MNR	CONDEPA	MAS
Cochabamba	ADN	MNR	MNR	ADN	MAS
Oruro	MNR	MIR	MNR	ADN	MAS
Potosi	MNR	MIR	MNR	MIR	MAS
Tarija	MNR	MNR	MNR	MIR	MIR
Santa Cruz	MNR	MNR	MNR	UCS	MNR
Beni	MNR	ADN	MNR	ADN	MNR
Pando	MNR	ADN	ADN	ADN	MNR

Cruz and Tarija both gave a majority of their votes to the MNR in the first three elections, and Pando consistently supported the ADN beginning in 1989. No region supported the same party in all five elections. In general, support for the MNR appears widespread and strong throughout the country, most notably in 1993, when the MNR won a plurality of votes in all but one region. This dominance dropped in 1997 when the MNR did not win a plurality in any single region, but rebounded significantly in 2002.

Using national-level votes disaggregated for each region to judge the strength of parties at the regional level poses some problems. Voters at the national level consider not only the presidency when casting their ballots, but also the distribution of legislative seats. Voters for a regional executive – one single officer – may vote quite differently from how they vote in national elections. Unlike the Colombian case, data are not available for subnational elections that might be used to more closely approximate regional-level voting preferences.

Local Strength

Rather than show strong regional divisions in the support for various parties, Bolivian parties differ in their support along urban/rural lines. As described above, the best available data to assess local support for parties comes from municipal election data covering only about forty municipalities in the most urban areas of the country. When decentralization occurred in 1994, over 200 new municipalities were created, raising the total to 311. Simple math indicates that 271 current municipalities were not included in the local contests that are discussed here. Due to this exclusion of new – and largely rural – municipalities, there will be a strong urban bias to the results before 1995. It was possible to disaggregate the results, separating out the vote totals for the nine regional capitals from the non-capitals. The non-capitals represent a slightly less urban sector of the country, and the difference between these two categories can help to identify urban versus rural voting behaviors. Table 5.6 displays electoral support for parties at the municipal level and disaggregated results for voting in capital cities and non-capitals from 1985 to 1989. The final column looks at the percentage of each party's vote deriving from non-capital municipalities.

TABLE 5.6: *Local Election Results, 1985–1989*

Party	Total	Capital	Not Capital	% vote not from capital
1985 Local Elections (% of the vote)				
MNR	31.4	24.5	35.0	73.3
ADN	25.1	33.7	20.6	53.9
MIR	10.1	10.2	10.0	65.3
1987 Local Elections (% of the vote)				
MNR	12.8	8.6	17.4	65.2
ADN	28.6	34.9	21.7	36.4
MIR	26.1	28.6	23.4	43.0
1989 Local Elections (% of the vote)				
MNR	19.3	18.4	23.5	43.0
ADN-MIR	33.6	36.2	33.7	35.4
CONDEPA	18.8	25.3	10.3	19.3
UCS	16.5	16.5	18.8	40.1

Note: Only parties gaining 10 percent or more of the vote are listed.

Parties with a higher percentage in this column derive a larger proportion of their support from more rural areas and may therefore be expected to perform well in rural municipalities newly empowered by decentralization.

Examining the 1985 results, one discerns that the MNR is strong overall but that its support is stronger in non-capitals (35 percent) than in capitals (approximately 25 percent). The ADN, in contrast, is much stronger in the capitals than in non-capitals, and the MIR gains 10 percent in each, making it the most balanced party in terms of its distribution of support.

The MNR performs quite poorly in the 1987 municipal elections – a midterm election in which it holds the presidency. Aside from the steep slide in MNR vote shares, the basic pattern of support holds from the 1985 results. In 1989, MNR support begins to rebound, two new parties enter the electoral arena, and the MIR and ADN combine to present a single political force. The MNR continues to be stronger in rural than in urban areas, CONDEPA shows the opposite composition of support, and the UCS appears largely balanced between rural and urban support. With the MIR as its partner, the ADN is able to pick up a striking percentage of the rural vote, contributing to a broader balance, although it continues to show a slight advantage in the capitals relative to its support in non-capitals.

Another way to tease out the urban/rural nature of party support is by examining the percentage of each party's support that comes from rural areas. The final column shows the percentage of the party's votes that came from outside the capital cities. Most parties show a significant divergence between their performance in and out of the capital cities, suggesting that areas that are more urban vote differently from areas that are more rural. Parties with a strong base of support in rural areas have higher values in the final two columns of the table.

The results confirm that the MNR enjoys a strong base of support in rural areas. It polls a consistently higher percentage of votes outside departmental capitals than within them and receives the largest portion of its support from non-capital votes. Of all the parties listed, it draws its greatest support from rural areas in each of these three, pre-reform periods.

Results from the 1993 elections for the office of *intendente* (intendent) at the cantonal level present the most proximate voting results to the passage of Bolivia's decentralization law. *Intendentes* wielded little real power and almost no resources, but the office was regularly filled through elections at the cantonal level – a level of government smaller than the provincial sections to which power would be devolved in the 1994 decentralization. By aggregating cantonal votes to the municipal level, a rough idea of relative party strength during 1993 can be obtained. This measure suffers from the lack of perfect coincidence between cantons and municipalities, but because the *intendentes* wielded little real power, the incentive to vote strategically for this office is almost nil. For this reason, the results should provide a fairly accurate read of voters' true preferences over political parties throughout the entire country at the time when the national government was earnestly considering decentralization. This measure also represents the most current information that would have been available to the actual political parties at the time in which they were deciding the shape of potential decentralization proposals.

In 1993 the MNR was not only a strong party at the local level, but the distribution of its support throughout the country garnered it a clear plurality of votes in almost 72 percent of the individual districts

TABLE 5.7: *1993 Local Elections*

Party	% of total vote	% of districts won
MNR	34.9	71.9
ADN	7.8	3.0
MIR-NM	9.4	3.0
CONDEPA	19.6	8.6
UCS	8.4	6.8

polled (see Table 5.7). If any party was poised to take advantage of municipalization in 1993, it was the MNR. This pattern continued in the 1995 and 1999 municipal elections, as well: In 1995, the MNR placed only one mayor in a small, provincial capital (the ADN won the mayoral position in La Paz, the capital); in 1999, the ADN won mayoral positions in two, small provincial capitals, while the MNR did not win any.[8]

Analyzing the local electoral strength of the parties reveals that the MNR has strong local-level support in the more rural areas of the country. This stems from its long association with the 1952 revolution, in which the MNR redistributed land to peasants and farmers and away from large landowners.

> The masses and leaders of the peasants (*campesinos*) viewed this party [the MNR] not only as an ally, but also as a savior from the situation of semi-slavery in which they lived prior to the Revolution [of 1952] and they supported it electorally on many occasions. (Molina and Arias 1996: 12)

If decentralization would increase the number and power of rural municipalities, the MNR would be the clear beneficiary, given its overwhelmingly rural basis of support. In the subsequent municipal elections of 1995, the MNR placed mayors in approximately 40 percent of municipalities, while ADN mayors governed only 12 percent of municipalities. In 1999, some 26 percent of municipalities chose mayors from the MNR – the largest percentage of any party contesting the election – 25 percent chose mayors from the ADN, while the MIR placed mayors in 19 percent of municipalities.[9]

---

[8] Results for 1995 come from Secretaría Nacional de Participación Popular (1996); results for 1999 come from the Corte Electoral Nacional website (www.cne.gov.bo), accessed March 2003.

[9] See note 8.

Summary

Having discussed each of the factors that should figure importantly in each administration's decision of whether or not to decentralize, this section attempts to draw together these pieces in the context of each administration to explain why decentralization is or is not adopted in each case. In most cases, the instability of electoral support across elections plays a central role.

The UDP came to office in 1982 on the basis of its 1980 election results, deferred two years by a series of coups. Though it had relatively strong national support at the beginning of its term, that support declined precipitously, leaving the party in complete disarray at the end of its term. It appears that the party not only ceased to exist at the national level, it disappeared as an electoral force at all levels, winning no municipal contests in 1985. In the face of this massive decline in support, decentralization was not an attractive option, since the party could not expect to win either subnational or national elections in the future.

The MNR's rise to the presidency in 1985 presents a slightly different case. Here the MNR has weak national-level support on gaining office (it is the second-highest vote-getting party in the national election, behind the ADN) and the highest subnational-level support of all parties in the system – with particular strength in rural areas. The change in its support at the national level based on the previous election's returns is somewhat high (it gains a 50 percent increase in votes), but this move is in a positive direction. One might guess that the MNR failed to decentralize because the party expected to regain the presidency, given the large increase in its national support. This hypothesis founders when one takes into consideration the electoral rules and, more importantly, the fact that the MNR began to lose support shortly after taking office.

Support for the MNR drops due to the party's drastic fiscal austerity program, implemented to stabilize Bolivia's skyrocketing inflation. Inflation in Bolivia set new records around the world, reaching an annualized rate of 8,000 percent. In fact, the economic chaos had forced the Siles Zuazo administration to step down and call early elections in 1985. The MNR's fiscal shock plan – Decree Law 21060 – proved effective but cost the party electoral support. Surprisingly, the MNR lost only four percentage points of support between the national elections of 1985 and 1989. At the local level, the drop in support was much steeper. Mid-term municipal election results from 1987 show this decline: The percentage of the vote won by the MNR fell by more than half from its 1985 level. In fact, it was the lowest of the three parties displayed in Table 5.6. This is true across the board, in both urban and rural areas. By the 1989 local elections, support for the MNR had begun to increase, but it was still down approximately 38 percent from its high level in 1985. The MNR may have rightly figured that it would gain little from decentralization as the drop in its support at the subnational level appeared steeper than the drop in its national support over the course of its administration.

The Paz Zamora administration that governed from 1989 to 1993 shied away from decentralization based on its weak electoral record at the subnational level, along with the overall decline in its support during its administration. The main factor that discouraged the MIR-ADN coalition from decentralizing was its weak support in the rural portions of the country. The ADN – a strong partner in the governing coalition – had the weakest support of the three major parties in rural voting, suggesting that it stood to gain little from a broad decentralization. The MIR fared poorly, as well. In addition, support for the MIR changed dramatically from election to election.

Strong support at the local level throughout its administration differentiated the MNR administration spanning 1993–1997 from its predecessors. Support at the local level had regenerated from its depressed level at the end of the Paz Estenssoro presidency, and this support remained stable while the administration debated decentralization. In the 1995 local elections, the MNR won a majority of votes in 37 percent of municipalities, winning roughly 39 percent of the mayoral positions. In 1996 and 1997, despite provisions that allowed for the removal of mayors by decision of the municipal council,[10] the MNR continued to hold between 37 percent and 39 percent of mayoral positions (Secretaría Nacional de Participación Popular 1996; Rojas Ortuste 1998). In all of these years the next strongest party had less than half the number of mayors claimed by the MNR. In addition, the MNR had the most stable support across time of any party in the system.

---

[10] Municipal councils may remove the mayor they have chosen after one year and choose a replacement from among the rest of the council members; this can occur each year of the mayor's term of office, allowing for the possibility of four different mayors over a four-year term.

A MORE DETAILED LOOK

My analysis focuses on the period beginning in 1982, although universal male suffrage was instituted by the revolutionary government beginning in 1952. The period 1982–2000 is the most interesting for several reasons. Between 1952 and 1964, the MNR won three elections with three-quarters or more of the vote (82 percent in 1956, 75 percent in 1960, and 86 percent in 1964), giving it little incentive to decentralize. After 1964, civilian and military regimes alternated at a furious pace with no civilian regime lasting longer than a year.[11] In the midst of this chaos, little reform could have been achieved by civilian regimes and no decentralizing reform would have been likely under authoritarian rule. In 1982, democratic contestation resumed with the election of Siles Zuazo, who began the twentieth presidential administration in as many years.

While I focus on this most recent period of democracy, it is worth noting that the division of power among national and subnational levels of government has been a much-debated topic throughout Bolivia's history. Bolivia's 1839 constitution attempted to decentralize political power by demanding that municipal councils be popularly elected. Despite the letter of the law, the issue lay dormant[12] for nearly a century until a 1931 referendum, inspired by Daniel Sánchez Bustamente, was carried out under military rule. This referendum found widespread support for decentralizing administrative powers to the regional level, and a new constitution in 1938 explicitly called for a political

---

[11] Mesa Gisbert (1990) classifies the 1966–1969 Barrientos presidency (and the subsequent 1969 Siles Salinas presidency) as civilian rather than military due to the elections that justified his rule. Barrientos had been a military leader of Bolivia between 1964–1965 and 1965–1966 during two military juntas. Upon his death – the circumstances of which were never fully clear – Siles Salinas served out the remainder of his term. In the 1966 elections, neither Paz Estenssoro (who had been president from 1952 to 1956 and 1960 to 1964 and who had been elected in 1964 before the military took over the government that year) nor Siles Zuazo (who had been president from 1956 to 1960) were allowed to run. For this reason, the civilian nature of Barrientos's presidency is dubious.

[12] That is not to say that the issue was completely absent from Bolivia's politics. For example, in 1857 the government called for decentralization but did not institute a workable plan to empower municipalities. In addition, central-regional tensions flared up at the end of the nineteenth century over natural resource rents, precipitating the transfer of the capital city from Sucre to La Paz (Urioste Fernández de Córdova 2002: 149–152).

decentralization that would reach down to the municipal level. Administrative decentralization to regions became formally incorporated into the 1967 constitution, but was largely ignored in practice, first by the elected general Barrientos, who was in power at the time, and then by his successors, who were mainly military dictators. Despite the paper progress made at both the regional and local levels, no laws were passed to put these ideas into practice until the decentralization law proposed by Sánchez de Lozada – the grandson of Sánchez Bustamente – in 1994 (Molina Monasterios 1997: 46).

In fact, during the democratic period beginning in 1982, several parties paid lip service to the idea of decentralization without making any real efforts to decentralize. During this period, the legislature considered more than twenty legal projects that proposed some level of decentralization (Molina Saucedo interview 1997). Many would credit the first MNR presidency of this period with having created a more decentralized state. Under the presidency of Víctor Paz Estenssoro (his third non-consecutive term) between 1985 and 1989, economic aspects of state power were deconcentrated through a series of neoliberal reforms that shrank the state's control over many economic activities and barred the state from intervention in public enterprises.

Despite breaking the state's near monopoly on large economic enterprises, no major steps were taken toward decentralizing fiscal and political power to subnational levels. In fact, Law 839, which was passed during this period, further centralized fiscal resources and exacerbated regional inequalities by redistributing federal funds. Law 839 eliminated several taxes (mainly taxes on businesses) collected at regional and municipal levels, allowing the national government to collect them instead. Proponents, who included Sánchez de Lozada (then Minister of Finance), argued that economies of scale at the central level would lead to more efficient collection. While this economic logic was sound, there was no concomitant measure to transfer the more efficiently collected taxes back to the subnational governments. Instead, the law stipulated that the collected taxes were to be spent within the regions where the businesses paying the taxes were located. In this way, a tax paid on gasoline in one region would benefit the region in which the gasoline company was registered. This law further concentrated resources in La Paz and Santa Cruz, the country's two largest centers of production.

Support for decentralizing political power to the regional level had grown quite strong by the 1989 election, and almost all parties included some reference to decentralization in their campaigns. The popularization of this issue can be credited to the Civic Committees of regional capitals, particularly to the efforts of the Civic Committee of Santa Cruz. These organizations function like chambers of commerce, composed of large business owners and other regional elites who band together to discuss and influence political and economic issues. One of their largest sources of power derived from their formal representation within the development corporations, which controlled 10 percent of national revenues. While these organizations had never been internally democratic, they rallied popular support for their proposal of greater departmental autonomy under the name of the "National Civic Movement." Specifically, this movement sought the direct election of departmental governments (a regional council and governor), stipulating that these regional elections should not be concurrent with national elections so that national issues would not influence these regional contests. It is likely that the civic committees believed they could more easily influence popularly elected regional governments than appointed prefects, particularly given their strong organization and proven ability to mobilize the public. This proposal resonated with regular citizens who clamored for a greater voice in local policy making.

Once in power, the MIR president, with strong support from his coalition partner, the ADN, began to devote more attention to decentralization, but with few consequences. Conferences were held throughout the country, but a cynical public expected few real results:

Nobody believed that anything would come from this effort. One group of deputies attended the opening session of the first meeting – which was supposed to last for three days – with return tickets for the following morning, anticipating that it would not be worthwhile to stay. (Molina Monasterios 1997: 135)

Toward the end of its term, the Paz Zamora government proposed a plan to decentralize financial resources to the country's nine regions. The proposal also anticipated a long-term, gradual process devolving responsibilities to municipalities as they proved their administrative capacity. The central government, of course, remained the sole judge of this capacity, deciding which municipalities would receive augmented powers on a case-by-case basis. The most urbanized areas of the country would be the most likely to prove their capacity to take on new responsibilities, and since the majority of MIR-ADN support resided in these areas, these parties could expect to continue controlling the vast majority of resources under a decentralized form of government. This law received a slight majority of support in the Senate but was thwarted in the lower chamber of the legislature, mainly due to MNR opposition.

In the end, president Jaime Paz Zamora, who had begun his term assuring the public that political decentralization was feasible in Bolivia, ended it expressing doubts about decentralization, causing one observer to ask: "Do unitarist fumes emanate from the presidential palace that nauseate and bewitch its inhabitants?" (Molina Monasterios 1997: 120).

The MNR presidency that followed approached the question of decentralization very differently from how the MIR-ADN government had approached it. While decentralization played a role in the party's platform of reforms called the Plan de Todos (Plan for All), few details had been spelled out before the MNR's inauguration. In fact, several experts invited to work on the outline of the reform were shocked to find that this lack of disclosure owed less to secrecy than to a fundamental lack of details:

It surprised me that there had not been a proposal. The Plan for All and so forth was there, but there was no proposal. We began to work almost from scratch. There were the idea of municipalizing and a couple of others, but there was nothing else. . . . The MNR did not have an idea of what constituted Popular Participation, even though they had invented the concept. (Rubén Ardaya, in Molina Monasterios 1997: 198)

Gonzalo Sánchez de Lozada – affectionately referred to during his term as Goni by the majority of the population – created a team of technical experts to examine the problem. Composed of highly trained politicians, technocrats, and a few economists, this team met frequently with the president to design the decentralization program. The policy team that drafted the LPP might be misperceived as a group of technocrats operating within a political vacuum; though its meetings were closed and the personnel were highly trained professionals, the nature of this committee was patently political. Meetings were closed not to ensure the purity of the resulting law but to keep political opponents from changing the president's very political agenda. Due to the already strong support by civic committees for a regional decentralization plan, the workings of this group were kept quiet for fear of opposition. In fact, leaked information incited such outrage from the Santa Cruz Civic Committee that the clandestine group was forced to distance itself from the uncovered proposal. This incident led to greater secrecy in the remaining meetings. According to Molina Monasterios (1997):

The President and the members of the committee met 36 times, between the 18th of November and the 20th of February in 1994. Many of the meetings were meetings of the cabinet. They discussed for 300 hours. The technical team worked 16,200 hours in developing the law. (196)

In this intense and secret atmosphere, the planners had to decide to which level of government power should be devolved. The most carefully crafted plan remained the proposal voted down under the previous government that would have strengthened regional governments. Regional decentralization was not the only idea to which the public had been exposed, however. Important works that proposed municipalization of the country had gained wide readership, including Rubén Ardaya's *Ensayo Sobre Municipalidad y Municipios* (Essay Regarding Municipalization and Municipalities), Ivan Finot's *Democratización del Estado y Descentralización* (Democratization of the State and Decentralization), and – perhaps most importantly – Carlos Hugo Molina's *La Descentralización Imposible y la Alternativa Municipal* (Impossible Decentralization and the Municipal Alternative). This last author played an important role on the policy team, but the ultimate decision fell to Goni. When asked how municipalization was chosen, Luis Lema, a member of the committee that drafted the law, replied: "In the talks that were held, throughout the entire period, with the leader of our party, Gonzalo Sánchez de Lozada" (Archondo 1997: 150).

Note that he refers to Goni as the party leader in this passage – underlining the important role party concerns played in the decision.

When asked why decentralization had not been advanced by an earlier administration, Carlos Hugo Molina Saucedo answered:

All of the government acts to try to improve effectiveness require two fundamental conditions: a legal framework and political will. As I mentioned, in
the last 12 years there have been 22 different legal projects to promote decentralization, but there was an absence of political will. This was the first
government to possess the political will. The discourse of decentralization is
something which brings applause and sympathy very rapidly so there is always
a popular will, but there was no political will on the part of leaders to act on
this. (interview, 1997)

ALTERNATIVE THEORIES

Theories linking decentralization to alternatives such as fiscal crisis
or international pressure have already been examined in Chapter 3.
Bolivian evidence suggested a particularly poor fit between these
economics-based theories and the timing of decentralization: Fiscal
deficits and the burden of debt were heaviest in the mid-1980s, but decentralization occurred during a period of relative fiscal stability and
improvement in the 1990s. In the section that follows, alternative theories arising from the Bolivian case are examined, including the role
of political ideology and the theory that pressures from below forced
innovation at the center. This section also explores a secondary impli-
cation of the electoral theory of decentralization: that electoral factors
should affect not just the timing of decentralization, but also the level
of government to which decentralized resources are targeted.

Ideology

A more parsimonious explanation for the MNR's adoption of decentralization might link decentralization to party ideology. The decision
of one party to decentralize and the decision of other parties not to
decentralize may simply reflect their different views on the value of decentralization more generally. By approaching the argument from two
sides, I argue that this is not the case. First and most broadly, modern
Bolivian history shows that no parties have held rigidly to particular ideological positions, making it unlikely that decentralization has
taken on particular ideological significance in inter-party competition.

Second and more specifically, the MNR has not always supported decentralization – in fact, they have been responsible for much of the overconcentration of power at the central level.

According to several experts, Bolivian parties gain support based not on ideological appeals but through patronage. Describing the state of the party system in 1985, Malloy and Gamarra (1988) state:

At its core Bolivia's was still a personalistic and patrimonial kind of political system in which institutional and programmatic considerations of all kinds were secondary to the dynamics of patron-client networks. (189)

The MNR is no exception to this generalization. Despite being Bolivia's oldest party, the ideological stance of the MNR has fluctuated wildly. The party began in 1941 as "antiliberal, anti-Marxist and anti-Semitic" (Gamarra and Malloy 1995: 402). It adopted a reformist stance in 1946, arguing for the nationalization of mines, the extension of suffrage, and agrarian reform. It championed state-led development and a centralist tendency throughout most of its lifetime, contributing greatly to the concentration of power at the central level. The same party began dismantling this power under the massive neoliberal shock engineered by one of its founders, Víctor Paz Estenssoro, in 1985, and the process concluded with the decentralization reforms signed by Gonzalo Sánchez de Lozada in 1993–1994:

The reign of state-ism in Bolivia lasted from 1952 until 1985 when Supreme Decree 21060 was approved (the neoliberal shock reform to stop the country's hyperinflation). Finally the mud crumbled from the giant which, as he fell, streamed away. The ultimate push was given by Victor Paz Estenssoro who, like Doctor Frankenstein, was both the father of the beast and also the one who eventually had to kill it. (Molina Monasterios 1997: 35)

The same party that had built the centralized power structure of the Bolivian state – in fact, the same party leader – struck the first blow against the centralized state.

Other parties also did not show a consistent ideological commitment to decentralization. While the MIR had campaigned on the issue, making promises to a population hungry for increased participation, little progress was made during its term in office from 1989 to 1993. In fact, the party showed little enthusiasm for decentralizing reforms during the period; its lip service to the idea far outweighed its effort to construct a decentralized reality.

A more convincing argument links decentralization not to party ideology but to party advantage. The MNR had no long-term ideological commitment to decentralization but was the party most able to benefit from municipalization. This was particularly true after the MNR restructured itself along territorial lines in the 1990s:

> It is known that the National Revolutionary Movement (MNR) which is the actual party in government, as a result of approving its last governing statutes in 1990, has become a territorial-based organization. It has an advantage over other parties in that it is the pioneer of ideas about this type of party organization. (Paredes Muñoz 1995: 96)[13]

Pressure from Below

Another theory that deserves attention explains decentralization in Bolivia as a response to pressures from below. Two possible sources of pressure are examined here: pressure from organized indigenous groups that sought greater autonomy from the largely non-indigenous controlled government (at times referred to as a "pigmentocracy"[14]) and more diverse and widespread pressure for increased democracy emanating from the grass roots and pressing for decentralization during elections.

While Bolivia is a country woven from several unique and rich indigenous cultures, attempts by indigenous groups to decentralize the government were weak in the period leading up to the LPP's passage. The two most prominent indigenous parties before the passage of the LPP – the MRTKL and Eje-Pachacuti – together polled less than 2 percent of the national vote in the 1993 elections, despite the fact that more than 70 percent of Bolivians self-identify as indigenous. In 1997 the Eje-Pachacuti obtained less than 1 percent of national votes. Between the 1997 and 2002 elections indigenous identity became an important factor in political organizing; two new parties, the MAS (Movement toward Socialism) and MIP (Indigenous Pachacuti

---

[13] See also Zegada (1996, 1998) on party organization in Bolivia.
[14] Marc Cramer uses this term in an editorial in the *Bolivian Times* lamenting the color divide between government and the governed in Bolivia in 1998.

Movement) together polled just over 27 percent of the national vote in the 2002 elections.[15]

Prior to this surge in indigenous party formation, indigenous groups could, of course, work within non-indigenous parties either internally as members or externally as potential voters to achieve decentralization if it was their goal. Several indigenous organizations did exist, even if they rarely formed political parties of their own. They play a significant role in Bolivian politics, but fragmentation and internal leadership struggles have handicapped their potential strength. Indigenous organizing centers around several poles, including the Tupac Katari Indian Movement (MITKA), the Bolivian Coordinator of Syndicates and Peasant Workers (CSUTCB), the Bolivian Confederacy of Indians of Eastern Bolivia (CIDOB), the Central Organization of Indigenous Peoples of the Bení (CPIB), and the Assembly of Guaraní People (APG). Evidence that indigenous groups pushed for decentralization appears weak, however.

One researcher, writing about indigenous groups in Bolivia and the decentralizing process, argues that, though they were beneficiaries of decentralization, indigenous groups were not responsible for the reform:

The exclusionary, managed, top-down process of [decentralization] can be attributed to the fact that there was no coherent political movement for the radical transformation of state-society relations from below, apart from the weak indigenous organizations and the writings of politically impotent intellectuals. (Van Cott 1998: 261)

Van Cott explains the indirect channels through which indigenous groups influenced the reform, as many of the technical consultants brought in to draft the law were either indigenous or sympathetic to indigenous claims.

Though Sánchez de Lozada spearheaded the decentralization effort, one might imagine that his vice president, Victor Hugo Cárdenas – Bolivia's first indigenous vice president, might have played a decisive role in its formation. In fact, Cárdenas distanced himself from playing any significant role in drafting the decentralization proposal.

---

[15] For an examination of why indigenous parties formed between 1997–2002, see Van Cott 2003b.

Finally, when Popular Participation became a political possibility in late 1993 and early 1994, many indigenous groups opposed it, most notably the CSUTCB. Several indigenous leaders felt that the law attempted to supplant existing indigenous institutions for self-governance with alternative structures outside their control. A large public relations campaign was required to convince the indigenous community otherwise.

In addition to indigenous pressures for decentralization, one might expect pressure for greater local democracy from a much broader segment of the population. If such support had existed, it is likely to have percolated to the surface during highly contested national elections. Decentralization had been a campaign issue in several elections and a topic of numerous conferences throughout the country. With pressure building in these ways, decentralization could have occurred as a capitulation. This story is a complex but rich one, and its nuances allow for the teasing out of one of the electoral theory's secondary implications.

REGIONALISM VERSUS LOCALISM

I argue that, even though there was pressure for greater participation, demands for decentralization focused on the devolution of power to the regional level – a level bypassed by the actual reforms adopted. Little to no pressure was exerted on the government to decentralize power to localities.

As already mentioned, pressure for regional decentralization came principally from the civic committees in each of the departmental capitals. These business and elite associations, not internally democratic, seem an unlikely source for pressure to democratize and extend popular participation in government; however, given their long history of civic organizing, civic committees stood to gain influence over regionally elected departmental governments who would have access to funds and political legitimacy.

While significant pressure was exerted for regional decentralization, almost no pressure was exerted to effect decentralization at the local level. A survey conducted in 1993 – just a year before the decentralization reform was adopted – asked whether local governments should exist or whether the existing municipalities were sufficient. Some 43 percent of respondents wanted more extensive local government, while 40 percent were satisfied with the status quo; 17 percent refrained from answering (Ministerio de Planeamiento y Coordinación 1993a: 21). Asked what was best about decentralization, respondents chose "*No sabe*" ("I do not know") almost two to one over the next most popular answer (ibid.: 22). No strong consensus on local government appears to have formed. On the contrary, although municipalities existed in a few enclaves of the country, they exerted little organized effort to increase their powers through a general decentralization law:

In contrast to the Civic Movement, the municipal governments never had success in creating a strong and cohesive association. In contrast it was characterized by its instability and its few proposals for limited reform of the Municipal Law. The municipal governments did not participate in the debates over decentralization because they were not invited and because they themselves considered the reform to be a change exclusively affecting the departmental level. (Paredes Muñoz 1995: 99)

In addition to disproving the hypothesis that decentralization occurred due to pressure from below, I also want to show how parties' electoral support at different levels of government shapes their preferences over decentralizing to regional or local governments. While the MNR was weak at the regional level, it enjoyed strong support at the local level, making the decision between federalism and localism a clear one.

According to Molina Monasterios (1997):

The LPP gave the municipalities much more than they had requested at that time. Their demands were more basic, there had not been a municipal consciousness. I believe that, based on their level of development, the municipalities would not have arrived at formulating a law like the LPP. It had to have come from above. (149)

Given that the vast majority of municipalities did not even exist prior to the decentralization law, there was no municipal unit to pressure for power from above. Rafael Archondo (1997) adds:

The provincial section did not have any jurisdictional authority whatsoever; it was a parcel of land without power, a product that was derivative, with no origin nor port of destination. (20)

Few would argue that pressure for municipalization caused the Popular Participation Law of 1994.

Looking back at the sections devoted to regional- and local-level support for Bolivia's political parties, it becomes clear that the MNR had the most to gain from decentralizing to the municipal level because of its widespread support throughout the country and particularly in rural areas. The MNR faced much weaker and more volatile support at the regional level; urban centers were much more likely to vote for the MNR's political rivals, especially the ADN. This data also reinforces the logic of the MIR-ADN plan to decentralize to regional levels, since the ADN would profit so greatly from winning regional capitals and major urban areas that would weigh heavily in regional-level voting. Given the constellation of their electoral support, both the MNR and the ADN have approached decentralization in ways that would provide them the greatest long-term benefits.

A final point worth noting is that the ADN reclaimed the presidency in 1997, placing itself in a position to effect changes in the Popular Participation program. Due to its popularity and the fact that decentralization was enshrined in the constitution (1994), the program was nearly impossible to reverse; however, the ADN was roundly criticized for slowing down the process of decentralization. The ADN's weak local support suggests that it would gain fewer benefits from local autonomy than the MNR, with its widespread local support. It also benefited less from decentralization than many smaller parties, such as the UCS and CONDEPA, in the early 1990s, and the MAS and NFR, at the start of the new millennium, that faced a small likelihood of gaining national power but that controlled several important municipalities.[16]

While decentralization remains alive and well in Bolivia, Banzer's administration adjusted several aspects of the decentralized framework set out in the LPP. These adjustments included administrative changes, fiscal changes, and efforts to increase the powers of regional prefects.

A subtle but significant way in which Banzer's administration downgraded Popular Participation resulted from an administrative restructuring of the program. While Sánchez de Lozada created a Secretariat of Popular Participation, Banzer reorganized the state apparatus, placing the responsibility for this program in the Vice Ministry of

---

[16] CONDEPA, in particular, had been successful at winning mayoral races in the department of La Paz, including its capital.

Strategic Planning and Popular Participation, within the Ministry of Sustainable Development and Planning.

More importantly, while the 1999 municipal elections were held on schedule and without any restrictions imposed by the central government, campaign funds were parceled out in an unusual series of payments (rather than as a lump sum). The government claimed that fiscal problems necessitated this change in previous practice. The change engendered a heated public debate in which the National Electoral Court demanded that at least half of the money be transferred to the parties at once. In addition to the controversy surrounding campaign funds, municipal governments criticized the government for failing to even out the payment of fiscal transfers promised by the Popular Participation Law. This, among other demands by Bolivia's Association of Municipal Governments, led to a twenty-four-hour strike in mid-August of 1999 that paralyzed the country (*Los Tiempos*, August 18, 1999). Again, the government explained its actions with reference to the central government's fiscal difficulties. It remains unclear to what extent monies were being retained in the center due to fiscal crisis and to what extent this was a strategic maneuver to keep financial resources in the central government's hands.

Finally, Banzer adjusted decentralization toward regional prefects and away from municipal councils (Böhrt Irahola 2001: 61–64). An early act of Banzer's government (undertaken in the first month of his presidency) liberated departmental prefects – all ADN partisans – from having to present written quarterly reports to the departmental assemblies (whose members are indirectly elected by the municipal councils). He also freed them of the necessity of obtaining the general director of the department's signature on administrative resolutions made by the prefecture. These measures, enacted in Supreme Decree 24833, also enhanced the prefect's power relative to provincial subprefects in the provinces and *corregidores* in the cantons (Urenda Díaz 1998: 83–85); it is particularly interesting to note that the prefects appointed to the two largest departments, La Paz and Santa Cruz, were not only ADN partisans but members of Banzer's own family.[17]

---

[17] For a good discussion of Banzer's appointments from within his own family, see Sivak 2001, esp. 270–277.

While none of these changes greatly damaged the impact of the LPP on devolving power to municipal governments, each represents a subtle but sure step toward reining in the process of decentralization.

CONCLUSION

While Bolivia's decentralizing reforms have not been in place for as long as Colombia's have been, scholars both within and outside Bolivia have begun to analyze their consequences for both economic and political development. The results are mixed. The most frequently cited benefits of decentralization refer to its structure for allowing citizen participation in local affairs (Urioste Fernández de Córdova 2002). These stretch beyond elections to include the crafting of participatory municipal development plans and the oversight of institutionally embedded committees made up from civic society organizations. Turnout in local elections has been relatively high since the LPP was enacted; in 1995 more voters turned out to elect local officials than had turned out in the national elections of 1993. Since then, there has been a consistent decline: 59 percent of eligible voters turned out in the 1999 municipal elections, compared with 71 percent in the 1997 national elections and 72 percent in the 2002 national elections.[18] In addition, municipal contests have created spaces for traditionally marginalized political forces to enter the governing arena. Remarkably, the 1995 elections brought 464 indigenous or campesino municipal councilors (and alternates) to office (representing 29 percent of the total); in seventy-three of 311 municipalities, these councilors represented a majority of councilors (Albó 1999: 16; Van Cott 2003a: 44). On the other hand, the election of female councilors dropped between 1993 and 1995 from 27 percent to only 8.3 percent (Secretaría Nacional de Participación Popular 1996: 10).

At the same time, critics find numerous faults, particularly in the mismatch between the structures imagined by the LPP and those that have actually been built in certain municipalities. Observers find oversight committees that have been coopted by traditional political parties (Andersson 1999), innumerable instances of corruption within

---

[18] These numbers come from Bolivia's Corte Nacional Electoral website (www.cne. org.bo), visited March 2003.

municipal governments (Seligson 1999, cited in Prud'homme, Huntziger, and Guelton 2000),[19] and policy incoherence where frequent turnover of mayors has become common (Rojas Ortuste 1998).[20] While municipal elections are open to all parties, candidates not affiliated with a recognized party have been barred from running, narrowing the range of electoral options. In addition, the first years of municipal spending have seemed to favor short-term projects such as beautifying the municipal plaza, rather than investment in infrastructure, education, or health (Urioste Fernández de Córdova 2002). Faguet (2001) finds that investment in education, water and sanitation, water management, and agriculture are, in fact, positively correlated with indicators of need. One assessment concludes: "Municipal governments remain weak, local taxes are embryonic, the transfer system is imperfect, local borrowing is excessive, [and] municipal accounts are unsatisfactory" (Prud'homme et al. 2000: 71). As in the Colombian case, the jury remains out on decentralization's contributions to political and economic development in Bolivia.

What seems somewhat clearer is that the impetus for decentralization in Bolivia responds to electoral incentives during the democratic period after 1982. Because the procedures for choosing the president leave each party uncertain of gaining or attaining the presidency despite potentially strong electoral showings, every party has some incentive to seek a decentralized system in which power is more disaggregated and therefore easier to grasp at many levels of government. To determine which parties will favor decentralization, one must look to their support at subnational levels and at the stability of their support over time. Both of these criteria shed a spotlight on the MNR, the system's most stable party across elections and the only party with consistent, widespread support throughout the country, particularly in rural areas. The ADN – the party with the second most consistent record of support in national elections – finds its support concentrated in urban areas and would be more likely to benefit from regional decentralization. Not surprisingly, the ADN-MIR coalition attempted

---

[19] Prud'homme et al. 2000 cite a survey carried out by Mitchell Seligson in 1998 in which, of 3,000 people surveyed, 23 percent reported paying bribes to municipal employees.

[20] Rojas Ortuste (1998: 32) notes that 29 percent of Bolivian municipalities replaced their mayors in 1997 and 25 percent replaced them in 1998.

a regional decentralization during the 1989–1993 period only to be stopped in the legislature by a strong MNR voting bloc. In its turn at the helm, the MNR redirected the country toward greater local decentralization.

The theory linking decentralization to the electoral motivations of political parties outperforms competing theories that seek to explain changes in power-sharing arrangements between levels of government tested in this chapter. Political ideology fails to separate parties adequately and seems rather fluid over time within parties, making it a weak motivator of policy. Economic crises and dependence on international creditors that peaked in the mid-1980s appeared mismatched with decentralization reforms passed in 1994. Finally, the reforms did not appear to result from grass-roots pressure for change. While dissatisfaction with the highly centralized structure of government was detectable, specific pressure for decentralization had not congealed before the reform occurred. What is more, indigenous movements failed to unify around this cause; instead, they exerted their energy to gain official recognition of their indigenous identity and to support programs such as bilingual schooling that would allow them to retain and enrich that identity.

In the first post-decentralization administration, ADN president Banzer slowed decentralization: He replaced nearly all officials within the National Secretariat for Popular Participation with his party militants and strengthened regional governments (all nine departmental prefects were ADN partisans) financially. One of Banzer's first acts as president, Supreme Decree 24833, modified the law governing prefects. Included in that decree, Banzer launched his first blow against the popular participation law, downgrading the Departmental Secretariat for Popular Participation from a Secretariat to an Operating Unit (Unidad Operativa), dependent on the Directorate of Social Development (previously the Secretariat for Human Development). Oporto Castro (1998) remarks: "This change related to the new government's intention to strip importance from everything related to Popular Participation" (49).

It would have been interesting to see how Gonzalo Sánchez de Lozada – elected to a second (non-consecutive) term of office – would have treated the process of decentralization that he began. Unlike the country's situation when he left office in 1997, when he returned to office, Bolivia faced an economic crisis; in early 2003 a series of demonstrations paralyzed the government, violence and looting occurred in the streets, and many opponents called for Goni to step down from the presidency. Sánchez de Lozada acquiesced to these demands, and stepped down in October 2003.

6

Ecuador, Venezuela, and Peru

INTRODUCTION

Colombia and Bolivia, despite extremely different party systems, levels of economic development, and experiences with democratic rule, both managed to decentralize in the last twenty years. Ecuador, Venezuela, and Peru add richness to this analysis by broadening the range of country experiences with national- and subnational-level power-sharing arrangements. Ecuador, a country whose parties experience wide swings in election results over time, provides the one example of a country that does not decentralize significantly during this time.[1] Venezuela, although it has a long history of extremely strong and stable parties and a long experience of democratic rule, decentralizes late and only partially. Peru provides the single example of a country where power has not only been decentralized, but also *recentralized* during democratic rule.[2]

This chapter analyzes whether the pattern discerned in previous chapters fits the experiences of these three countries. More specifically, it seeks to determine whether decentralization occurs during periods when the party in power is uncertain of its chances in national elections, gains strong support at subnational levels, and has a fairly

---

[1] For a good discussion of Ecuador's decentralizing experience, see Frank 2003.

[2] You may recall from Chapter 5 that Hugo Banzer (1997–2001) in Bolivia has made some effort in the direction of recentralization, but he has not been successful enough to classify Bolivia as "recentralized." A further comparison of Banzer and Fujimori is elaborated below in this chapter.

steady level of support across time periods. Parties that fit this profile are expected to support decentralization because it offers them an opportunity to win a large proportion of positions contested through subnational elections when they are unsure of retaining power at the national level. Large changes in support for parties across elections frustrates a party's ability to predict its electoral prospects, shortening its time horizons and diminishing the appeal of decentralization's long-term electoral benefits. This hypothesis is supported if the parties that display these features when in power attempt to decentralize and if the parties that do not display these features do not attempt to decentralize. The same logic can be extended to predict partisan positions within legislatures and other governing bodies.

The following analysis concludes that extreme changes in the electoral support of Ecuadorian parties hinders decentralization reform throughout the period studied. It also finds that, despite relatively constant levels of electoral support across elections, Venezuelan parties do not decentralize until the late 1980s because they believe in their ability to win or retain national power. Finally, I find that electoral incentives work in the opposite direction, as well – parties with strong national-level support, weak subnational-level support, and high variability of their support over time seek to recentralize power. This is evidenced by the experience of Peru between 1990 and 1995 during Fujimori's first term in government. These features are also shared by Hugo Banzer's ADN (Democratic National Action party) in Bolivia between 1997 and 2001 and, to some extent, by Venezuela's Hugo Chávez presidency (beginning in 1998); not surprisingly, these administrations have all been accused of recentralizing behavior.

This chapter provides short summaries of each country's experience with decentralization over the entire period of its most recent democratic experience. In keeping with the format of the previous country-based chapters of this book, the discussion here pays particular attention to the national electoral support of parties, their subnational support, and the stability of their support across elections. Where additional information is available to gauge the party's support between elections, those data are included to shed more light on the party's strategic thinking over the course of its term. This is particularly important in cases where party support changes dramatically over the course of an administration. This chapter also allows for a closer look at party behavior outside the executive, in appointed commissions, legislatures, and within factions of parties, where these played important roles in decentralization.

ECUADOR

In 1978, Ecuador's ruling military junta eased the country back to democracy. Swaddled in a new constitution that strongly resembled its 1967 predecessor, the new Ecuadorian democracy emerged with a complex system governing its subnational territories. In some ways Ecuador appears politically decentralized at the start of this period. Each of its twenty-one provinces elected a prefect and provincial council. Its 193 districts[3] had municipal status with elected councils, and twenty-five of them – the provincial capitals and a few other major cities – directly elected their mayors, as well. The political power of these provincial and municipal executives, however, consisted solely in controlling a decisive vote should their councils encounter a deadlock.

Shadowing the elected, subnational executives, the president appointed a governor in each province (who was tasked with coordinating national policy at the provincial level and was an agent of the president), and a municipal president in each canton to perform the functions of the mayor in cities that either were not provincial capitals or did not have at least 50,000 inhabitants. The financial resources of both provincial and municipal governments were severely circumscribed by the central government.[4] In 1991, municipal income accounted for only 1.5 percent of GDP; transfers from the central government made up two-thirds of that figure (Ribadeneira 1995: 145). This

---

[3] It is worth noting that, with only 193 municipalities and a population of 10.6 million in 1994, this translates into an average of nearly 55,000 people per municipality (Nickson 1995: 32). (By the end of 1999 there were 214 municipalities.) This is higher than the population per municipality in Bolivia, Colombia, or Peru, suggesting little direct contact between municipal residents and the official local government. Of course, numbers alone are a crude measure of accessibility (Cameron 2000).

[4] Nickson (1995) notes that municipal budgets must pass through the national planning body (CONADE) for approval before receiving funds and also that most of the money received by subnational levels derives from legislators' "district" budgets that allow them to greatly control these districts, using local officials primarily to mobilize local voters in their favor. In addition, the executive can funnel money to subnational levels through the appointed offices he controls at each level, bypassing mayors and prefects he finds unfavorable.

system – maintained until at least 1998 – simply does not qualify as effectively decentralized, as subnational levels lack real fiscal power and most of the country cannot elect real local executives.[5] Despite amendment of the constitution in 1984, this fundamental structure of power sharing changed little, and Ecuador ended the period with a rather centralized government. Legislation promoting both political and fiscal decentralization advanced after 1996, but its implementation became a low priority in the midst of the country's worst financial crisis in decades; these issues are considered below.

The next section explores whether or not political parties holding power during this period faced electoral incentives to decentralize or whether, in contrast, they faced incentives to maintain the centralized system. Looking at the national level of support for parties, the change in party support over time, and the support parties receive at subnational levels, this section concludes that Ecuadorian politicians have faced few incentives to decentralize from 1978 to 1996. The period 1996–2000 receives special attention due to the extreme volatility of this period. Touched off by the ouster of President Abdalá Bucarám, this five-year period witnesses the rotation of six different presidents, a military-aided coup, and a severe financial crisis. In the midst of this turmoil, small but significant steps were taken to advance decentralization on paper, but few policy changes have been implemented.

Although Ecuador experienced extended periods of democracy before 1978, this section focuses on the latest democratic period spanning 1978–1996. It was the 1978 constitution that finally instituted universal suffrage,[6] making democratic contestation for office fully participatory, in contrast to the battle within the elite that had decided officeholders before the dictatorship. These earlier periods receive brief comment in the concluding section.

---

[5] Lautaro Ojeda Segovia (1993) goes further, noting, "Local governments have been losing their role as managers, intermediaries or mediators of social demands for social services.... This erosion or loss of the social role of local governments has converted them into mere executors of works and actions conceived or begun by groups with local, regional or national power, reducing in this way municipal action for small works, and, what is worse, [turning them into] conduits of central government funds (upon which they depend to an incredible degree) to cover current expenses, especially wages and salaries" (25).

[6] In the presidential election of 1968, some 30 percent of the population who were able to vote in 1978 were barred from voting due to the enforcement of literacy requirements.

TABLE 6.1: *Presidential Election Results and Vote Change, Ecuador 1978–2002[a]*

Party[b]	1978	1984	1988	1992	1996	1998	2002
CFP	27.7	13.5	7.9	–	–	–	–
PSC	23.9	**27.2**	14.7	25.0	27.2	–	12.2
PLRE	22.7	–	–	–	–	–	–
ID	12.0	**28.7**	24.5	–	–	15.9	14.0
PRE	–	–	17.6	22.0	**26.3**	26.9	11.9
DP	–	6.7	11.6	–	13.5	**35.3**	–
PUR	–	–	–	**31.4**	–	–	–
MUPP-NP	–	–	–	–	–	14.3	20.4[c]
MIRA	–	–	–	–	–	5.2	–
PRIAN	–	–	–	–	–	–	17.4
RP	–	–	–	–	–	–	15.4

Note: A dash indicates that the party received less than 5 percent of the vote. Boldface type is used to distinguish the president's party.

[a] These figures represent first-round voting results for presidential candidates. The winners of second-round contests are set in bold. For the second-round results, see Chapter 2.

[b] CFP: Concentración de Fuerzas Populares (Concentration of Popular Forces); PSC: Partido Social Cristiano (Social Christian Party); PLRE: Partido Liberal Radical Ecuatoriano (Liberal Radical Party of Ecuador); ID: Izquierda Democrática (Democratic Left); PRE: Partido Roldosista Ecuatoriano (Ecuadorian Roldosist Party); DP: Democracia Popular (Popular Democracy); PUR: Partido Unión Republicana (Republican Union Party); MUPP-NP: Movimiento Unidad Plurinacional Pachakutik – Nuevo País (Plurinational Unity Movement – New Country); MIRA: Movimiento Independiente para una República Auténtica (Independent Movement for an Authentic Republic); PRIAN: Partido Renovador Institucional Nacional y Acción Nacional (Party of Institutional Renewal and National Action); RP: Independent candidacy of Leon Roldos Aguilera.

[c] For the 2002 elections, the party coalition is PSP/MUPP-NP.

National Strength and Vote Change

The results displayed in Table 6.1 summarize first-round voting[7] results for parties in Ecuador's current, democratic period – the longest in its history. Two points jump out from the table: First, no party has won the presidency more than once during this period, and second, party support at the national level is extremely changeable. These features conspire to create a context of extreme uncertainty in which parties

---

[7] Ecuador's electoral system requires a second round of voting if first-round results do not confer a majority of votes to any party.

cannot reliably predict future political support at the national level from election to election. In fact, given the short average life span of parties, many cannot say whether or not they will play a significant role in future elections. Incumbent parties face steep declines in their vote shares over the course of their terms in this period, losing nearly half of their support in the best cases – CFP (Concentration of Popular Forces) and PSC (Social Christian Party) – and disappearing almost entirely (at least in the short-term) in the worst – ID (Democratic Left) and PUR (Republican Union Party). Looking to previously discussed cases, Ecuador most resembles Bolivia, but without the stability lent to its system by a party such as the MNR (National Revolutionary Movement), the ADN (Nationalist Democratic Action), or the MIR (Movement of the Revolutionary Left).

If weak national-level support translates into a fear of isolation from central power in future elections, it should increase a party's support for decentralization. If this were the only factor to consider, every party in the Ecuadorian system should support decentralization. If the high level of change in support for parties across elections aggravates their ability to predict future support and shortens their time horizons, there should be little support for decentralization. Table 6.1 shows that these conflicting forces act on all the parties in Ecuador's system. Among its many parties – nineteen gained an appreciable percentage of the vote in elections between 1978 and 1986 alone (León Velasco 1987: 7) – no party wins a substantial level of support in all seven elections shown in the table; however, the PSC (with substantial support in six elections) and the PRE (with substantial support in the five elections since 1988) come closest. If one had to predict which party would be most likely to decentralize in Ecuador, the PSC (with strong coastal support based in Guayaquil) or the PRE stand out as the best candidates, based on their weak national-level support and the relative stability of their vote shares over time. All other parties, although they face weak national-level support, do not enjoy a comparable level of stability.

Subnational Strength

In addition to national vote considerations, the geography of a party's support also helps to determine the attractiveness of decentralization. Parties that can expect to win a substantial proportion of decentralized

TABLE 6.2: *Percent of Districts Won by Parties in Votes for Prefects (Councils), Ecuador*

Party[a]	1978	(1980)	1984	(1986)	1988	1992	1996	1998
ID	–	37	53	47	84	–	14	9
DP	–	32	–	5	–	10	5	5
CFP	27	5	–	11	–	–	5	–
PSC	42	–	–	5	–	40	19	18
PRE	–	–	–	5	11	–	29	18
PLR	21	11	–	11	–	5	–	–
PCE	–	5	–	–	–	–	5	–
PD	–	–	16	–	–	10	–	–
FADI	–	–	11	5	–	8	–	–
AL214							9	–

Note: A dash indicates that the party received less than 5 percent of the vote. Boldface type is used to distinguish the president's party. Results for elected provincial prefects appear under the years 1978, 1984, 1988, and 1992. Results displayed under the years in parentheses reflect the percent of provinces in which each party won a plurality of votes for provincial councilors elected in those years.

[a] See Table 6.1; FADI: Frente Amplio de la Izquierda (Broad Front of the Left); AL214: Alianza 2–14 (Alliance of Lists 2 and 14).

power based on their record of subnational support should be more willing to decentralize. Tables 6.2 and 6.3 demonstrate that few parties have gained a significant proportion of support at the provincial or municipal level during periods in which they have controlled the presidency. The CFP in 1978 enjoyed some support at the provincial level when it won the presidency, but much of that support had evaporated midway through its presidential term. While this clarifies the party's failure to decentralize during the second half of its term, it is not clear why decentralization did not occur during the first half, unless its popularity declined from the beginning. High levels of change in its vote share may provide the answer; it is clear from the CFP's electoral record before 1978 that it had experienced erratic support over its lifetime. Founded in 1946, the CFP won no appreciable percentage of presidential votes in either 1948 or 1952; it won a respectable 24 percent of the vote in 1956's presidential election, then declined to 6.0 percent of the vote in a combined ticket with the PCE (Ecuadorian Conservative Party) in 1960; it ran no candidate in the 1968 contest.

In contrast to the CFP, which won significant support in local contests simultaneous with its accession to the presidency, the PSC would

TABLE 6.3: *Percent of Districts Won by Parties in Votes for Mayors (Councils), Ecuador*

Party[a]	1978	(1980)	1984	(1986)	1988	(1990)	1992	1996	1998
ID	10	45	24	55	32	**11**	15	10	9
DP	–	20	12	5	8	11	7	14	5
CFP	20	5	8	5	–	6	–	–	–
PSC	–	–	8	5	8	21	19	43	18
PRE	–	–	–	5	20	24	19	19	18
PLR	20	10	–	10	8	9	–	–	–
PCE	25	5	–	–	–	–	7	–	–
PUR	–	–	–	–	–	–	4	–	–
PSE	–	–	–	–	–	–	–	5	–
MUPP-NP	–	–	–	–	–	–	–	5	–
Lista21	–	–	–	–	–	–	–	5	–

Note: A dash indicates that the party received less than 5 percent of the vote. Boldface type is used to distinguish the president's party. Results for elected municipal mayors appear under the years 1978, 1984, 1988 and 1992. Results displayed under the years in parentheses reflect the percent of provinces in which each party won a plurality of votes for municipal councilors elected in those years.

[a] See Table 6.1.

not have won even a meager 5 percent of provincial contests based on its performance in the 1984 elections of provincial prefects. By mid-term, it won a plurality of the vote in a scant 5 percent of provinces during the mid-term elections for provincial councilors. According to León Velasco (1987), the PSC was not only weak in subnational contests, but also declining during the period of its presidency.[8]

Another potential decentralizer is the ID (which draws its strength mainly from the highlands). In the same year it won the presidency, the ID enjoyed victory in the overwhelming majority of prefectures. Despite its strong showing in 1988, its provincial prospects weakened precipitously and very quickly thereafter, not unlike the CFP's pattern of support after 1978. Generalizing from these examples, it appears not only that Ecuadorian parties have weak support at the provincial level, but also that support at the provincial level does not display

---

[8] "Finally, it is necessary to point out two cases of marked decline for this party. These are in the prefect elections along the Coast, excluding Guayas, and in the elections of mayors in the Sierra, excluding Pichincha, between 1978 and 1984" (León Velasco 1987: 26).

strong continuity across electoral periods. Support at the provincial level appears even more mercurial than national-level support during this period.

While municipal results appear slightly less volatile than results at the provincial level, they also do not give presidential parties strong incentives to decentralize. The modest local-level support enjoyed by the CFP on its presidential victory in 1978 all but evaporated within its first two years in office. The PSC in 1984 and the PUR in 1992 faced meager prospects for controlling local-level offices during their presidencies. The ID, with the strongest and most stable support across local-level elections during this time span, experienced a severe drop in its local-level support after taking the presidency in 1988. Two years into its term, the ID had lost nearly two-thirds of its strength at the local level.

Given the extreme changeability of party support at all levels of government and the weak support that parties in the presidency have faced at subnational levels, it is no surprise that decentralization was not furthered between 1978 and 1996. Experts on the Ecuadorian party system attribute the party system's chaos to the tendency of voters to vote for candidates rather than parties (León Velasco 1987, 1992; Conaghan 1995; Mainwaring and Scully 1995). This is true even for the ID, whose electoral success appeared inextricably joined to the personal appeal of its founder, leader, and president from 1988 to 1992, Rodrigo Borja. In fact, commenting on *personalismo* in Ecuador's party system, Jamil Mahuad stated: "In Ecuador, parties have a last name and a first name" (interview, August 2000).

A More Detailed Look at Ecuador, 1978–1996

Strong regional differences between its coastal and inland regions have seasoned the cauldron of Ecuadorian politics from the beginning. Calls for federalism have bubbled to the surface throughout its political history – most notably in 1939 and then again twenty years later. With sharply different economic sectors, the two regions have fought over trade policy and over the correct method for allocating federal funds among the regions. These regional rifts have rarely developed into active political fault lines, largely because the main political cleavages have not formed around these issues. Prior to the most recent period, most political players coalesced around their common membership in Ecuador's political elite.

Under pressure to federalize the system in 1939, the Central Bank decided on a more generous policy of lending outside Quito; afterward, discussion of federalism muted considerably. In addition to economic issues, politics affected the volume of calls for federalism. Quintero and Silva (1991) argue:

But what decisively helped to weaken the regional movement was not the exact and relatively isolated incident of the arrangement with the Bank . . . rather it was the general occurrence on the same day of the Assembly: the imminent accession to the presidency . . . of a native representative of the dominant interests of the Guayaquileños, Dr. Arroyo del Río. (48)

Furthermore, in the period 1952–1968, most of the politicians controlling the presidency had been strongly supported by voters in the coastal region, largely owing to its impressive population explosion after 1950 (Larrea 1986: 106). With their own representatives in the executive and the hope of regaining that office at least in alternating terms (if not indefinitely), the incentives to press for greater autonomy were much reduced.[9]

If regional animosities failed to provide the main line of political cleavage in the pre-1978 period due to the solidarity of the elite, the tendency of voters to elect on the basis of candidate charisma rather than policy platforms or even party identity continued to drown them out. Menendez-Carrión (1991) observes:

The patterns of preferences detected revealed an electorate that was far from being generally "reliable," not for candidates or even for any type of political tendency. The absence of a level of sustained support not only at the regional level, but also at the provincial level and in urban areas for candidates or political tendencies over time is clear. (261)

Similarly, León Velasco (1992) claims that while there is a general correlation between regions and support for particular parts of the ideological spectrum, those differences do not translate into stable support

---

[9] This is not to say that they were completely extinguished, however. Menendez-Carrión (1991) notes that between 1979 and 1984, regional movements for better services and against centralized government caught national press attention in Santa Rosa, Ambato, Lago Agrio, Riobamba, Orellana, Esmereldas, Chone, Machachi, and several other areas.

for particular parties. Furthermore, "between the highland region excluding Pichincha and the coastal region without Guayas the contrasts are much less" (125).

Looking at particular presidencies during this period, it appears that few enjoy the kind of strong support in subnational contests that might encourage them to decentralize and win regional or local offices when they inevitably lose their fleeting national power. Only the ID enjoys strong support at the local and provincial levels on winning the presidency (in 1988), although its local support was in a slight decline from its high in 1986. In fact, according to Velasco's classification, "[T]he ID is the only party that has achieved national coverage in a rather stable fashion, whether complete or incomplete" (León Velasco 1992: 125). Unfortunately, its support evaporated almost immediately thereafter, giving it little hope of winning a significant share in future subnational elections.

Interestingly enough, the issue of decentralization arose during the ID presidency of Rodrigo Borja, when partisans of Febres-Cordero (*febrescorderistas*) in the Guayaquil region protested the insufficiency of centrally provided public services at a time when the country was fighting to emerge from one of its worst financial crises. Instead of creating a more decentralized system, Borja responded by creating a municipal development fund (Programa de Desarrollo Municipal, PDM) within the nation's Development Bank (BEDE) that conferred $300 million targeted to projects in municipal governments. This measure quieted the civic strikes whose numbers spiraled upward in 1989 and earned Borja popularity, even among the opposition mayors in the coastal region.[10]

Still, the ID, with its uncertain national support and strong local support, in 1988 appeared the strongest candidate to decentralize on taking power. In fact, in Figure 3.2 showing predicted values of decentralization based on the statistical analysis in Chapter 3, the predicted probability that Ecuador would decentralize in 1988 was 44 percent,

---

[10] Rodrigo Rangles Lara (1995) writes: "Close to the end of his administration, mayors of the opposition like the Christian Democrat 'Chicho' Centanaro, of Milagro, the most belligerent and aggressive during the initial months of the government, honored and thanked the president because 'you, Doctor Borja, have helped us, without focusing on the fact that we are political opponents and because you have shown above all that service to the community comes first' " (131).

putting it close to the 50 percent cutoff line. The ID's failure to decentralize appears tied to the rapid decline in ID support at all levels of government shortly after it took office.

Decentralization lay dormant for many years before bursting on Ecuador's political stage in 1995, as part of a referendum spearheaded by President Sixto Durán Ballén to bypass the opposition-controlled legislature and impose a series of reforms that would shock the economy back from the brink of disaster. Although several key civic organizations supported the idea of decentralizing power, popular pressures (led by the indigenous group, CONAIE, the unions associated with Ecuador's Institute of Social Security, IESS, and the leftist Popular Democratic Movement, MPD) lobbied the electorate for a "no" vote on all of the referendum's eleven points.[11] These groups interpreted the referendum as a push for neoliberal reforms, construing the decentralization measure as a government strategy to shirk its responsibilities for providing public services.[12] This claim was supported by the proposal's vague language regarding implementation.[13] The "no" vote prevailed in the national plebiscite.

A More Detailed Look at Ecuador, 1996–2000

Since 1996, Ecuador's political situation has become yet more muddled with the victory of the PRE's Abdalá Bucarám in 1996 and his quick ouster in 1997. After a controversial handover of power that

---

[11] Polls taken just two weeks before the vote by Cedatos showed strong support for all measures and predicted an overwhelming victory in the polls (*Vistazo*, November 16, 1995).

[12] *The Economist*, January 28, 1995; The *Financial Times*, November 28, 1995, reported: "Mr. Bolivio Cordoba of the polling group Cedatos said most voters used the referendum to express disapproval of the government. Even such issues as administrative and financial decentralization, backed by a majority in independent polls prior to the referendum, were rejected."

[13] Question 1 of the referendum read: "*El Estado transferirá progresivamente competencias y recursos a los organismos seccionales, preferentemente en los sectores de educación, salud, vivienda, vialidad y saneamiento ambiental, a fin de garantizar una efectiva descentralización administrativa y financiera.*" [The State will progressively transfer responsibilities and resources to the sections, giving preference to the sectors of education, health, housing, roads and environmental cleaning, to the purpose of guaranteeing an effective administrative and financial decentralization.] *Vistazo* (November 16, 1995) notes, "Nevertheless, the proposal seems merely declarative, since there is no talk of mechanisms (for implementation)."

included two changes of government, elections were held for a new executive in 1998. After a DP (Popular Democracy) victory in the second round, Jamil Mahuad became president, but was ousted in a coup in January 2000. His vice president, Gustavo Noboa, replaced Mahuad and remained in office until the 2002 elections were won by Lucío Gutiérrez, who had played a leadership role in ousting Mahuad. With these frequent changes and the onset of a severe fiscal crisis, decentralization has taken a back seat to more pressing matters. It has not disappeared, however, and some significant changes were accomplished both through legislation and within a constitutional reform. The extreme political and financial turbulence of this period recommends its separate consideration.

After Bucarám's ouster and before the 1998 elections, the national legislature moved toward a more fiscally decentralized system. On March 20, 1997, the legislature passed a law to increase fiscal transfers to subnational governments; on October 29 of the same year, a legal plan for putting this law into action was approved. The "Law of 15%" (Ley Especial del 15% del Presupuesto) proposed the transmission (on the basis of several fixed criteria) of 15 percent of the national budget to subnational governments without any increase in the responsibilities of these subnational recipients.[14] Why would the central government give away financial resources to subnational governments without tying them to greater spending responsibilities? One must look within the legislature, where the main proponents of this law were the PSC. In fact, the movement toward greater fiscal decentralization was spearheaded by one legislator, in particular: Susana Gonzáles, a PSC delegate who ran for and won a legislative seat after losing a municipal election in her home city. To see why the PSC desired a more decentralized system, one need only look at the electoral fortunes of the PSC in the period leading up to the law's passage. As mentioned earlier, the PSC is the only party to win a substantial percentage of the vote in every election during the period 1978–1996. It is also the party with the lowest average change in its vote share across elections. Looking closely at the numbers in Table 6.1, it becomes clear that changes in vote share remained fairly small and steady across all (pre-1996) periods except

---

[14] The funds were to be split as follows: 10.5 percent to municipalities and 4.5 percent to provinces.

for 1984–1988, the period in which the PSC held the presidency. After a harsh rejection of the PSC in 1988, support rebounded to levels similar to its pre-presidency level in 1992 and stayed about even in 1996. Thus, by 1996, support for the PSC was relatively stable. At the same time, the PSC had one of the highest levels of national support among the Ecuadorian parties in both 1992 and 1996. Despite making it to the second round of national presidential elections in both of those years, the PSC lost the second round, first to the PUR and then to the PRE. The second defeat was particularly painful for the PSC because it had polled more votes than the PRE in the first round of the election. Given the party's inability to clinch national electoral victory, decentralization may have seemed an attractive way to distribute resources to its partisans who had won important posts at the subnational level. What did PSC support look like at the subnational level in 1996? In 1996, PSC partisans filled the prefect position in almost 20 percent of the provinces (four out of 21); they also made up roughly 43 percent of the mayors (nine out of 21) in provincial capitals – by far the greatest number of mayors of any party in the system (Freidenberg 2000: 23).

In the midst of the chaos surrounding Bucarám's expulsion, a referendum to create a national assembly to reform the constitution gained strong support.[15] This assembly institutionalized the Law of 15 Percent while reining in some of its more extreme features and increased political decentralization. The vote to elect constituents awarded positions in the following manner: 20 seats to the PSC, 10 to the DP (Popular Democracy), seven to the PRE (Ecuadorian Roldosist Party), three each to the ID and MPD, and two to the NP (New Country, an indigenous party). These positions translated into a majority right block made up of the PSC, DP, and FRA (Radical Alfarista Front) and a minority left block composed of the ID, NP, MPD, and PSE (Ecuadorian Socialist Party). Little work has been published analyzing the process of reform within the assembly,[16] but the resulting 1998 constitution improves on earlier versions by allowing direct election of mayors in all municipalities (previously, this had occurred only in

---

[15] In several provinces, however, less than half the electorate turned out to vote (*The Economist*, December 13, 1997).

[16] For an excellent discussion of the politics of indigenous reaction to the assembly, see Andolina 1998.

provincial capitals and in cities with populations greater than 50,000). On the fiscal side, the constitution changed the basis on which central government transfers (including those transferred under the Law of 15%) would be distributed. The Law of 15% called for distribution based on equal parts to each canton (10%), an index of unsatisfied basic needs among the population (50%), and the population of each canton (40%). The constitution dropped the first criterion, and added three: financial capacity, improvement in level of life betterment, and administrative efficiency. Finally, the criticism that the Law of 15% transferred funds without responsibilities led to a change in the wording of the constitution; Article 226 now reads, "There cannot be a transfer of responsibilities without a transfer of equivalent resources, nor a transfer of resources without (corresponding) responsibilities." The decentralization law also allows for the decentralization of funds and responsibilities to occur through a bargaining process between the central and subnational governments; only subnational governments that would like to increase their responsibilities and funds may do so.

The constitution's political innovations have been implemented, but its financial aspects have been stalled as the country grapples with the worst financial crisis in its history. One positive move was the creation of a National Decentralization Commission aimed at processing autonomy claims, but the commission's progress fell short of expectations. In my interview with Jamil Mahuad, the former mayor of Quito and elected president from the DP in 1998 (August 2, 2000), he explained:

When I got to power, there was a lot of talk about decentralization and I wanted to do something to further it, but it just did not seem like an immediate priority. The country was facing so many problems that were really urgent, like its external debt, so decentralization had to wait.

Indeed, the magnitude of the financial crisis was astounding. In 1999, inflation reached an annual rate of 60 percent, the sucre (the national currency) fell 65 percent against the U.S. dollar, and economic output fell 7.3 percent. Although fiscal decentralization had reached only about 9 percent[17] (less than half of the 15% required by law), critics argued that the government simply could not "afford" to transfer these

---

[17] This figure obtained from a conversation with Jonas Frank, Ph.D. candidate and worker at a Quito-based NGO, October 2000.

funds to subnational levels during a period of such national crisis. The economic problems contributed not only to the removal of Ecuador's president but to the first ever default on Brady bonds and the adoption of the U.S. dollar as the nation's currency. In the government's attempts to deal with these problems, decentralization has been set aside as a major issue.[18] In addition, the focus of the decentralization debate has shifted away from the kind of municipal decentralization of political and economic resources that has been at the heart of this book toward a debate over granting autonomy to ethno-linguistic groups in specifically defined indigenous territories and to granting autonomy to provinces (Cameron 2000).

VENEZUELA

Despite having the longest period of democratic contestation in the Andean region, Venezuela's decentralization reforms occurred relatively late and continue to advance slowly toward a more decentralized state of affairs. Why does this pioneer among democracies lag behind in the decentralization of power to subnational governments?

Venezuela's central government has long exerted dominance over its subnational governments. Though its 1961 constitution technically clings to the language of federalism, that document initiated a centralization of power that left almost no resources or offices of note to be contested at the regional or local levels. Until 1989, the president appointed Venezuela's twenty-one governors and all of its mayors.[19] States received 15 percent of federal budgetary funds, through a less-than-automatic transfer system giving the central government ample opportunities to disperse funds according to political favoritism. Some portion of the percentage accorded to states was to be funneled toward

---

[18] In 1999–2000, debate over decentralization shifted from increasing transfers to provincial and municipal governments to a debate over provincial autonomy, particularly focused on the potential autonomy of Guayas, the coastal province that includes the city of Guayaquil. Led by former president and PSC member Febres-Cordero, the movement succeeded in getting the issue on a national referendum held during the summer of 2000. Sufficient support was not gained for this move, which would have turned tax bases in Guayas that had formerly contributed to the national tax base into the sole ownership of the state, disadvantaging other states in the country that are net recipients of national tax redistribution.

[19] As of the end of 1998, Venezuela had twenty-three states and 333 municipalities.

municipalities – again through a discretionary process that left many municipalities without significant funding.

Prior to 1979, a single ballot determined the election of national legislators, regional assembly members, and municipal councilors; voters could select only between closed lists of candidates ranked by each party's leadership. This procedure changed slightly in 1979 when municipal councilors were elected in a separate election – not concurrent with national elections – that continued to use closed party list balloting.[20]

In 1989 new legislation ushered in a much higher degree of decentralization by allowing the popular election of governors and mayors. The mechanisms governing financial transfers also changed, requiring that 20 percent of the national budget be transferred to regional governments and that 20 percent of state budgets be transferred to municipalities by 1999. Venezuela's Decentralization Law (Ley Orgánica de Descentralización, Delimitación y Transferencia de Competencias del Poder Público a los Estados) was a principal piece of legislation regarding fiscal and administrative decentralization. This law allows state governors to determine when different responsibilities will be transferred to the states and also allows governors to return responsibilities to the central government. Because implementation has been slow and transfers to both states and localities remain uncertain, I categorize these reforms as an intermediate degree of decentralization.[21] Recent events in Venezuela, including Hugo Chávez's rise to power in 1998, the approval of a new constitution in 2000, and a new round of elections in 2000, have also led to slight changes in the status of decentralization in Venezuela. This chapter examines these events systematically.

This chapter focuses on Venezuelan presidential administrations spanning the period 1958–1998, ending with a discussion of more recent Venezuelan politics. The analysis finds that few incentives for decentralization existed over this time period because one party, Democratic Action (AD), largely dominated power. Other parties occasionally faced opportunities to influence the power-sharing arrangements

---

[20] Regional assemblies continued to be determined by the national legislative votes during this period.

[21] In the statistical analysis, however, Venezuela in this period receives a "1" for decentralizing.

of the government – most notably, COPEI (Social Christian Party) between 1968 and 1973 and again between 1978 and 1983. The following discussion demystifies why decentralization did not occur until an extra-presidential commission, with the ruling AD party in the minority, pushed decentralization into the limelight and why it was finally an AD administration that pushed decentralization forward – at least on paper. The rest of the discussion focuses on how the fractures in the two-party dominant system and the subsequent rise of Hugo Chávez to the presidency have slowed Venezuela's decentralization process.

National Strength and Vote Change

Table 6.4 reveals the transition of Venezuela's party system from a multi-party system dominated by the AD in the 1950s and 1960s to a two-party system dominated by the AD in the 1970s and 1980s to a system where traditional parties are in disarray. AD's electoral victories

TABLE 6.4: *Presidential Election Results and Vote Change, Venezuela 1958–2000*

Party[a]	1958	1963	1968	1973	1978	1983	1988	1993	1998	2000
AD	**49.2**	32.8	27.5	**48.6**	43.3	**55.3**	**52.9**	23.6	–	–
COPEI	15.2	20.2	**28.7**	35.3	**45.2**	32.6	40.3	22.7	–	–
URD	34.6	18.9	22.3	–	–	–	–	–	–	–
IPFN	–	16.1	–	–	–	–	–	–	–	–
FDP	–	9.4	–	–	–	–	–	–	–	–
MEP	–	–	19.4	5.1	–	–	–	–	–	–
CN	–	–	–	–	–	–	–	**30.5**	–	–
MAS	–	–	–	–	5.2	–	–	–	–	–
Causa R	–	–	–	–	–	–	–	22.0	–	19.0
MVR	–	–	–	–	–	–	–	–	**56.2**	**56.9**
PRVZL	–	–	–	–	–	–	–	–	40.0	–

Note: A dash indicates that the party received less than 5 percent of the vote. Boldface type is used to distinguish the president's party.
[a] AD: Acción Democrática (Democratic Action); COPEI: Partido Social Cristiano (Comité de Organización Política Electoral Independiente) Social Christian Party; URD: Unión Republicana Democrática (Republican Democratic Union); IPFN: Independientes pro Frente Nacional (Independents for the National Front); FDP: Frente Democrática Popular (Popular Democratic Front); MEP: Movimiento Electoral del Pueblo (People's Electoral Movement); CN: Convergencia Nacional (National Convergence); MAS: Movimiento al Socialismo (Movement Toward Socialism); Causa R: Causa Radical (Radical Cause); MVR: nine-party coalition, headed by the *Movimiento V. República* (Movement for the Fifth Republic); PRVZL: four-party coalition, including the AD and COPEI.

in 1958 and 1963 are accomplished with a comfortable margin over its closest competitor. In 1968, the AD split deeply over its choice of presidential candidate; those who supported Luís Beltrán Pietro formed the MEP (People's Electoral Movement) and garnered nearly 20 percent of the vote. In the wake of this split, AD lost the presidency – by a single percentage point – to COPEI, a party whose support had been growing steadily at the expense of smaller parties in the system. By 1973, AD had once again coalesced behind a single candidate, winning the elections by more than ten percentage points. At this point, the field of parties had narrowed to two contenders: the AD and COPEI. COPEI won the presidency in 1978, but with a slim margin of victory; this was the only contest that the AD lost until 1993, when the traditional parties faced fierce competition from more populist parties.

Looking at national-level support and the change in support over time for each party during the period 1958–1988, the dominant position of the AD is striking, although the COPEI gains power occasionally, in 1968 and 1978. Given the proposition that weak national support should encourage parties to decentralize, the AD had few incentives to decentralize during this period since it could reasonably expect to hold the monopoly of power at the center often. COPEI, on the other hand, gained national power both infrequently and by a small margin. In 1968 COPEI won the presidency by a single percentage point and fell short of winning a plurality in legislative votes by slightly more than one percentage point. In 1978, its victory margin was just over 3 percent and it won 39.8 percent of the legislative vote compared with AD's 39.7 percent – an extremely close contest. Explanations of COPEI's reluctance to decentralize must rely on either its overestimation of future support at the national level – overconfidence – or a lack of substantial support at the local level that would allow it to benefit from decentralized power.

It is notable that COPEI's support was rising sharply through 1978, on a trajectory toward dominance. Between 1963 and 1968, support for COPEI rose 44 percent, and between 1973 and 1978, it rose 27 percent, representing the fourth consecutive period in which support grew by more than 25 percent over the previous election result. With its national support rising rapidly on its taking control of the presidency during its first term, one might reason that COPEI simply overestimated its future ability to control national power. During the second period, when COPEI support had continued to grow but at a slower pace, this explanation is less convincing. It is also notable that COPEI's Herrera lost support quickly during his 1978–1983 term, so that, by the end of his presidency, it was clear that COPEI could not expect an easy re-election. Why did Herrera and COPEI not decentralize during this second time period? To answer this question, it is necessary to examine subnational support.

Subnational Strength

Venezuela's electoral system affords few opportunities to gauge the support parties would receive in subnational elections until they were actually contested in 1989. Regional votes were nonexistent during this period, and although the separate election of municipal councils began in 1979, voting occurred by closed lists on which candidate names did not even appear (De la Cruz 1995: 316). Results from national legislative elections (*votos pequeños*) disaggregated by region and then by municipal district are shown below for the period 1958–1988, as they represent the most comparable information on subnational level support available. From 1992 onward, results reflect voting in gubernatorial and municipal elections (see Tables 6.5 and 6.6).

Subnational results partially illuminate COPEI's reluctance to decentralize during each of its presidential terms. Across all election years at both regional and local levels, AD always outpolls the COPEI. Not only does COPEI always receive less support than AD in subnational tallies, but it also gains a greater percentage of the national vote than

TABLE 6.5: *Regional Support for Parties, Venezuela*[a]

Party	1958	1963	1968	1973	1978	1983	1988	1992	1995	1998	2000
AD	75	70	60	95	55	100	87	32	55	33	18
COPEI	10	15	35	5	45	0	13	50	14	17	5
MAS	–	–	–	–	–	–	–	14	9	13	18
MVR	–	–	–	–	–	–	–	–	–	29	5

Note: A dash indicates that the party received less than 5 percent of the vote. Boldface type is used to distinguish the president's party.

[a] 1958–1988 values show the percentage of regions in which the president's party won a plurality of the votes for president; 1992–2000 values show the percentage of gubernatorial contests won by each party. Results for 2000 are from Lalander 2002.

TABLE 6.6: *Municipal Support for Parties, Venezuela*[a]

Party	1958	1963	1968	1973	1978	1983	1988	1992	1995	2000
AD	80	60	54	85	58	94	81	45	58	25.5
COPEI	10	26	37	14	42	6	19	43	31	10.4
MAS	–	–	–	–	–	–	–	7	4	–
MVR-MAS	–	–	–	–	–	–	–	–	–	25.3
CN	–	–	–	–	–	–	–	–	3	–

Note: A dash indicates that the party received less than 5 percent of the vote. Boldface type is used to distinguish the president's party.

[a] 1958–1988 values show the percentage of municipalities in which the president's party won a plurality of the votes for president; 1992–1998 values show the percentage of mayoral contests won by each party. Results for 1995 are from Lalander 2002: 212.

of subnational districts after 1958. The AD appears poised to win the vast majority of subnational positions should elections occur there. Still, once out of the presidency, even a small number of subnational positions would represent a net increase in the COPEI's power.

With subnational votes tied to national legislative votes prior to 1979 and with municipal elections sequenced closely behind national elections thereafter, the linkages between presidential and all legislative voting are tight. In fact, Sosa (1984) notes that 93 percent of voters vote for the same party in both presidential and legislative elections. It may have been an attempt to weaken this linkage that propelled the COPEI to push for the slight staggering of municipal contests from national contests during its second term. In the municipal elections of 1979, the COPEI won 54 percent of local council positions compared with AD's 36 percent; in 1984 COPEI won 24 percent versus AD's 66 percent. The comparison of this second figure to the percentage of municipalities in which it won a plurality of the national vote in 1983 shows a striking difference in COPEI strength. At least in this one case, COPEI performs better at subnational levels when their elections are delinked from national contests. Things change substantially for all parties after 1992, and though the AD and COPEI slip from national dominance, they continue to exert a strong hold on subnational elections.

A More Detailed Look at Venezuela, 1958–2000

Venezuela's uninterrupted experience with democratic elections has earned it glowing recognition as an exceptional example in a region

beset by numerous authoritarian experiments. Its most recent democratic period originates from the Pact of Punto Fijo, in which the three
major political parties at the time – AD, COPEI, and URD (Republican
Democratic Union) – pledged to limit the range of their disagreement
in an attempt to avoid future military interventions in government (the
Pérez Jiménez dictatorship had just ended). In contrast to the much
more formal and specific National Front agreement in Colombia, this
agreement represented a set of priorities – with maintenance of constitutional rule at the top of the list – not a set of specific arrangements
for achieving them. Given the priorities listed, however, centralization
of government was implicit for carrying them out. Several mechanisms
were adopted to control intra-party conflict, including the use of closed
lists for voting at all levels and strict control by a few party elite over the
placement of candidates within those lists. The pact did not, however,
explicitly commit parties to maintaining centralized government structures. A more detailed look at party politics is required to determine
why Venezuela decentralized in the late 1980s.

This section begins with a more detailed analysis of the two COPEI
presidencies sketched earlier, before turning its attention to the establishment, trajectory, and successes of the presidential commission set
up to propose reforms to the state, COPRE (Comisión Presidencial
para la Reforma del Estado) – the organization that finally brought decentralization to the forefront of Venezuela's politics. The 1989 laws
allowing election of both regional governors and municipal mayors
can be traced to the recommendations of this group. To understand
decentralization, one must look inside this institution.

COPEI won national power in 1968 by a slim margin of votes over a
divided AD. COPEI's support at all levels of government was growing
and it was a formidable political power in the Andean region of the
country – factors that line up with the characteristics of a decentralizing
party. To understand why COPEI did not decentralize in this period,
it is important to focus on COPEI's evaluation of its future national-
level prospects. I argue that COPEI believed that its national power
was not wholly attributable to temporary splits in the AD; on the
contrary, it believed that it was becoming the dominant national power
in Venezuelan politics.

COPEI entered the presidential elections of 1973 confident of victory. This assessment rested on extensive public opinion polls, as

COPEI conducted an extraordinarily expensive and technologically advanced campaign. One assessment of the COPEI's 1973 campaign noted that "party planners, confident of victory from the outset, were influenced less by concern over retaining the presidency than with maximizing the margin of victory" (Martz and Baloyra 1976: 105). Their confidence rested on two assumptions: that Rafael Caldera's presidency was the best in living memory and that the AD was "the deteriorating vestige of a once-great party, its vitality and popularity sapped by three internal divisions" (ibid.: 105). When COPEI's presidential candidate was not elected president, COPEI leaders were "stunned" and "disbelieving":

> None had seriously entertained the possibility of defeat, given the brilliance of the government record, the size and magnitude of Fernández crowds, the support of influential independents, and the technical brilliance of the electoral organization. (ibid.: 235)

It seems likely that COPEI did not decentralize during its first presidential term because it fully expected to continue wielding the centralized power vested in the executive office.

During its second presidential term, hopes for imminent COPEI dominance did not delude the party's strategic thinking. After Herrera Campíns won the presidency in 1978, support for COPEI began to decline, inspiring little confidence of a national victory in the 1983 presidential campaign. Why did COPEI not decentralize power in this period? Two plausible hypotheses emerge: First, the COPEI may have expected that its subnational support was weak; second, it may have perceived an inability to push decentralizing reforms through a legislature it did not control. While no conclusion can be drawn without further research, I briefly sketch each of these explanations.

Venezuela's electoral landscape was substantially reshaped by the 1968 and 1973 elections. Prior to 1968, party support exhibited clear regional trends with the AD winning strong support in the east and COPEI winning strong support in the Andes. The 1968 elections, in which supporters of Luís B. Prieto broke with the AD and formed the MEP, marked an end to AD's domination of Venezuela's eastern electorate. MEP took a large percentage of the votes in that region. In 1973, eastern voters discouraged by MEP weakness but unwilling to return to the AD voted for COPEI in record numbers. Also in

1973, COPEI's strength in the Andean region diminished when the AD ran an Andean-born candidate, Carlos Andrés Pérez.[22] By 1978, both the AD and COPEI enjoyed nation-wide bases of support, with regional differences much diminished. As a result, parties could no longer rely on sure support from regional bases. Since municipal votes continued to be dominated by parties' reputations for national governance, declining national support pointed to a probable decline in local support, as well. It seems plausible that COPEI failed to decentralize because it perceived that its chances of winning subnational contests were low.

A second reason that COPEI may not have decentralized depends on its perception that it could not push reforms through a legislature it did not control. With strong AD representation in the legislature, COPEI may have perceived that an attempt to decentralize power would only encounter opposition in the legislature. This hypothesis appears less convincing for two reasons. First, initiatives to decentralize power often become so popular that legislators opposed to them on principle find casting a "no" vote nearly impossible, regardless of the party's long-range electoral incentives. Second, Herrera Campíns never mentioned decentralization as a priority during his annual presentations to Congress. Instead, Herrera listed the installation of a merit system within the public administration and increasing control over the public administration as his top priorities. His proposals for moving the government closer to the people were limited to the strengthening of regional development corporations. These corporations, popular throughout the region during the 1970s and 1980s, funneled resources for subnational development through highly centralized bureaucracies controlled from the national capital.

Decentralization did not occur in Venezuela until a presidentially appointed commission began to circulate the idea. To understand decentralizing reforms, it is necessary to look at the genesis, composition, and effects of this organization.

In 1984, shortly after gathering the reins of government, AD president Jaime Lusinchi created the COPRE (the presidential commission

---

[22] COPEI's campaign tactic of questioning Pérez's citizenship (claiming he was truly Colombian) served only to alienate Andean voters, proud of their home-town candidate.

for the reform of the state), extending its mandate to study the causes of, and suggest solutions to, the rising anomie of Venezuelans toward their political system. Composed of thirty-five members with the AD in the minority, COPRE fulfilled its mission with an unintended effectiveness. Urdaneta, Martínez Olvarría, and López Maya (1990) note:

> It was notable that, just two short months into the Lusinchi administration, the obstacles impeding the realization of the reform as they were conceived in their entirety, emerged fundamentally from two actors: the government and the party in government. (64–65; see also Coppedge 1994: 7–8 and 163–4)

COPRE consisted of nine members from the AD, five from COPEI, one member each from MAS (Movement toward Socialism), URD, and MEP, nine Independents, six Independents leaning toward the AD, two Independents leaning toward the left, and one Independent leaning toward MAS. Its 1986 announcement of five proposals for immediate reform included such sweeping policies as popular election of governors and party financing of political party campaigns. The extension to the formal model elaborated in Chapter 2 provides a useful tool for thinking about the COPRE's incentives. Extending the logic of the model beyond presidential administrations to think about the incentives faced by commissions and constitutional assemblies, one should expect decentralization when the assembly is composed of individuals with strong incentives to decentralize. Given the strong representation of groups unlikely to gain access to the presidency – such as the URD, MEP, MAS, and several independents that did not self-identify as leaning toward the AD (and, at this point, this could include COPEI, which had seen its support decline sharply after the presidency of Herrera) – this should not be surprising. More illustrative of how party concerns affect decisions on reform is the reaction of parties to COPRE's suggestions.

COPRE's 1986 announcement marked a new era in politics as political parties attempted to regain control of the political agenda, while the press and public rallied around COPRE's proposals. Rather than renounce these instantly popular proposals,[23] the AD responded with

---

[23] A survey published in *El Nacional* (January 17, 1988) indicated that 82 percent of those polled counted themselves as proponents of the direct election of governors.

official silence. Suggesting that they were studying the proposals in depth, the AD did not offer an official response to the call for reforms for the better part of a year, until the party head, Manuel Peñalver, spoke out against the direct election of mayors. Several other party leaders argued against the reforms in their own personal statements:

[T]here emerged an obstacle from the least likely place: President Lusinchi. Some initiatives of COPRE, especially those pertaining to political and economic reforms, produced strong resistance within the highest levels of the Executive that was expressed in three ways: first, in the constant reminders to COPRE of its position as an advisor and not a promoter of policy; second, in advising that the reforms should not be approved as an excuse to attack the political parties or to question their role in the Venezuelan institutional system; and, finally, in the paralysis or retardation of a good portion of the initiatives proposed by the Committee to the Executive. (Gómez Calcaño and López Maya 1990: 201–202)

In sharp contrast, COPEI, whose hopes of winning the executive had continued to drop over the Lusinchi term, vociferously advocated adoption of the reforms,[24] as did MAS, MEP, FEDECAMARAS (a conservative business group), and FACUR (Federation of Associations of Urban Communities). COPEI's efforts in particular helped to put these issues at the forefront of the 1988 elections:

The pressure exercised by this party should not be underestimated. This pressure was repeatedly manifested in the form of challenges to the AD candidate in terms of putting into question his possibility of winning the December 1988 national elections. (Gómez Calcaño and López Maya 1990: 172)

The workings of the COPRE generated a society-wide focus on the issue of decentralization, but it was not drafted into law purely through popular pressure. The COPEI seized on the popularity of decentralization, gambling that the AD would continue to oppose such a measure strongly, given its political interests in maintaining centralized power. COPEI hoped that making decentralization a central part of its campaign platform would nudge it ahead of the AD in the 1988 election. The AD leadership, particularly the national executive committee (CEN) that controlled the ranking of candidates, would probably have

---

[24] As far as decentralization was concerned, COPEI went further, calling for a "new federalism" (Gómez Calcaño and López Maya 1990: 115).

obliged in continuing to oppose such a change, but there was a contest going on within the AD over the party's presidential candidate. The
party leadership and outgoing President Lusinchi backed the candidacy
of Octavio Lepage for president, but Carlos Andrés Pérez began a
strong campaign to win the nomination. Using the same logic that
had led the COPEI to back decentralization, Carlos Andrés Pérez embraced several of the reforms called for by COPRE. This strategy won
him widespread popular support, and all but forced the party to select
him as its candidate (for an excellent game-theoretic treatment of this
topic, see Penfold Becerra 1999).

Due to these cross-cutting tensions within the party, the AD put forward a presidential candidate committed to decentralization. Carlos
Andrés Pérez signed a pact with leaders of the other major parties
agreeing to enact reforms encompassing COPRE's suggestions on gaining office. At the same time, however, the administration in power failed
to make forward strides on the issues at hand. In fact, it was popularly
perceived to be hindering reform:

[I]n the final months the hegemonic actors have proceeded to tame down the
proposals to the maximum admissible point. This situation has undermined
the work done by COPRE. (Urdaneta et al. 1990: 81–82)

In Venezuela, an extra-presidential commission with strong representation from parties that would benefit from decentralization helped
to put this issue at the top of the 1988 campaign agenda. Strategic
calculations regarding their electoral prospects prompted the COPEI
and later a faction within the AD to champion decentralization as a
way to attract the votes of a public eager for change.

Carlos Andrés Pérez and the AD fulfilled their campaign promises
of furthering decentralization through passing legislation[25] that allows
for the election of governors and mayors and assures them financial
resources. Still, the AD appeared begrudgingly compliant rather than
enthusiastically supportive of reform.[26] Worse still, while they enacted

---

[25] These include the Ley Orgánica de Régimen Municipal, the Ley Orgánica de Decen-
tralización, and the LODT – all passed in the first year of the Pérez presidency.

[26] This reluctance of AD legislators to embrace decentralization in the same way that its
presidential candidate had done reflects how Pérez used the issue of decentralization
to force his candidacy on the party. The AD party leadership had been very much
against his candidacy initially, endorsing Octavio Lepage instead.

paper reforms, legislators were perceived as trying to undermine the effectiveness of those reforms:

Like Penélope besieged by her suitors, the Venezuelan elite promised to acquiesce to the annoying demands of opening and renovation made by the upstarts. By the light of day they wove the reforms which, to be sure, would be the death of clientelistic and exclusive democracy. And, in the darkness they unraveled what they had done, perhaps hoping for a political boss who could confront the task of ejecting the intruders. (Gómez Calcaño and López Maya 1990: 207)

Given that governors have a great deal of discretion in determining the timing and extent of the transfer of responsibilities from the central to state governments, it is interesting to look at the evolution of decentralization over its first ten years.[27] In a report sponsored by the Inter-American Development Bank, Moritz Kraemer argues that decentralization has advanced further in states governed by the MAS party than in those governed by either COPEI or AD. This is particularly true in the earliest period of decentralization, from 1992 to 1995. In addition, he notes,

The only state that was held by the central government's party (Convergencia) in the 1995–98 electoral period . . . made the second fastest progress in decentralization. . . . [T]his frenzy might have been a reaction to the minimal chances that Convergencia could be returned to power in the presidential elections of 1998, when the incumbent, Rafael Caldera, is constitutionally barred from running again. (Kraemer 1999: 22 n. 13)

It appears that an electoral logic guides the pace of decentralization undertaken by state governors. Those parties that hold governorships and have low presidential prospects attempt to take on more decentralized power than those with stronger opportunities to win national power.

In the two most recent presidential periods, since the passage of decentralizing laws, decentralization has been contested by national governments led by presidents with weak and uncertain bases of support at subnational levels. In 1993, Venezuelans elected Rafael Caldera, the one-time head of COPEI, who ran this time as the leader of a new party, Convergencia Nacional (National Convergence). This victory marked the first presidency not held by either AD or COPEI in over

---

[27] For a good discussion of the process of transferring resources and responsibilities to regional governments, see De la Cruz 1992: 17–73.

four decades. Though this new party captured the presidency, the traditional parties continued to dominate legislative positions as well as regional and municipal executives (see Tables 6.4–6.6). Given the party's strong position in the presidency, its uncertainty of winning the next election (due to its recent origin), and its inability to win subnational elections, Caldera's party faced incentives to centralize power. In the prologue to his book on decentralization, Oswaldo Angulo Perdomo notes the shift toward recentralization initiated by Caldera:

Behind it all there were some who did not oppose the initiation of decentralization because they were overwhelmed by the phenomenon of intense public opinion that supported the process between 1987 and 1993. However, pro-center sectors returned to power in 1994 and continued the process of discrediting decentralization. The reason for this is clear: decentralization implies the redistribution of power in society. The political and economic elite who controlled the country were not prepared to lose one inch of their power or influence. (Angulo Perdomo 1997: 21)

During this period, the Caldera government clashed often with popularly elected governors and mayors, delayed the transfer of resources to subnational levels, and began a campaign to turn public opinion against the decentralization process (Angulo Perdomo 1997). In fact, during the banking crisis and economic decline of his first years in office, the national press swirled with rumors that Caldera would assume authoritarian powers (Bland 1998). No major reversals of either public opinion or legislation occurred, however.

The 1998 elections brought Hugo Chávez to power, at the head of an uncertain coalition of new parties. The two traditional parties joined a larger coalition supporting his challenger, and though they were unable to break Chávez's hold on the presidential slot, they did manage to win a good proportion of legislative seats as well as the majority of gubernatorial positions (the *Financial Times*, September 13, 1999); they also placed mayors in many important regional capitals. Like Caldera in this respect, Chávez came to office with high national popularity (as evidenced by his fairly easy victory in both the 1998 and 2000 elections), but without co-partisans in subnational seats of power and with quite a bit of uncertainty about his political coalition's ability to stand the test of time. Indeed, in the 2000 elections, Chávez's main rival arose from within his own coalition, in the person of his former co-conspirator in the 1992 coup attempt, Francisco Arias Cárdenas.

Under Chávez, Venezuela has embarked on an ambitious political restructuring, with a new constitution. Although approved by a wide majority, arguments against the reformed charter focused on the damage it would do to the decentralization process (Ellner 2001). In fact, when the constituent assembly briefly considered imposing a state of emergency on the country's mayors and governors, several thousand people took to the streets chanting, "Dictatorship no, democracy yes" (*Financial Times*, September 13, 1999). While local and regional elections were still held, "the authority of governors and mayors has been curtailed" (*New York Times*, July 28, 2000).

In sum, a commission composed mainly from non-AD adherents proposed an opening of the political system to greater levels of participation at all levels. The AD leadership, seeing its access to national power jeopardized by popular calls for reform, was forced to agree to the reform package. The party found a silver lining in the fact that the AD's strong support at subnational levels meant that the party could expect to win a large percentage of the newly electable governorships and mayoralties. Not surprisingly, parties with less access to the presidency (all parties except AD) enthusiastically supported the opportunity to compete for subnational positions. Finally, those parties with the smallest perceived chances of gaining the presidency have gone the farthest toward claiming decentralized power in states where they have won elected governorships. The two most recent administrations, led by Caldera and Chávez, have attempted to curtail subnational power to some extent (Lalander 2002). In both cases, these executives came to power at the head of new alliances that had much less success in advancing the candidacies of their subnational partisans. In addition, future support for both parties was extremely uncertain at the time of election. Given this combination of factors, decentralization's stagnation in Venezuela is unsurprising.

PERU

The Peruvian cases dramatically illustrate how political fortunes shape power-sharing arrangements between central and subnational governments. Between 1978 and 2000, power was decentralized to local governments on paper, decentralization promises were converted into practice, decentralization to regions was attempted but not fully adopted, and, finally, power was substantially recentralized. Each instance bears out the prediction that decentralization occurs when the party (or parties) in a position to effect its adoption enjoys weak national support, strong subnational support, and stable support over time. Recentralization occurs when the party in power is characterized by strong, but unstable, national support and weak support in subnational contests. Finally, it is interesting to note that Peru held new regional elections in 2002, suggesting a new round of decentralization; however, the resources and responsibilities of these positions remained unclear at the time of the election (Tanaka 2003b).

In 1978, Peru decentralized power to local governments through a Constitutional Assembly dominated by Peru's oldest and most institutionalized party: APRA (American Popular Revolutionary Alliance). Despite its endurance, APRA had never controlled executive power. The first elected government of the new democratic period implemented the decentralizing provisions of the new constitution and passed additional decentralizing reforms. This government, headed by Fernando Belaúnde Terry of the AP (Popular Action), was voted into office with a plurality but not a majority of the vote. The AP benefited from strong subnational-level support in municipal elections, and its national vote share had changed little compared with the previous presidential election – despite the fact that nearly twenty years of military rule intervened between the two. Finally, Peru provides the only case in this volume in which power was substantially recentralized. Alberto Fujimori created the Cambio 90[28] (Change 90) party as a personal vehicle for his 1990 presidential bid and rode it comfortably to the presidency. When he encountered resistance in the legislature – which his party did not control – and his party failed to win a significant portion of the 1993 municipal elections, Fujimori shifted power back toward the center, in

a total offensive, an attack that diminished corruption, but that also poked holes in the autonomy of local government and in its capacity to operate. It was a real counterreform that erased, without looking back, that which had been won regarding municipal development during the decade of the 1980s. (Delgado Silva 1995: 27)

---

[28] Fujimori headed the Cambio 90 party in 1990, the Cambio 90/Nueva Mayoría party in 1995, and the Peru 2000 party (which included original Cambio 90 elements) in 2000. To minimize confusion, I refer to Fujimori's party as the Cambio 90 throughout this chapter.

TABLE 6.7: *First-Round Presidential Results and Vote Change, Peru 1963–2000*

Party[a]	1963	1978[b]	1980	1985	1990	1995	2000
AP	39.1	*c*	**45.4**	7.3	–	–	–
APRA	34.4	35.3	27.4	**53.1**	22.6	4.1	–
UNO	25.5	–	–	–	–	–	–
PPC	–	23.8	9.6	11.9	–	–	–
FOCEP	–	12.3	–	–	–	–	–
IU	–	29.3	–	24.7	8.2	–	–
FREDEMO	–	–	–	–	32.6	–	–
Cambio 90	–	–	–	–	**29.1**	**64.4**	49.8
UP	–	–	–	–	–	21.8	–
PP	–	–	–	–	–	–	40.3

Note: A dash indicates that the party received less than 5 percent of the vote. Boldface type is used to distinguish the president's party. Peru also holds a second round if no party gains a majority in first-round voting. Winners of second-round voting are shown in boldface type.

[a] AP: Acción Popular (Popular Action); APRA: Alianza Popular Revolucionaria Americana (American Popular Revolutionary Alliance); UNO: Unión Nacional Odriísta (National Odriíst Union); PPC: Partido Popular Cristiano (Popular Christian Party); FOCEP: Frente Obrero Campesino Estudiantil y Popular (Popular Front of Workers, Peasants and Students); IU: Izquierda Unida (United Left); FREDEMO: Frente Democrático (Democratic Front); Cambio 90: Cambio 90 (Change 90); UP: Unión por el Perú (Union for Peru); PP: Peru Posible (Peru Possible).

[b] This column presents national-level results for Constituent Assembly elections.

[c] The AP boycotted these elections.

This section analyzes these changes to understand how political forces acting through the parties in power shaped each instance of reform.

National Strength and Vote Change

As in Ecuador and Bolivia, party support at the national level in Peru is changeable and fleeting, as shown in Table 6.7. Only APRA maintains support across this period, though it nearly disappears in the 1995 elections. The average percentage change for Peru's parties across elections is the highest of any country studied in this volume. The party with the most stable support over this period is the APRA, with an astounding 78 percent average vote change over successive elections. This high aggregate result masks periods of relative stability, however. Surprisingly, the least volatile period is the one spanning almost twenty years of dictatorship: From the final election of the previous democratic period in 1963 to the first election under Peru's new constitution, APRA and AP gain and lose less than eight percentage points of support. In the 1978 election for seats in the Constituent Assembly, APRA's percentage of the vote lies within one percentage point of its 1963 total, demonstrating remarkable stability. In fact, APRA's vote share in its first bid for the presidency in 1931 was 35 percent, and in its only other legal run for the presidency, in 1962, it won 33 percent of the vote. Over the long period stretching from 1931 to 1978, APRA's national-level support remained virtually constant in the aggregate, despite two substantial interludes in which it could not contest power.

When the AP gained the presidency in 1980, its percentage of the vote had changed only six percentage points since the last presidential election – a low rating given twenty intervening years without democratic contests and the party's decision not to participate in the Constituent Assembly. In 1980, the AP president was the same Fernando Belaúnde Terry who had been elected in 1963 and was overthrown by the military in 1968. This was to be the pinnacle of party stability in Peru.

The 1980s ushered in a period of extreme shifts in party support, owing mainly to the inability of either the AP from 1980 to 1985 or APRA from 1985 to 1990 to cure the country's economic ills or to stanch the flow of violence caused by the Shining Path and other rebel movements. These worsening problems weakened the governing party's credibility; by the end of the decade, both APRA and AP were largely discredited. Anticipating the 1990 national elections, new parties emerged to capture the votes of those dissatisfied with both conventional alternatives. In fact, the mere taint of association with traditional parties helped to turn Mario Vargas Llosa's 1990 first-round victory for the FREDEMO (Democratic Front) party into a second-round defeat to Alberto Fujimori and his Cambio 90 party.[29]

Subnational Strength

Peru is divided into twelve regions (including the special region of Lima/Callao), which are subdivided for administrative purposes

---

[29] Of course, many other features contributed to the electoral defeat of Vargas Llosa in 1990, including the breakdown of traditional parties, his personalistic style, and the fact that most people viewed him as a member of a discredited class (see Cameron 1997).

TABLE 6.8: *Percentage of Regions in Which Each Party Won a Plurality, 1980–1995*

Party Level	1980 Nation	1980 Muni	1983 Muni	1985 Nation	1986 Muni	1989 Muni	1990 Nation	1993 Muni	1995 Nation
AP	**85.2**	69.2	15.4	–	–	–	–	8	–
APRA	11.1	11.5	65.4	**88.9**	100	8	22	4	–
FREDEMO	–	–	–	–	–	58	41	–	–
Cambio 90	–	–	–	–	–	–	33	–	**100**

Note: A dash indicates that the party received less than 5 percent of the vote. Boldface type is used to distinguish the president's party.

into twenty-five departments. Further down the hierarchy, Peru has 189 provinces and 1,809 districts; both provinces and districts have municipal status, and each elects local officials (Nickson 1995). To examine regional political strength, it is possible to look at either national election results disaggregated by region (these are found under the column heading "Nation" in Table 6.8) or to look at municipal results aggregated up (these are found under the column heading "Muni" in Table 6.8). In practice, the results do not differ substantially.

In the 1980s, regional volatility is reflected in the rapidly changing fortunes of the parties that controlled the presidency. While the AP won a large percentage of regional pluralities in both national and municipal voting in 1980 – the same year it was elected to the presidency – that support dropped sharply by 1983 and was all but gone in 1985. Similarly, APRA won strong support by region in both the 1985 national election (which installed its candidate, Alan García, in the executive) and in the 1986 municipal elections; however, it won a plurality in only 8 percent of the regions in 1989 municipal elections – a steep decline. Cambio 90 wins a plurality of votes in one-third of the regions in 1990 national elections and a plurality in 100 percent of the regions in 1995 national elections but wins no appreciable number of municipal elections in between. A look at local results explains the underlying weakness of the Cambio 90 in subnational contests.

Mirroring the regional results, municipal contests tell a story of quick changes in the political fortunes of parties (see Table 6.9). Both the AP in 1980 and the APRA in 1985 entered the presidency with strong support at the municipal level in local contests; both parties watched that support wane. Cambio 90 presents a very different constellation of support, however. Despite the party's hegemonic victories

TABLE 6.9: *Percent of Municipalities in Which Each Party Won a Plurality 1980–2002*

Party[a]	1980	1983	1986	1989	1993	2002
AP	**65.4**	23.2	–	–	5.0	6.4
APRA	15.6	**47.7**	**91.8**	16.0	12.0	12.9
IU	–	20.0	–	–	–	–
FREDEMO	–	–	–	46.0	–	–
Cambio 90	–	–	–	–	–	–
PP	–	–	–	–	–	10.8
AEUN	–	–	–	–	–	8.5
PDSP	–	–	–	–	–	9.0

Note: A dash indicates that the party received less than 5 percent of the vote. Boldface type is used to distinguish the president's party.

[a] See previous table in this chapter; AEUN: Alianza Electoral Unidad Nacional (United National Electoral Alliance); PDSP: Partido Democrático Somos Peru (Democratic Party We Are Peru).

in the 1990 and 1995 national elections, the party enjoyed almost no success in local contests. This seemingly odd outcome owes to the personal popularity of Alberto Fujimori in presidential contests and the inability of Cambio 90 to institutionalize itself and gather popular support for its candidates at other levels of government. John Crabtree (1995) labels Cambio 90 a "non-party," highlighting its ephemeral nature. In 1993 political independents or "others" not identified by party won the vast majority of municipal contests:

On 29 January 1993, the government party, Change 90/New Majority, won only about 2.8 percent of all districts in the country. In Lima, Fujimori withdrew his candidate when the polls indicated that he would lose by a wide margin. The other new parties that appeared for the CCD (Constitutional Assembly) elections in 1992 (almost all were more electoral lists than political parties) were not a factor. None of them, including Change 90/New Majority, has a national structure to enable it to present candidates in the 1,800 electoral districts, or even in the 180 provincial capitals or 25 departmental capitals. (Rospigliosi 1994: 47)

Post-Fujimori municipal elections in 2002 reaffirm this pattern, with various non-traditional parties winning more than 40 percent of the contests; the more traditional APRA and AP won 13 percent and 6.4 percent of the contests, respectively, while Toledo's PPP won 11 percent (ONPE 2003).

The theory proposed in this volume predicts that decentralization will occur when parties in power face weak national electoral prospects, strong subnational support, and stable support over time. The strong showing of APRA in Constituent Assembly elections in 1978 and the AP victory in 1980 fit these characteristics: Neither won a majority at the national level, both had strong support in subnational level elections, and both had fairly stable support across previous elections leading up to their victories. Indeed, the new constitution of 1978 strengthened local government and the AP presidency not only converted constitutional promises into reality, but also enacted laws to further decentralization.

The opposite set of features characterizes Fujimori's Cambio 90: strong support at the national level, but weak support for the party at lower levels of government and extreme change in levels of support over time. Fujimori systematically gathered power back toward the center, crippling local governments both politically and financially in an attempt to retain his monopoly on power at the center. The next section explores these topics in more detail.

A More Detailed Look at Peru, 1978–2000

In a country that traces its independence to the *Cabildo* (local governments under the Spanish colonial system that provided many seats for American-born Creoles),[30] the fate of local government has followed a bumpy trajectory. Throughout most of the twentieth century, constitutional language allowing for the election of local officials has been disregarded. Only two local elections took place in the 1960s before military rule abolished the practice, increasing central power. The constitution of 1979 reestablished local elections. This new constitution was drawn up by an elected constituent assembly dominated by APRA and the conservative PPC (Popular Christian Party).

On June 18, 1978, Peru elected a constituent assembly to rewrite its constitution in preparation for the return to civilian rule after a decade of military intervention. The AP did not participate in the elections,[31]

---

[30] See the discussion in Elías Jiménez 1990, esp. 28–31.
[31] The AP tried to distance itself from the Constitutional Assembly called by the outgoing military government in an attempt to avoid political contamination by association

but the APRA won a plurality of the seats. When it allied with the strong bloc controlled by the conservative PPC, this coalition controlled a majority of the seats in the assembly. Although parties of the left won a surprising third of the vote, they did not take an active role in crafting the new charter and, in the end, refused to sign it. Their role was weakened first by their factionalism – they represented over twenty parties that had banded together into five coalitions for the sake of the elections – and second by their refusal to focus on the work of building a constitution.

The position of these parties was that the Assembly was only part of a larger political struggle and should be used to promote the demands of unions and other lower-class groups. . . . The main goal of the Left was radical social change and not a return to civilian rule. (Mauceri 1997: 25)

The same author notes:

With AP abstaining and the Left intent on using the new Assembly as a forum to challenge regime legitimacy, only the conservative PPC and APRA saw in the assembly a means to create a new political system. Both also had hopes of designing such a system to their own political advantage. (21)

To determine the shape of their political advantage, it is important to focus on their bases of support. APRA's support in the assembly vote drew heavily from rural areas of the country, while the PPC gained stronger support in the urban areas of Lima, Callao, and Arequipa (Medina Garcia 1980). APRA's rural strength is not surprising, since its historical appeal had been "tied to agricultural extension and capitalization and the marginalization of the small farmer. . . . APRA's support base consist[ed] primarily of the middle classes, workers, and certain groups of campesinos" (Graham 1992: 25). Although APRA operated in coalition with the PPC, APRA was perceived as dominant.

With its strong support across the country, particularly in rural areas, its strong institutionalization,[32] and its earned reputation as Peru's

---

with it. Instead, the AP argued that constitutional revision should occur after the first democratic election, under the auspices of an already democratic system (Saba 1987).

[32] Graham (1992) notes that APRA's "hierarchical structure . . . was in part responsible for the APRA's exceptional capacity to organize and to mobilize, which rivaled that of the army" (27). McClintock (1998) notes, "The APRA was the only party throughout Peru's history that can be said to have achieved institutionalization" (53).

"quintessential opposition party" (Graham 1992: 127), APRA had clear incentives to decentralize power. It had never won (or been allowed to win) the presidency but consistently won subnational elections, and its support was nearly unwavering in the period preceding the 1978 Constituent Assembly.

As we have seen, decentralization language on paper may not coincide with effective decentralization within the country. APRA pushed to decentralize power in the 1978 constitution, but these provisions remained ineffective until the AP breathed life into them. In fact, the AP furthered decentralization during Belaúnde's term by adopting legislation to increase the financial autonomy of local governments. This was principally accomplished through passage of the 1984 Municipal Finance Reform (Reforma Financiera Municipal) and through the Ley Orgánica de Municipalidades (Law no. 23853).

In 1980, President Belaúnde came to office with a comfortable victory margin over his nearest competitor. Support for reinstating municipal elections was high among the population who sought to shed the practices of the authoritarian period. Belaúnde's previous presidency (1963–1968) had brought municipal elections back from their dormancy under previous democratic governments, making it difficult for him now to stand in their way. This is particularly true given the new resonance they had acquired through their inclusion in the new constitution. In addition to the widespread expectations of decentralization raised by the constitution, the AP expected to do quite well in municipal elections, given its subnational strength in municipal contests prior to the authoritarian period. These expectations were borne out in the 1980 municipal contests:

The AP-PPC alliance gained control over more municipalities than did their APRA-UNO rivals, and the Alliance candidate, Luis Bedoya Reyes, a Christian Democratic leader, easily won the mayorship of Lima. Overall, Belaúnde's supporters received 46.6 percent of the total vote, while the Coalición had 44.4 percent. Compared to the proportion of votes received in the presidential election of June 1963, this represented a net gain for Belaúnde's alliance and a net loss for the combined forces of the APRA-UNO Coalición. (Saba 1987: 50)

After these initial successes, however, the AP began to lose support at all levels. This can be seen in its poor showing in the 1983 subnational contest in which "Acción Popular was soundly defeated throughout the length and breadth of the Republic" (Saba 1987: 74). "By 1983–1984, President Belaúnde's popularity was reaching an all time low and Acción Popular's diverse bases of support were crumbling nation-wide" (ibid.: 72). Given this decline at all levels, why did the AP deepen fiscal decentralization in 1984, when its inability to win subnational elections had already been evidenced? To understand this seemingly paradoxical reform, one must consider its trajectory through the policy-making process. The new municipal code, passed in May of 1984, had first been issued as a presidential decree in 1981 – before the AP began to lose substantial support. The National Congress considered the decree and eventually rejected it, finally allowing an amended version to be passed late in the term.

When the AP submitted decentralizing measures, it enjoyed fairly strong support at the national level, significant subnational support, and steady support at all levels of government. Except for its strong national level support on winning the presidency, these features made decentralization attractive. Given President Belaúnde's previous presidency and its sponsorship of municipal democracy, along with the expectations created by the freshly printed constitution, reinstating municipal elections was a necessary reform. By the end of his term, Belaúnde and the AP had seen their support dwindle to a new low. The deepening of fiscal decentralization after the AP's poor showing in 1983 municipal contests owed to the legacy of the AP's initial sponsorship of the measure. At the end of its term, the AP was weak at all levels and uncertain of its future electoral prospects at all levels.

In the 1985 national election, AP won less than 10 percent of the presidential vote; it dropped from a Senate plurality of twenty-six seats in 1980 to just six seats in 1985. After controlling a majority of ninety-eight seats in the legislature's 180-person lower house, it won only ten in 1985. Capitalizing on what was perceived as an utterly failed orthodox approach to mend the economy, APRA's Alan García rode a wave of support for heterodoxy[33] into the presidency, marking APRA's first presidential win. Despite his different approach, García failed equally

---

[33] For an excellent discussion of these economic programs and the attempts to implement them in Peru in the 1980s, see Pastor and Wise 1992.

in his attempts to rescue the economy. "Relative to Belaúnde, Alan García raised hopes much higher and dashed them more completely" (McClintock 1998: 28).

As APRA's turn in the executive drew to a close, its diminished support in the 1989 municipal contests mirrored its waning national-level support. The 1989 municipal elections also evidenced the rise of strong new parties, such as FREDEMO. In what was seen as a conscious attempt to create a refuge for *apristas* thrown out of national power, Alan García pushed through legislation (Law no. 24792) to strengthen regional governments.[34] This attempt was neither wholly successful nor broadly popular, but the attempt by a party losing national power to create sources of power at subnational levels should not be surprising. This motive seems to have been quite clear to Peruvians, as well:

The reasons were more political than technical: they predicted then an incredible electoral defeat for the APRA at the national level, due to which the exiting President – also the President of the party – intended to compensate the national reversal at the regional level, establishing a type of *political counterweight*. (Thedieck and Buller 1995: 219)

This seems particularly reasonable in light of the fact that APRA could count on strong party organizations within each of the regions to help it win gubernatorial elections. In fact, in the regional elections held in 1989, APRA won control of ten of Peru's eleven regional governments (Buller 1993: 151). While the election of regional governors suggests that decentralization occurred during this period, this decentralization did not include a clear transfer of fiscal resources, perhaps due to the haste of the reform effort.[35]

Experiments in regional government and municipal strengthening soon drew to a close as Peruvian politics entered a new decade and a new era. With Peru's major parties discredited after ten years of economic chaos, Alberto Fujimori's Cambio 90 party emerged victorious

[34] Regional power was principally increased by the Basic Law of Regionalization (Law 24,650).

[35] "Principally, the legal regulations for the creation of regional taxes had not been spelled out, such that the regional government was financially completely dependent upon transfers from the central government and, with that, was subject to the political whim of the central government" (Thedieck and Buller 1995: 212).

in second-round elections against FREDEMO's Mario Vargas Llosa; this election christened both of these parties into Peruvian politics. Remarkably,

[T]he combined 1995 congressional vote for all parties that had participated in the 1978 Constituent Assembly – namely the APRA, Acción Popular, Partido Popular Cristiano, and Izquierda Unida – was 15 percent. It would be hard to imagine a more complete breakdown of a party system. (Cameron 1997: 68)

Having helped to topple the discredited party system, Fujimori overturned a series of institutions and traditions, gaining popular support with each resounding thud. His masterstroke occurred when he dissolved the Congress on April 5, 1992, postponed the municipal elections scheduled for November of 1992, and called for the election of a new constituent assembly to write him a new constitution.[36]

As part of this institutional reengineering, Fujimori first withheld transfers from regional governments in the first two years of his presidency, then appointed prefects to head regional governments after 1992, abrogating the regional elections initiated by APRA. One author suggests a political motivation: "[I]t could not count on representatives of its own party in any of the regional governments or assemblies" (Thedieck and Buller 1995: 220). Fujimori's ability to overturn the election of regional executives was successful partially because citizens had little experience of electing governors (just one regional election occurred, in 1989). In addition, many Peruvians saw APRA's push for regional elections as a ploy to improve its access to power after its inevitable loss of the presidency:

There then appeared a new subnational political stratum, without a good administrative structure, without sufficient financial bases and without an institutionalized relationship with the other political-administrative levels (national and local) and, even worse, without having been anchored in the conscience of the population. (ibid.: 219)

---

[36] While Fujimori won the second round of the 1990 presidential elections by a wide margin, his first-round results had not won his party a majority in the legislature, causing several of his reforms to become deadlocked in that body.

Riding on Fujimori's popularity, the 1993 referendum to confirm the new constitution won a slim victory, substituting a much more centralized power structure for the more decentralized one guaranteed in the 1979 constitution. In the postponed municipal elections that occurred in the same year, Cambio 90 faced its first major defeat when its candidates won less than 3 percent of the vote. This weak showing of support at the local level gave Fujimori little incentive to perpetuate a system that decentralized power to a level he and his party did not control. Under Fujimori, power was taken back from local governments both through political and economic reforms (Dammert 1999). In contrast to the celebration of regional elections, however, local elections enjoyed greater legitimacy and more frequency throughout Peru's history. Fujimori employed a more subtle strategy to enfeeble local governments than he had used at the regional level. This is largely because local governments were accorded a great deal of respect for their role in sparking a move toward independence from Spain, and autonomous municipal governments were also envisioned in Peru's constitutions in 1823, 1828, 1856, 1871, and 1933. Due to neglect, municipal elections did not occur until 1963 and then were discontinued under military rule. Still, the idea of electing local governments took root early on in the national psyche and Peruvians were able to elect local leaders throughout Fujimori's tenure in office.

Politically, Fujimori eroded the ability of opposition parties – already weakened by the end of the 1980s – to organize strong candidacies in municipal elections. This was accomplished by lowering the number of signatures required on petitions for candidacy, thus leading to a proliferation of candidates that would split the vote. Lima's 1993 municipal election illustrates this phenomenon particularly well: A staggering thirty-eight candidates competed for the position of mayor. Decree Law 776 (Nueva Ley de Tributación Municipal), passed on the final day of 1993, represented Fujimori's most effective weapon in the battle to reclaim central government discretion over financial transfers to municipalities. This law abolished the resources previously guaranteed to municipal governments, replacing them with the Municipal Compensation Fund (FCM), which was centrally administered. Through its modification of property and sales tax rates and their distribution to municipalities, municipal budgets shrank almost

80 percent in the law's first year of operation (Kay 1995: 14). One author describes the law's effects:

[I]t not only asphyxiated them economically, it severely restricted their autonomy, without having to expropriate the financial resources that corresponded to them by law, but by establishing new criteria for their distribution, designed to sow aggravation in the municipal atmosphere. (Delgado Silva 1995: 14).

Of the FCM, the same author argues that it

introduces the most gross arbitrariness, the most obvious verticalism, the most absolute subordination and the most blatant manipulation into the relations between the Central Government and the Municipalities. (27)

It seems that the law itself may have been tied to particularistic political motivations:

A clear objective of changing the municipal fund allocation seems to have been to reduce the power of one of Fujimori's main rivals, Ricardo Belmont, the mayor of Lima. (Graham and Kane 1998: 90)

Finally, the law was also described as a "thinly veiled attack against the provincial mayors and politicians who helped to mobilize 'No' votes in the constitutional referendum" (Kay 1995: 15).

Municipal elections in 1995 reinforced the fact that Fujimori's personality was the key to Cambio 90's national-level victories. These results "confirmed two trends evident in the 1993 municipal elections: the surge in support for independents, and the inability of Cambio 90 to operate as a national-level coalition" (Graham and Kane 1998: 81).

Sitting atop a party with strong support at the national level but without a level of institutionalization that might enable it to win elections at any other level, Fujimori faced strong incentives to draw power toward the center. From there he could frustrate opposition parties hoping to build electoral strength from a base of subnational victories. With strong discretionary control over financial resources, he could reward subnational politicians and constituencies that supported him and punish those that did not; alternatively, he could use access to this money as a bribe to win over reluctant or recalcitrant constituents.

A study conducted by Graham and Kane found that "high levels of FONCODES (discretionary social fund) expenditures are associated with significant increases in support for Fujimori from 1993 to 1995, particularly in the departments where support for Fujimori was lowest in 1993" (Graham and Kane 1998: 89). More importantly, "discretionary public expenditure clearly responded to voting trends, being redirected to areas where Fujimori lost in the 1993 referendum" (99). These conclusions were sharpened and reaffirmed by Schady (2000).

Since Fujimori's departure from power, Peru's president Toledo has reinstituted regional elections, but the newly elected positions remain vaguely defined. Given that Toledo's party won only one of the twenty-five regional governorships, while the APRA won nearly half and no other party won more than two,[37] there seems little reason to expect Toledo to champion strengthening regional governments in the remainder of his term.

ECUADOR, VENEZUELA, AND PERU IN CONCLUSION

Examining the experiences of these three countries with decentralization provides strong evidence that the electoral prospects of parties in power conditions their support for decentralization. Each country's experience reinforces the prediction that parties are more likely to decentralize when their hold on national power is weak, when they have strong subnational bases of support, and when the changeability of their electoral support across elections is relatively low. Ecuador's chaotic party system and its lack of decentralization during this period underscore the importance of stability in making decentralization attractive to parties. COPEI's support of decentralization in 1989 Venezuela looks a lot like the APRA's support of decentralization in 1978 Peru: Both were parties with strong subnational bases of support and weak national-level support relative to their rivals. COPEI's reluctance to decentralize during its 1968–1973 term reinforces the importance not just of achieved national power but of perceived future

---

[37] APRA won twelve governorships; the UPP won two; and one governorship was won by each of the following parties: Perú Posible, Frente Independiente Moralizador, Movimiento Independiente de Campesinos y Profesionales (MINCAP), Movimiento Independiente Luchemos por Huanuco, Unidos por Junín Sierra y Selva, Unidos por Loreto, Movimiento Nuevo Izquierda, Partido Democrática Somos Peru, Concertación en la Region para la Descentralización, Movimiento por la Autonomía Regional Quechua Aymara, and the Movimiento Independiente Nueva Amazonia (www.jne.gob.pe, accessed April 2, 2003.).

access to national power. This party's prediction that its future national support would improve overwhelmed the impact of its weak victory in 1968, its strong regional basis of support, and its relative stability over time to keep it from pushing for reform during this period. Finally, the fact that Alberto Fujimori recentralized power in Peru after creating a new party with strong support for its leader in national elections but minimal support for its candidates in subnational elections provides an extra check on the theory. If parties with weak national support, strong subnational support, and stable support over time should decentralize power, surely parties with the opposite characteristics should gather power back to the center. This exactly characterizes Fujimori's Peru.

The next chapter draws comparisons across cases from all five countries to provide a more thorough discussion of the theory set forth in this book. In the context of all of the rich information that has been presented in Chapters 4 through 6, it is time to revisit the discussion of the theory and statistical results laid out in Chapters 2 and 3. This allows for an exploration of the points where the in-depth case studies complement, and where they contradict, the evidence laid out in those earlier chapters.

PART III

COMPARISONS, CONCLUSIONS, AND EXTENSIONS

7

Comparisons, Conclusions, and Extensions

The last several chapters have explored the relationship between decentralizing policies and the electoral concerns of political parties. Using multiple methods, a theory linking the two was developed and tested against alternative theories. Using statistical and case study analysis of Bolivia, Colombia, Ecuador, Peru, and Venezuela, strong support has been marshaled for the hypothesis that political parties in a position to shape the contours of center-subnational power-sharing arrangements are heavily influenced by their electoral prospects at different levels of government. This chapter briefly synthesizes the results from the statistical and case study analyses before taking advantage of a few focused, cross-country case comparisons to address some remaining questions. It ends with a brief sketch of some theoretical and empirical extensions.

This volume opened with a formal model, which added precision to the general theory that electoral concerns affect decentralizing decisions; the model allowed me to check the exact relations between key factors. This led to the testable hypotheses that decentralization becomes more attractive to parties who perceive greater electoral opportunities at the local level than at the national level based on their constellation of electoral support. The formal model also singled out the importance of stable support over time in parties' decision calculus. Parties discount future time periods heavily when the volatility of their past support makes predicting future support difficult. Because the benefits of decentralization accrue in the future, higher discount rates on future periods greatly depress the incentives of parties to reform in this way. Parties will give up power today only if they can be reasonably confident of reaping the benefits at the newly empowered subnational levels in future time periods.

Hypotheses generated in the modeling exercise were put to statistical tests to determine their validity across administrations over time in all five countries. Logit regression verified that the expected relationship held in the cases: The probability that an administration would decentralize increased as the party in power experienced less support at the national level, more support at local levels, and lower levels of change in support at the national level between elections. Using the regression results to generate predicted values and comparing these with the actual behavior of each administration, the model correctly sorted all but one of the twenty-six cases, correctly identifying twenty-one cases in which decentralization was not adopted, as well as five cases in which decentralization occurred. This method misidentified one case of decentralization as a nondecentralizing case – Colombia 1990–1994 – a case of decentralization initiated by a popularly elected constitutional assembly. These results point to the large degree of generalizability of the statistical results, while also pointing out the important limitations of a purely statistical approach.

COMPARATIVE LESSONS

Having analyzed decentralization experiences by country in the previous three chapters, exploring each administration within each country, I am now in a good position to answer some lingering questions by drawing on the rich detail of these individual country experiences. Why does Colombia decentralize early and Venezuela decentralize late when they are both fairly stable, two-party systems? Why does Bolivia decentralize when Ecuador – also a multi-party, multi-ethnic state – does not? Why do constitutional conventions in Peru (1979) and Colombia (1991) and a presidential commission in Venezuela (in the mid to late 1980s) play such strong roles in decentralizing power, while constitutional conventions in Peru (1992–1993) and – to a lesser extent – Venezuela (1999) draw power back toward the center? Why do both Colombia and Bolivia decentralize even when their political party systems appear so different? And why do some individual countries – Peru and, to a lesser extent, Venezuela and Bolivia – first decentralize power and then recentralize power within a relatively short period of time? It is only by disaggregating country experiences to the administration level that the above questions can be satisfactorily answered. Comparing cases across countries helps to tease out the importance of each factor in determining a governing party's incentives to decentralize. Through carefully chosen comparisons, it is possible to explain why cases that appear broadly similar on the surface differ in their outcomes and also why cases that seem quite dissimilar experience similar outcomes.

This set of comparisons is divided into three parts, crafted to take advantage of the "method of agreement" and the "method of difference." These two analytical tools, dating back to the work of John Stuart Mill, can be especially useful when dealing with a small number of observations because they allow the researcher to pinpoint key similarities and differences in a systematic way.[1]

Similar Features, Different Outcomes

The first comparison contrasts the Colombian decentralizing administration of Betancur (1982–1986) with Venezuela's nondecentralizing Caldera administration (1968–1973). The second contrasts Bolivia's decentralizing administration under the leadership of Gonzalo Sánchez de Lozada (1993–1997) with Ecuador's nondecentralizing Febres-Cordero administration (1984–1988).

On the surface, Venezuela and Colombia appear broadly similar during most of this period: Both have relatively stable two-party systems of electoral competition in which both parties have deep ties in society and a relatively stable record of electoral support over time (at least until the early 1990s in Venezuela). Why does Colombia decentralize so much sooner than Venezuela? In search of an answer, it is necessary to disaggregate both country experiences into individual administrations. Two cases that exhibit deep similarities are Colombia's 1982–1986 administration and Venezuela's 1968–1973 administration. In both countries, a dominant party had emerged in a (roughly, in the case of Venezuela) two-party system, but in each of these administrations, the smaller party had acceded to the presidency – largely

---

[1] See Przeworski and Teune 1982 and Collier and Collier 1991 for discussions of these methods.

due to a split within the dominant party. In both cases, the parties in the presidency held strong support in a substantial number of local governments, and in both countries the stability of their vote shares across elections was relatively high. In Colombia, under the Conservative Betancur, decentralization was enacted; in Venezuela under the *copeyano* (Social Christian Party) Caldera, decentralization remained largely absent from the government's agenda. This difference in outcomes may derive from the different prospective beliefs of the two parties about their ability to retain control over the central government. In Colombia, Betancur won the presidency without a strong increase in the Conservative vote total, and the split in the Liberal party was considered temporary from the start. In Venezuela, in contrast, COPEI won the presidency with a significant upward swing in its vote total and the belief that the AD was a party in decline. Because both parties had similarly strong local support, similarly low volatility of support, and historically weak national support relative to their main partisan rival, this example helps to highlight a crucial difference between two cases: the important role played by parties' interpretations of the historical trends of their national-level support when determining the governing party's support for decentralization.

Two other countries that appear very similar on the surface are Ecuador and Bolivia. If Colombia and Venezuela resemble each other in having stable, two-party competition through much of their history, Ecuador and Bolivia present an opposite comparison: Both have multi-party systems with rather unstable support for parties across elections. To compare why one multi-party, multi-ethnic system decentralized and the other one did not, again it is necessary to disaggregate the country experiences to the level of individual administrations. A pair of presidential administrations that showed striking similarities on the surface and yet experienced different outcomes are the Febres-Cordero administration in Ecuador (1984–1988) and the Sánchez de Lozada presidency in Bolivia (1993–1997). In Ecuador, the PSC placed second in the first round of presidential voting, edging out its main contender in the second round by a slim, three-percentage-point margin. In Bolivia, the MNR had won a plurality of votes in the previous presidential election, only to be denied the presidency under Bolivia's presidential election rules. It won the presidency in 1993 with a plurality at roughly 35 percent of the vote (Sánchez de Lozada was the presidential candidate in both elections). In both Ecuador and Bolivia, national-level support for the victor was weak. In both cases also, the change in support for the party between national elections was low. In Bolivia power was decentralized, while in Ecuador it was not. The crucial difference between these two cases is that the MNR in Bolivia possessed widespread popularity in local contests, while the PSC in Ecuador was extremely weak at the local level, winning just over 6 percent of local contests. Decentralization therefore offered rich rewards to MNR partisans at subnational levels, while it offered little to members of the PSC, despite their weak hold on national power and the stable support they enjoyed across elections.

A final set of cases that show broad similarities but very different outcomes are the five cases of extra-presidential commissions and constitutional assemblies that influenced the trajectory of decentralization in their respective countries. Three of these – Peru (1979), Colombia (1991), and Venezuela (late 1980s) – furthered decentralization, while two – Peru (1992–1993) and Venezuela (1999) – did not. In all cases, the extra-presidential bodies wielded powers autonomous from the president's administration, and each of these bodies addressed the issue of intergovernmental power sharing. Taking a closer look at these assemblies, it becomes clear that those assemblies in which non-administration parties gained a high percentage of the positions increased decentralization, while those assemblies that were heavily controlled by the party that also controlled the presidency increased national powers relative to subnational powers. In the latest instances in Peru and Venezuela, these were presidential parties that had a centralizing constellation of electoral support: strong support for the presidential candidate at the national level, little electoral experience, and much weaker support for subnational candidates running on the party's label.

Different Features, Similar Outcomes

Within the Andean region, two countries could hardly be more different than Bolivia and Colombia. Bolivia is widely known for its political instability and its economic turbulence (it holds the record for the region's most severe bout of hyperinflation in 1985), while Colombia has the region's most stable party system and its record for constitutional longevity; Colombia also experienced the longest continuous growth of GDP of any country in the world until 1999. Most importantly, given the primacy of stability in determining decentralization's attractiveness to parties, it seems strange that decentralization occurred both in the most stable party system studied here and also in the party system with the highest volatility.

Despite the overall differences in their political systems, administrations in both Bolivia and Colombia instituted decentralizing reform and under broadly similar circumstances. Colombia decentralized in the early 1980s when the Conservative party, led by Belisario Betancur, came to power due to a temporary split in the historically stronger Liberal party. In addition to having generally weak national support, compared with the Liberals' record of national success, the Conservatives enjoyed pockets of support throughout the country in local contests and had extremely stable support over time. Though Bolivia's party system has been categorized as "inchoate" (Mainwaring and Scully 1995) due to its high volatility and the short average life span of its parties, one party within that system has enjoyed relatively stable support over time: the MNR. Decentralization occurred in Bolivia under the leadership of this, its most stable party. Decentralizing legislation was passed during the presidency of Gonzalo Sánchez de Lozada; he was in a unique position to appreciate the difficulty of gaining national power given that he had won a plurality of the votes in the previous (1989) national election, only to be denied the presidency through Bolivia's complex electoral rules. Decentralization was adopted when the party had gained significant subnational strength compared with its 1985–1989 presidency. Comparing these two instances, Betancur's and Sánchez de Lozada's administrations have three things in common: parties that did not expect to control the executive in the long term based on their weak national support, widespread support at the local level, and relatively stable vote shares over time.

Variation within One Country: A Lens for Examining Recentralization

When outcomes across time within one country differ dramatically, the number of explanatory variables that explain that variation is narrowed considerably. Because they share the same cultural and historical context, comparing two administrations within one country affords a particular type of controlled experiment. This section attempts to explain decentralizing and recentralizing tendencies within individual countries over time, looking first at Peru – the only country that has substantially recentralized power in this sample – and then turning to Venezuela and Bolivia.

Comparing Peru in the late 1970s and early 1980s with Peru in the early 1990s pairs two cases with remarkable similarities; these two cases also happen to be the two administrations in the sample with the most different outcomes. In the first period, power was decentralized; in the second, power was recentralized. Peru began the 1980s with a new constitution, a constitution crafted in a constitutional assembly guided largely by the APRA, Peru's longtime opposition party. Throughout Peruvian history, Haya de la Torre's APRA party had attracted significant and consistent electoral support, without ever gaining control of the national government. The resulting constitution enshrined the institution of local elections in the national charter. The subsequent AP presidency headed by Belaúnde Terry breathed life into this decentralizing reform by overseeing the first local elections in the 1980s. The AP, with less than dominant national support, strong local support at the beginning of its term, and stable support (comparing its 1980 vote total with the vote it received in 1963 – the last election before Peru's authoritarian government) perceived decentralization's long-term advantages. In contrast, Fujimori's rise to the presidency ushered in a period of recentralization. Just over a decade after the new constitution's adoption, Cambio 90 came to power with strong support in national presidential elections but with weak support for the party's candidates in subnational contests. Fujimori realized his party's poor (and unpredictable) performance at all levels of government and acted to conserve power within the one area where his control was assured. Fujimori not only curtailed local government autonomy through severe fiscal recentralization, he also postponed municipal elections at the beginning of his term, abolished the election of regional officials, and slashed fiscal transfers to the regional level. Peru's recent history provides the perfect circumstances for both the decentralization of power – as seen in the Constitutional Assembly of 1978 and the first democratic term (1980–1985) – while also creating the ideal context for power's recentralization in the 1990s. By the 1990s, the stable party system that made decentralization possible in the previous period had given way to near chaos as Peru's traditional two parties crumbled. In the absence of predictability and with the president's party grossly under-institutionalized, Fujimori faced every incentive to bring power back toward the center.

The tendency to recentralize power can be detected to a much lesser extent in both Venezuela under Chávez and Bolivia under Banzer. In both cases, these presidents came to power at the head of parties with weak support in subnational contests.

Like Fujimori, Banzer led a party widely viewed as a personal political vehicle; unlike Peru's Cambio 90, the ADN has been in operation since 1979 (the last year of Banzer's eight-year dictatorship). While often among the top three vote-getting parties, the ADN has not been hegemonic like Cambio 90 and its 1997 victory was not overwhelming (21% of the vote – a margin of 4.6 percentage points over the MNR). Still, the ADN shares with Cambio 90 the strong electoral draw of its leader (and presidential candidate) at the national level and its lesser strength in subnational contests. Both the ADN and Cambio 90 also display large swings in their vote shares across elections. In Bolivia, the change in the ADN's vote share across elections has been relatively low compared with other Bolivian parties, but it is well above the average across countries in the region. The short time horizon this implies was exacerbated for the ADN by Banzer's very advanced age and the lack of a clear successor. Given these features – the ADN's weak local support and short time horizons – it is no wonder that Banzer was no great fan of decentralization. It is telling that, after Banzer's death, the ADN polled only 3.4 percent of the vote in national elections.

Likewise, Hugo Chávez, while continuing to be highly popular among his core constituency, can be seen as more of a personal political phenomenon than as part of an organized party. Though he has managed to control the national government by cobbling together coalitions in Venezuela's legislature, opposition to Chávez is most visible at the regional and local level, where traditional parties were able to consolidate control over several key governments. One of the most frequent criticisms of Venezuela's new constitution, largely drafted by Chávez, is that it draws power back toward the center, reversing the highly popular decentralizing program of previous administrations.

BROAD LESSONS

The insights gained from this analysis extend beyond explaining the causes of political and fiscal decentralization. Lessons can be drawn not only from the conclusions of this analysis but from the methods employed to reach them. In particular, this project has sought the impetus for reform not in external factors but in the electoral incentives of policy makers; it has taken political parties as its primary actors; and it has utilized several different methodological approaches, combining the benefits of each to bolster the overall strength of the analysis.

Social scientists seeking to explain political outcomes have gained considerable leverage from explanations that focus on economic forces acting through political institutions. This approach makes the most sense when the impetus for reform is some type of external shock – such as an economic crisis – affecting the whole region. Responses to such an external shock will be mediated through political and economic institutions. Not all reforms, however, represent institutional responses to external forces. This project has demonstrated how political and economic institutions can be strongly affected by political forces, particularly electoral forces.

This analysis has focused on political parties as important actors in political and economic reform. Where parties have been taken seriously in political science work, the focus has often remained at the level of the party system. By disaggregating party systems, as this work has done, it is possible to unlock the diversity of incentives faced by individual parties within those systems. For example, individual parties within unstable party systems may act more like stable parties within stable party systems (the MNR in Bolivia, for example). Likewise, unstable parties may act opportunistically within stable party systems depending on their own electoral prospects.

Finally, the methodological approach taken in this investigation has combined the strength of several different investigative strategies. Formal modeling techniques were used to specify the variables that affect the ultimate decision to decentralize (or not) and the relationship between those variables. Statistical analysis was used to provide a basic test of the model using comparable data across countries and time periods. Because the statistical test required comparable data across the cases, it assured that each case was analyzed according to the same standards when determining whether or not a case fit the profile of a decentralizing administration. The fact that the statistical analysis strongly supported the hypothesis that decentralization follows an electoral logic increases my confidence in the overall results. In the statistical analysis it is not possible to fit each case analysis to the theory through ad hoc reasoning. While this is an immense benefit of using statistical analysis, there are drawbacks as well. Because the requirements of the statistical model inhibit the inclusion of all the data available, in-depth country analyses were used to flesh out the experiences of each of the administrations covered in this project. One of the most serious limitations of the statistical model is that it did not allow the inclusion of data that bear on changing perceptions of each party's strength throughout the course of each administration. For parties that experienced swift and sharp changes in their support, a sole focus on retrospective measures of electoral strength is particularly problematic because predictions of future support often bear little relation to previous results.

Case studies drew on fieldwork in Bolivia and Colombia, archival investigation, and interviews with key policy makers to bring more evidence to bear on the relationship between reform and electoral concerns. In addition to allowing me to add a greater variety of data on party support for each administration, the in-depth analyses also allowed me to extend the theory's logic to cases in which decentralization occurred not by presidential initiative but through the use of extra-presidential bodies such as constitutional assemblies.

Each of these methodological approaches on its own provides important leverage on the question and on the theory's ability to answer it. Taken together, the findings from the statistical analysis and the case studies can be compared with one another to assure a more complete and consistent analysis of the available information and therefore a better test of the theory's predictive power. Triangulating these methods (Tarrow 1995), the project found strong evidence that decentralization of political and fiscal resources occurs when political parties in positions to affect power-sharing arrangements between levels of government see an electoral advantage in a more decentralized system.

Each piece of the analysis points to the same conclusion: Parties seek to decentralize power when they face weak national-level support and strong subnational level support and when their share of the vote changes little across elections. This is not to say, however, that these are the only factors that affect the decision to decentralize political and fiscal resources; however, they play a significant and consistent role across instances of decentralization and one that has been underappreciated in the literature attempting to explain these phenomena.

THEORETICAL AND EMPIRICAL EXTENSIONS

For the purposes of my analysis, I defined decentralization rather narrowly as the coincidence of political and fiscal decentralization, presented graphically in Figure 2.1. Having explained the combination of fiscal and political decentralization as the result of electoral pressures, it seems logical to ask whether this theory can contribute to an understanding of decentralization along either the political or economic dimension alone (the off-diagonal boxes in Fig. 2.1). What leads to political decentralization without fiscal decentralization? Why would political decentralization occur without fiscal decentralization? Finally, how does decentralization change over time as new administrations come to power?

Political Decentralization

Political decentralization in the absence of fiscal decentralization creates political spaces for opposition parties at subnational levels of government, without guaranteeing them access to financial resources. Because most of the power still lies at the center, this policy appears primarily to benefit parties that hold central government power and expect to continue holding it. If the party in power controls central government power and expects to continue in that position, why decentralize at all? The most likely suspects are pressure from below, pressure from the international community concerned with democratization, or electoral pressures to embrace decentralization in order to win national office. Decentralization under these conditions provides nice window dressing but an almost meaningless degree of change in power-sharing relations between levels of government in the short term. Pure political reform may also be used strategically by a party that wishes to determine its subnational support in a highly insulated political system. By allowing subnational elections for officials who hold little real power, the party gains valuable information about its regional or local support. This type of motivation appears most likely for parties with strong but declining national support.

While political decentralization may occur without fiscal decentralization initially, fiscal decentralization is often deepened in the longer run as elected officials at the subnational level use their political positions to stir popular support for more automatic transfers (Eaton 2004).

Fiscal Decentralization

Increasing the fiscal resources of subnational governments without allowing the popular election of subnational government officials also continues to favor the center. Parties that already hold central power and expect to continue holding it are the only ones that benefit from decentralizing fiscal power while continuing to appoint those who wield it.

Why would a party in firm control of a strong centralized government give away fiscal power at all? In contrast to the case of pure political decentralization, it is unlikely that pressure from below and from the international community concerned with democratization constitute the impetus for this reform. Simply moving financial resources away from the central government without extending political choice over who will control those resources does not have the mobilizing quality of a call for political decentralization. Few local groups pressure for pure fiscal decentralization, but international pressure for increased government efficiency may lead to this type of reform. Because it does not increase the ability of opposition parties to come to power at subnational levels, pure fiscal decentralization simply moves fiscal resources closer to constituents, which follows more of an efficiency/fiscal crisis logic than an electoral logic for incumbent parties. Fiscal decentralization appears most likely when a government that is strong at the central level faces severe fiscal crisis or international pressure to improve its efficiency.

The Nature of Fiscal Transfers

If political decentralization is irreversible – or at least extremely difficult to reverse – as I believe that it is, then the fiscal dimension becomes the line along which we might expect to see most of the future variation in decentralizing reform. While the debate about pure fiscal or pure political decentralization teased out some of the factors that contribute to each piece of decentralizing reform independent of the other, the discussion of both of these contributes to an understanding of why the central government might tinker with the formulae for fiscal transfers.

Once political decentralization has been introduced, political parties can much more clearly determine their ability to hold subnational positions. With this advantage, they can predict their future electoral prospects with more accuracy, and it is likely to affect their attitudes toward decentralized fiscal policy when they control the presidency. Consistent with the discussion of fiscal decentralization above and with the theory developed in this project that decentralization corresponds to electoral incentives, the shape of fiscal decentralization should change with the constellation of power of the party or parties in a position to reform the revenue-sharing formulae governing fiscal transfers to subnational governments. More specifically, parties in power face incentives to increase the proportion of discretionary transfers relative to automatic transfers and/or to adjust the formulae used to distribute automatic transfers to reward subnational governments controlled by their allies. This incentive to increase the discretionary nature of transfers should be overwhelmed by the incentive to increase automatic transfers (relative to discretionary transfers) for parties that do not expect to hold on to central power, if they care about the future.

Systematic statistical analysis of fiscal decentralization is hindered by the lack of comparable data across countries and over time on the amounts and the nature of transfers to subnational governments from the center. Even without this data there is some support for the theory from evidence collected both within the countries studied in this project and from countries not included. As discussed in Chapter 6, Fujimori increased discretionary transfers relative to automatic transfers of fiscal resources in Peru. This also seems to have been the case in Argentina in the 1990s under Menem, when the Peronists gained strong control of the central government. Mexico experienced a similar process in the 1980s and 1990s, when the nationally strong PRI (Institutionalized Revolutionary Party) kept tight control over fiscal transfers. It is certainly too early to draw any conclusions about the predictive power of this hypothesis, but it appears to be a promising avenue of future research.

EXTENSIONS TO OTHER CASES

Focusing on the Andean region, I was able to hold relatively constant the initial level of decentralization at the point of democratization. Brazil, Argentina, and Chile were excluded largely because decentralizing reforms adopted in each were closely tied to the return to democracy after authoritarian rule. Because each of these countries had a long history of local (and sometimes regional) elections before the authoritarian period, returning the country to a decentralized structure was part of the return to democracy – not necessarily a choice over which the first democratic governments of the new period could exert control. This does not mean that electoral considerations play no role in these cases. In fact, decentralization at the beginning of the new democratic period went well beyond a mere return to the old decentralized system in many cases. In the next few pages, I briefly survey decentralization in Argentina, Chile, and Mexico.[2]

Examining the deepening of decentralization at the return to democracy in both Argentina and Chile, it is clear that electoral considerations of political parties importantly shape the nature of power sharing between levels of government. In transitions back to democracy after authoritarian rule, however, the restoration of previously decentralized mechanisms appears to overshadow immediate electoral considerations. In these cases, it is important to understand the combination of past legacies of decentralization and long-term electoral concerns to understand the restoration of decentralization and, most importantly, its extension.

The extent and nature of decentralization in both Chile and Argentina corresponds to power struggles between parties with different bases of support. In Chile, the Concertación (Alliance of Democratic Parties) pushed for decentralization to local governments, while the parties of the right pushed for decentralization to the regional level. A two-tiered structure resulted from these opposite pressures as each

---

[2] Other authors have done a much more thorough job discussing these cases. For an excellent treatment of these cases, see Rodríguez 1997; Eaton 2002 and 2004.

political group pushed for its own advantage. The Concertación was strong at all levels of government but pushed for a return to the pre-authoritarian practice of local elections; the right championed the appointment of regional and provincial officials with some fiscal power, confident of its ability to control the Senate, which must approve these appointments. Importantly, as the Concertación enjoyed central power, it kept regional government finance under largely discretionary control, while making transfers to local government much more automatic. In Argentina, the Peronists pushed for decentralization while in the opposition from 1983 to 1989, but Menem began to increase the level of discretion in inter-governmental transfers once he gained the presidency. In negotiations with the UCR (Radical Party) for a constitutional reform in 1994, the Peronists agreed to greater decentralizing language, but Menem used a number of tools to postpone the actualization of those reforms.

Mexico's decentralization of political power while maintaining central government discretion over fiscal resources corresponds to tension between pressure for democratization from below and the PRI's long hold on central power. This began to change as PRI confidence in national victory declined under Zedillo. Zedillo's New Federalism (Nuevo Federalismo) program increased the transparency of fiscal transfers in the period before the PRI's first presidential loss in nearly a century.

Argentina

Argentina's 1853 constitution institutionalized provincial elections (Argentina's twenty-two regions are referred to as provinces), but they have been interrupted several times by authoritarian rulers. When constitutional rule resumed in 1983, these regional governments were reinstated.[3] The 1994 constitutional reforms increased provincial autonomy to an even greater extent. Despite the language of the constitution, however, power sharing between central and provincial governments became decidedly tilted toward greater presidential control of funds in the 1990s. This section explores trends in power sharing

---

[3] Local power is more difficult to determine, since provinces create municipal laws, spawning a great deal of variety across local governments. Due to this variety, I discuss only central-provincial government power sharing here.

between central and provincial governments from 1983 to 1995. It describes how, as the political fortunes of the two major parties changed, so too did their positions vis-à-vis the decentralization of power to the provinces. These changes corresponded loosely to the trends we might expect based on preceding chapters. This discussion can be most profitably divided into three periods: the period of Radical rule from 1983 to 1989 under Alfonsín, the Menem presidency (1989–1995) that followed, and the specific instance of the 1994 constitutional reform.

Opportunities for political decentralization have been limited in Argentina since the state was founded as a federal republic. As a result, this discussion focuses on fiscal decentralization. One political area of power sharing that has notably changed is the president's ability to remove provincial governors. The 1994 constitution requires legislative approval of the president's decision to remove provincial governors. Most other changes in power sharing have occurred on the fiscal side, with several changes in the laws governing the transfer of funds from the central government to the provinces providing a range of variation in need of explanation.

Due to a lapse in the 1973 law (Law 20221) that had established fixed criteria for automatic transfers from the center to the provinces, transfers occurred primarily through the central government's discretion after 1984. This led to severe economic problems as provinces ran up large deficits in the expectation that the central government would cover their expenses – a practice that largely paid off for them, much to the economy's detriment (a classic example of moral hazard). As a result, pressure grew for a reinstatement of more transparent and automatic mechanisms for transferring funds (World Bank 1990). The desire for more automatic transfers to the provinces resonated most strongly with the Peronist party in the early years of the new democratic regime. At that time the Peronists controlled a majority of the provincial governorships but did not control the presidency; as a result, they stood to gain the most from greater decentralization. The UCR, in contrast, controlled the presidency and, from 1983 to 1985, a majority of the lower chamber of the legislature (the upper chamber is elected through the provinces and was thus controlled by the Peronists), but it controlled only two provincial governorships. Not surprisingly, decentralization did not advance greatly during the Alfonsín administration, except where the Peronists could push through reforms.

In 1987, the Peronists supported a law (23548) that would restore greater transparency to the transfer process, but the law was weakly enforced.

Support for greater decentralization became a key Peronist cause during Alfonsín's presidency, from 1983 to 1989. Peronist activism during this period culminated in the 1988 Federal Pact that was signed by Peronist governors and called for greater provincial power relative to the central government. The issue was prominent in the Peronist 1989 electoral platform, and in May of 1990 the party's governors and high-ranking party officials signed the Accord for Federal Reaffirmation (Acuerdo de Reafirmación Federal), re-emphasizing their support for increased decentralization. Once Menem came to power, however, his government's position toward increased decentralization changed. Interestingly, the UCR, which held a couple of provincial governments and no central control after 1989, became more sympathetic to the idea of greater transparency in fiscal transfers. The newly reversed positions of the two major parties can be most clearly seen in their interaction over constitutional reform in 1994.

The Pact of Olives, whereby Menem and Alfonsín designed the framework for the 1994 constitutional reforms, was widely viewed as a negotiated agreement to allow Menem's re-election bid. In exchange for the opportunity of a second term, the UCR extracted several concessions that placed checks on the president's power relative to both the legislature and the provinces (Jones 1997). The constitution made three major changes pertinent to federalism: It called for greater transparency and automaticity in fiscal transfers; it required congressional approval of presidential intervention in provincial governments (a privilege that Menem on his own authority used five times during his first term); and it allowed for the popular election of the mayor of the city of Buenos Aires (a UCR stronghold). Suddenly, the UCR had become the champion of greater decentralization.

The greatest moves toward decentralization during the democratic period that began in 1983 were extracted by the opposition – first the Peronists in 1987 and then the UCR in 1994 – in both cases the party controlling the presidency opposed the reforms. Menem's reluctance to decentralize fiscal power to the provinces was evidenced in his actions: In a 1992 fiscal pact with the provinces, Menem bypassed the 1987 law that his own party had pushed into place to make transfers more automatic, rerouting 15 percent of the revenues slated for provincial governments toward social security. Because of this pact, the transfers to provinces remained nearly constant despite the large increase in tax revenues during Menem's term of office (Eaton 1998: 7). To cement the deal, he negotiated with individual governors, "replac[ing] the distribution criteria legislated in the 1987 revenue sharing law with criteria that reflected little other than political deal making" (ibid.: 8).

In 1993, Menem arranged a second fiscal pact that increased the dependence of provincial finances on the central government; it also increased the discretionary nature of fiscal transfers. In fact, a study by the Ministry of Finance in 1994 found that the portion of funds transferred to provinces from the central government without restrictions on their use declined in 1987, increased between 1987 and 1989 as a result of the 1987 law governing transfers, and then declined after Menem came to power in 1989. It reached its lowest point in the years studied (1983–1993) in 1993 (Secretaría Hacienda 1994: 17). One might have expected the 1994 constitutional reform to reverse this trend. However, despite the fact that the constitution requires a new revenue-sharing law (along the lines of the 1987 law) to have been enacted by the end of 1996, "Menem was successful in getting Congress to delay discussions of a new bill and to extend the current, more discretionary system until the end of 1998" (Eaton 1998: 10–11). Menem was able to exert strong influence over Peronist governors and the party rank-and-file due to strong party discipline and the fact that the *menemista* party leadership controlled nomination to legislative candidate lists in a closed-list PR system (Jones, Sanguinetti, and Tommasi 2000).

In its most recent democratic period, Argentina has returned to the levels of political and fiscal decentralization that existed before authoritarian rule. Changes in the level of political decentralization have been small: new constitutional limits on the president's ability to remove provincial governors and the direct election of the mayor of the city of Buenos Aires. Both occurred in the constitutional reform and were championed by an opposition with slim chances of regaining the executive in the short term; they were granted by Menem, a president hungry for another term of office. This accords well with the two parties' electoral strength: The UCR – out of national power and holding a few provincial governments with a strong chance of winning the mayor's race in the city of Buenos Aires – acted to strengthen its position vis-à-vis the Peronists. To improve their chances of retaining the presidency with Menem as their candidate, the Peronists agreed to several limitations, hoping to capitalize on their strength at the national level. On the fiscal side, both parties sought greater discretion over intergovernmental transfers when they controlled the presidency. Both parties in opposition have fought for greater transparency.

Chile

Like Argentina, Chile has a long history of subnational electoral contests (Valenzuela 1977). These were suspended during the military government spanning 1973–1990, and in June of 1992, mayors and local councilors were democratically elected for the first time in twenty-one years. The relationship between local elections and authoritarian rule is not as simple as these two facts may make it appear. During Pinochet's rule, though political decentralization was shunted, fiscal decentralization achieved a remarkable increase in local government spending. Return to democratic rule after the election of Patricio Aylwin led not only to a reinstatement of local elections, but also to decentralization that increased the power of regional governments. In addition, a third level of government was established between regions and municipalities at the provincial level. During the authoritarian period, fiscal decentralization advanced without political decentralization. Under Aylwin, political and fiscal decentralization advanced together. This wealth of variation in central/subnational power-sharing arrangements provides yet another test of the theories explored in this project. The next few pages tease out the currents leading to each of these changes.

During the Pinochet dictatorship the election of local officials was suspended. Instead, mayors were appointed and worked with local development committees established along corporatist guidelines. On the fiscal side, however, local governments became truly powerful. Through reforms enacted in 1979 and 1980, Pinochet established a formulaic system for transferring funds to local governments.[4] Along

---

[4] The main source of funds for most municipalities comes through the Common Municipal Fund (Fondo Común Municipal), distributed on the following basis: 10 percent equally distributed to all municipalities; 20 percent distributed according to the number of inhabitants; 30 percent accorded on the basis of the number of properties in the municipality that are exempt from the land tax (this is largely redistributive); 40 percent

with funds, he transferred responsibility for primary health care and primary and secondary education to local governments. According to Sergio Boisier (1994):

> None of this had anything to do with decentralization, which was always present in the [government's] discourse and always absent in reality. (18)

He goes on to quote another analyst of the situation:[5]

> The model of decentralization of the Military Government is more an instrument to reaffirm autocratic power than an arena for the participation of the governed. Technically it becomes a process of political and administrative centralization with the deconcentration of decision making, always subject to the previous authorization of the higher hierarchical authority and to their control over its correspondence with their policies, plans or programs approved by the superior levels. (18)

When the dictatorship ended it bequeathed a fiscally decentralized system in which real municipal spending between 1970 and 1992 had multiplied almost threefold (Yañez and Letelier 1995: 141). Under the first democratically elected administration, the popular election of mayors and local councilors was passed, along with a reform that granted decentralized power to regions and provinces. What forces conspired to create this outcome?

It is difficult to explain political decentralization under Aylwin because evidence for two competing theories overlaps and is hard to disentangle during this time period. One might argue that political decentralization represented a piece of the overall return to democracy since local elections had been held prior to the military dictatorship. One might also use the presidential voting results that elected Aylwin to predict that the Concertación would stand to win a great proportion of the locally elected positions under a decentralized system (Echenique and Rolando 1991). While this is true, the Concertación's widespread victory does not suggest that the coalition should have expected a loss at the national level in the near future. It seems that the revival of

---

distributed in direct proportion to the lowest permanent personal income per inhabitant for each municipality as compared with the national average (also redistributive); and 10 percent kept aside by the Ministry of the Interior (who oversees distribution of these funds) as an emergency fund to cover recurrent municipal deficits.

[5] Cumplido 1992.

decentralization owes more to the democratic restoration than to the electoral considerations of the Concertación.

Shortly after Aylwin's inauguration, he sent a bill to the legislature calling for increased decentralization of political power to local governments. His proposal passed in the Chamber of Deputies (controlled by Concertación parties), but the Senate (controlled by parties of the right) refused to consider the measure without some additional decentralization of power to the regional level. In 1991, Law 19097 modified Article 13 of the constitution to create a system in which power was decentralized not just to local governments but to regional and provincial governments, as well. The resulting law granted greater fiscal power to the thirteen regional and fifty-one provincial governments, while retaining appointed executives at both levels. The law granted the 335 *comunas* municipal status with popularly elected mayors and councilors. Did redemocratization or electoral motivations most clearly propel the two parties toward this outcome?

During the debates over these issues, the right pushed for regional and provincial decentralization, while the Concertación promoted local decentralization. The extension of decentralized power to two new levels of government goes beyond the status quo level of decentralization established before the authoritarian period, indicating that this reform marks more than a simple return to the pre-dictatorship system. In fact, not only were new layers of government granted more decentralized power; the Concertación also increased the level of political decentralization enjoyed by local governments in comparison with what it had been before the dictatorship.[6] It is also interesting to note that the push for regional and provincial decentralization arose not from the Concertación, the more pro-democracy party, but from the opposition parties on the right who were most closely associated with the dictatorship.

If decentralization reflects merely the desire to democratize, the right's championship of these measures appears anomalous. Interpreting the outcome through the lens of electoral advantage suggests that

---

[6] Prior to 1973, mayors were indirectly elected by councilors, the heads of the largest municipalities were appointed by the president, and municipalities were not granted legal autonomy until the constitutional reform was adopted in November of 1991 (Nickson 1995: 132–133).

the Concertación had stronger pockets of support at the local level than at intermediate levels of government and that the right expected it could win appointments at these intermediate levels, while it would be less likely to win local elections. In addition, the Concertación's move to decentralize suggests that it did not expect to continue holding a monopoly on power at the center. Do these expectations make sense in light of the results of the presidential elections that brought Aylwin to office? In fact, the support for Aylwin was both deep and widespread at all levels of government, suggesting that the right would not benefit from regional decentralization any more than it would from decentralization to the local level. The Concertación vote outweighed the vote for the right in all of the regional totals and in all of the big and medium cities. In fact, the decentralization plan adopted for the regions did not include the popular election of their executives, so it is not clear that they could have benefited even if they had shown greater strength at these levels. Despite this observation, Sergio Boisier claims:

Politically, the opposition acted with an impeccable logic. On the one hand, they took an emerging national demand (even though key sectors were very restrained[,] they had a strong capacity for exerting pressure), stealing the initiative from the government and forcing them to modify their position. On the other hand . . . the opposition made very simple political and electoral calculations that permitted them to predict the long term difficulties of winning a presidential election and the short term difficulty of confronting the almost certain possibility of losing a large part of their control of the municipalities (a concern that was borne out in reality soon afterward). From there sprung the logic of creating new political spaces (the regions) in which to test their presence in the State apparatus. (Boisier 1994: 18)

Given the strong turnout for the Concertación at all levels, it is also not clear why they would have expected to lose future national-level elections. These two concerns point away from motives based purely on electoral motivations.

It appears that a theory based neither solely on redemocratization nor on pure electoral motivation can adequately explain Chile's decentralizing reforms. A combination of the two plus a sharper look at the right's influence in the Senate, however, may provide more perspective on the situation. While the Concertación had strength at the national level and might have expected to win future elections, pressures to return to the old system of governance prior to Allende's overthrow were strong. In addition, the Concertación's strength in local-level voting made this a relatively costless strategy. Opposition to further decentralization – decentralization that would go beyond resuscitating democratic practices associated with the predictatorial system – may have sprung from the lack of an electoral incentive to decentralize further given their apparent national strength.

Gaining insight into the right's motivation for pushing decentralization to intermediate levels of governments is difficult, given their poor electoral prospects at all levels. However, because these intermediate-level officials were to be appointed by the president – and confirmed by the Senate – what really matters is the right's representation in the upper house of the legislature. Due to new electoral rules put in place on Pinochet's departure (Siavelis and Valenzuela 1996), the right is over-represented in the Senate relative to their share of the vote. In addition, the 1980 constitution established several permanent senate seats (including one that was held by the ex-dictator, Pinochet) to be filled by individuals sympathetic to the right.

The contours of decentralizing reform in Chile appear to follow an electoral logic to some extent, but also appear closely tied to the redemocratization of Chilean politics at the end of authoritarian rule. Though enjoying strong support at the national level, the Concertación government of Patricio Aylwin reintroduced local elections as part of a return to the status quo ante. Concertación strength at the local level reduced the cost of this measure. The Concertación did not, however, seek to extend decentralization to other levels of government that had not enjoyed popular elections before authoritarianism. The right, faced with a small likelihood of attaining the presidency in the near future but enjoying strong support in the Senate, pushed for a more decentralized system of power in which the Senate would exert significant power over the appointment of intermediate-level officials.

Mexico

Despite its formal founding as a federation,[7] power has been centralized in the Mexican presidency since the 1910 revolution. This centralization of power faced decentralizing pressures in the 1980s and 1990s,

---

[7] Mexico has thirty-one states, the federal district, and 2,412 municipalities.

particularly under the presidencies of Miguel de la Madrid (1982–1988), Carlos Salinas de Gortari (1988–1994), and Ernesto Zedillo (1994–2000). On the political side, Mexico enjoyed a long history of regional and local elections. The main advance along this dimension was the recognition of opposition victories in municipal and gubernatorial contests once monopolized by the PRI. On the fiscal side, a variety of programs tinkered with intergovernmental financial relations. Although a high degree of federal discretion persisted in the allocation of funds toward municipal and state governments, Mexico's political system went some way toward decentralization. Given the PRI's historical hegemony within national politics, why did PRI presidents give power away to subnational levels during this period, and why did decentralization take the particular form that it did in Mexico?

To understand why PRI presidents began decentralizing, it is important to understand the evolution of support for the PRI. Decentralization coincided with declining support for the party. As the PRI's support in national contests waned, subnational governments were strengthened. The fact that the PRI retained its federal monopoly for so long helps to explain why the decentralization of fiscal resources remained strongly controlled through the federal government's discretion. In some instances, opposition election victories imposed decentralization that could have been avoided only at great cost to the president. Given the PRI's strong control of the national government, political decentralization in Mexico must be seen as a controlled opening from above caused by pressures from below.

Why did the PRI allow this controlled opening? Perhaps the government used decentralization to "test the waters," allowing for greater political contestation at subnational levels, while keeping fiscal resources sharply constrained. Perhaps the government was strengthening subnational governments in order to increase its legitimacy and thereby strengthen its hold on national power (Molinar Horcasitas 1995; Rodríguez 1997). Alternatively, the government may have been laying the groundwork so that, in the event of a presidential loss, the PRI could take advantage of its regional and local-level strength to win subnational positions. All of these explanations point to the same phenomenon: the attempt by a once hegemonic party to hold onto power (either at the central level or at subnational levels) through decentralizing reforms.

Mexico took its first steps toward decentralization in 1980, during the Lopez Portillo presidency. Lopez Portillo gained the presidency in 1976 through an election without opposition; the PAN (National Action Party) refused to field a candidate as a protest against electoral fraud. In the face of this challenge to the system's legitimacy, the PRI began to reform the political system. The first decentralizing measures advanced along the fiscal dimension, creating clearer guidelines to govern the transfers of funds between the central government and state and municipal governments. Under this system, instituted in 1980, a share of central government tax revenues would be distributed to the states through the Fund for General Disbursement (Fondo General de Participaciones, FGP) using a specific formula that took into consideration population, each state's contribution to federal tax receipts, and some redistributive criteria.[8] Twenty percent of state receipts from the FGP were to be transferred from the states to municipalities, but the basis for the transfers was left to the states' discretion. Finally, the central government established the Municipal Development Fund (Fondo de Fomento Municipal, FFM) which transferred 1 percent of federal tax revenue to municipal governments, distributed on the basis of where municipal property taxes and water charges had risen fastest (to encourage greater local resource collection). The bulk of funding to municipalities continued to come from the central government through more discretionary investment funds targeted to specific projects.

Political decentralization increased under the de la Madrid administration. De la Madrid came to power in 1982 with only 74 percent of the vote. While this outcome still represented a huge margin of victory over the opposition PAN candidate (who won 16 percent of the vote), it was the lowest percentage of the vote won by the PRI in its history. Shortly after taking office, de la Madrid passed an amendment to Article 115 of the constitution that spelled out municipal responsibilities for basic urban services and changed the procedures for selecting local leaders. This took effect in 1984.

In 1983, the government recognized the first significant number of opposition victories in municipal contests. These victories were not confined to small municipalities in the countryside but extended to

---

[8] Of the FGP, 45.17 percent was to be distributed by population, 45.17 percent in proportion to each state's contribution to federal tax receipts, and 9.66 percent in inverse proportion to the receipts per person within each state.

large and important cities, including five state capitals. This recognition of opposition victories represented a significant increase in municipal autonomy from the PRI-controlled central government. This power should not be overstated, however. According to the Mexican constitution, the Senate can declare the powers of state governments null and void and can also remove governors, municipal presidents, and legislators at subnational levels of government. Several presidents have used their partisan power to persuade PRI senators to employ these powers. During de la Madrid's presidency, the governors of both Guanajuato (Enrique Velasco Ibarra) and Chihuahua (Oscar Ornelas) were

removed from office for reasons that were clearly political. . . . Ornelas was removed because he had "allowed" too many PAN victories in his state; Velasco Ibarra was removed because he supported the wrong candidate to succeed him as governor and openly opposed the party. (Rodríguez 1997: 25)

By the end of the de la Madrid presidency, some political and fiscal decentralization had occurred, but the great majority of power remained in the president's hands.

In 1988, Carlos Salinas de Gartori won the presidency with an unprecedentedly low 51 percent of the vote. A splinter of the PRI led by Cuauhtémoc Cárdenas won 31 percent of the vote (although some argue that he actually won the presidency and that the official totals reflected vote rigging and electoral fraud), while the PAN won 17 percent of the vote. Despite this drop in support for the PRI, the margin of victory remained substantial. Nonetheless, the waning support for the PRI was a real cause for concern. By the mid-term elections in 1991, however, the PRI had dramatically reclaimed its strength, climbing from 50 percent of the vote in 1988 congressional voting to 61 percent, not far from its 65 percent in 1985 midterm elections and far ahead of its competitors.

During the Salinas government, opposition victories were recognized for the first time in gubernatorial contests. In addition, municipalities enjoyed a sharp increase in fiscal resources through the president's Solidarity program (PRONASOL). By the end of this term, however, the central government continued to control most of the political and fiscal resources available to subnational governments.

In the wake of the PRI's presidential victory, the government acknowledged the first opposition victory in the gubernatorial contest in

Baja California, won by the PAN in 1989. Other opposition victories followed. Of course, the president continued to enjoy the constitutional privilege of replacing elected governors if he could get the Senate to play along; sixteen governors were removed during the Salinas presidency (but none of them from the PAN). On the fiscal side, municipalities enjoyed a flood of funding from the central government, but the funds were distributed purely at the central government's discretion through the PRONASOL program. This program bypassed the transfer system already in place, instead targeting money directly to municipal committees that had drawn up development plans in the prime years of the government's fiscal austerity program. When it was founded in 1989, the program distributed U.S. $500 million; in 1993 it had grown to U.S. $2.2 billion (Rodríguez 1997: 81). By 1992 this highly discretionary program had become the largest source of funding for most municipalities. Several authors have suggested that PRONASOL's (National Solidarity Fund) primary motivations were electoral:

> The main effect of the program is to reconstruct the image and powers of the presidency, which had been so badly tarnished in the succession of 1987 and the general elections of 1988. Assuming power under allegations of fraud, and confronting thirty-one governors – many of doubtful loyalty and even competence – President Salinas needed an immediate and potent response. (Bailey 1994: 117–1178)

> PRONASOL's expansiveness, particularly during electoral contests, dovetails nicely with "political survival" arguments that explain policy options as choices that rational policymakers undertake to maximize their goals. (Dresser 1994: 151)

In fact, the PRI appeared to target specific communities where support for the opposition had grown (Centeno 1994). It seems as if the PRI hoped to buy back support for its candidates through PRONASOL patronage: "[R]eversing the 1988 electoral victories of the PRD appeared to be a significant part of PRONASOL's political agenda" (Dresser 1994: 155).

Despite these measures, opposition victories continued. By 1994, some 238 of Mexico's 2,392 municipalities were governed by the opposition. In 1996, the PRI had clear control of 1,551 of Mexico's 2,412 municipalities, with the PAN controlling 225, the PRD controlling 181, and 455 municipalities in the hands of "others"[9] (Rodríguez 1997: 55).

Ernesto Zedillo came to power in 1994 with 50 percent of the vote, close to the low total won by Salinas in 1988. Again, the PRI held a wide margin of victory over its opponents – the PRD with 17 percent of the vote and the PAN with 27 percent. Zedillo inherited a system in which the opposition parties won an increasing share of subnational power and in which subnational governments increasingly enjoyed access to fiscal resources, though most were subject to the central government's discretion. Near the beginning of his term, the Mexican economy collapsed during the 1994 peso crisis, the Zapatista movement gained strength in the southernmost areas of the country, and the PRI was rocked by scandal as several high-ranking PRI officials (including members of the ex-president Salinas's family) were linked to various crimes. If the administration entered office with a sense of dwindling power, its first years served only to weaken its grip on that power.

In the face of dwindling PRI support, Zedillo instituted changes in the relationship between the central and subnational governments. Before he left office, Salinas incorporated the PRONASOL program into the new ministry of social development (SEDESOL). Zedillo moved to create a much more transparent system of transfers, in which the state governments exercised greater control over the distribution of funds to municipalities. PRONASOL funds were divided among three separate funds in 1996. The largest of these, the Municipal Social Development Fund (FDSM), was distributed to the states based on poverty measures applied to both the state and its municipalities. According to Rodríguez (1997):

Thus, the mechanisms for the distribution of resources from the federal government to the states appear to be more transparent and equitable, given that they favor the poorer states; however, the precise mechanisms of decision making for the allocation of these resources from the states to the municipalities remain unclear, which may sustain the patterns of state and federal discretionary power that have existed in the past and that have caused inequitable development both among states and among municipalities of a given state. (105–106)

---

[9] Some 413 of these 455 others were leaders chosen within Oaxaca according to the traditions of indigenous communities there.

The criteria for distribution would also give the greatest share of the resources to Oaxaca, Chiapas, Veracruz, and Puebla, states in which support for the PRI was quite high at the time. By cutting the degree of discretion involved in distributing funds to states and municipalities, this reform could constrain future administrations to continue providing transparent sources of funding to states, and particularly to states with traditionally strong PRI support. This last measure goes the farthest toward actually putting into place a system of inter-governmental transfers that would benefit the PRI after its presidential loss in 2000.

The PRI did not act alone in strengthening municipalities and regional governments. During the 1998 federal budget negotiations in the National Congress, the PAN pushed stridently for greater fiscal revenues for municipalities. In fact, after several weeks of stalemated discussions without budget approval, the PAN made its support for the PRI budget contingent on greater funding for municipalities. The formula outlined for the distribution of these new resources also strongly depended on the size of a municipality's population, a criterion that dovetailed with the PAN's dominance of several large municipalities (Peredo 2000).

It is not surprising, in light of the theories developed in this chapter, that a formerly hegemonic national party would increase the transparency of intergovernmental fiscal transfers in the period preceding a national election in which it perceived it might have the lowest chance of victory in its history. The PAN's support for these programs and its role in crafting the criteria used for resource distribution that match the attributes of the areas where it has demonstrated electoral strength, are also not surprising.

In Mexico, decentralization deepened as the PRI lost national-level support. Although support declined throughout this period, the PRI remained fairly secure at the national level until the turn of the century. As its confidence of continuing to win the presidency weakened, the PRI increased the transparency of fiscal transfers to subnational governments to capitalize on the party's strength at the state and local levels. It appears that Zedillo began to institute such changes in his New Federalism (Nuevo Federalismo) program as the party's approval ratings reached their all-time lows.

COMPARISONS

This project has demonstrated that electoral considerations shape the support of political parties for the combination of political and fiscal decentralization in democratic, centralized countries. This last discussion of Argentina, Chile, and Mexico shows how regime transition complicates a straightforward application of this approach where political systems have once been politically decentralized and experienced an authoritarian interlude. Even parties that should not support decentralization based on the strength of their national electoral support face strong pressures to return to the previously decentralized system as part of a democratic restoration. Chile provides the greatest illustration of this. It is difficult to see why the nationally strong Concertación government of Patricio Aylwin would have sought greater decentralization from an electoral standpoint without considering Chile's long history of local government. This finding gives strong support to the idea that, once political decentralization has occurred, it tends to persist, even after a long period of military rule.

Adoption of new decentralizing measures continues to follow an electoral logic, however, as all three cases demonstrate. Support for decentralization within both the UCR and the Peronist parties corresponds to their rising and falling expectations of winning or maintaining national control. The parties of the Chilean right pushed for greater political decentralization to regional and provincial levels, correctly judging that they would not be able to gain the presidency in the near future. The PRI's waning national-level support appears to have led to its willingness to empower governors and mayors of all parties.

In this concluding chapter, I also began to theorize about pure political and pure fiscal decentralization. I argued that both seemed most likely to occur under parties in central government with strong expectations that they would continue to control national power. Decentralization along each of these dimensions alone occurs for different reasons, however: Political without fiscal decentralization seems most likely to occur as a response to either popular or external pressures from below, while fiscal without political decentralization appears to result from economic pressures from either within or without. Mexico in the 1980s and early 1990s provides the best example of pure political decentralization, as it recognized opposition victories in subnational elections but kept fiscal power extremely centralized. Within the Andean cases, decentralization in Venezuela, as well as Peru's two attempts to empower regional governments (under García and Toledo), have also contained elements of this. On the other hand, Pinochet's fiscal decentralization in Chile during the 1970s and 1980s, even as he discontinued local elections, appears to be part of a greater economic project to streamline expenditures in the face of fiscal deficits.

Some of the most intriguing insights drawn from this examination of Argentina, Chile, and Mexico bear on the hypothesis that the nature of fiscal transfers will be shaped by the electoral fortunes of political parties. Exploring the extent and nature of fiscal decentralization in Argentina, Chile, and Mexico generates clear evidence that political parties with strong national-level support push for more discretionary means of allocating intergovernmental transfers, while parties in opposition favor more automatic transfers, particularly if they hold significant subnational posts. Peronists in power in Argentina sought out mechanisms to avoid the formulaic nature of intergovernmental transfers that they themselves pushed into law while in the opposition before Menem's rise to the presidency. In Mexico, highly discretionary transfer mechanisms – most notably, PRONASOL – popular during the 1980s were replaced with more formulaic, block grants under Zedillo as the PRI's national support waned.

These extensions of both the theory and the case discussions demonstrate the strength of electoral considerations among the many items that influence politicians' decisions. In countries that have experienced long periods of centralized, democratic rule (Colombia and Venezuela) or in those that have transitioned from military rule without a prior tradition of decentralized government (Bolivia, Ecuador, and Peru), electoral considerations appear to be the greatest determinants of political and fiscal decentralization.[10] In countries returning

---

[10] Mexico does not fit easily into these categories. One may consider it a country that has experienced a long history of centralized democracy, but its one-party system often lands it in the authoritarian category. In addition, it has a very decentralized framework politically, allowing for the possibility of opposition victories even though they did not occur (or were not recognized) until the last couple of decades. It may also be considered a case that has transitioned or is transitioning from authoritarian (but not

to decentralized rule after an authoritarian interlude (Argentina and Chile), democratic restoration tends to trump electoral considerations where the two do not coincide. However, even in these cases of democratic revival, extensions of decentralization along both the political and fiscal dimensions appear to be strongly tied to electoral considerations.

Of course, decentralization in its many forms has become a worldwide phenomenon and is not confined to the countries of Latin America. While this project has focused intently on the experiences of Latin American countries, many of the same electoral considerations have played a role in recent decentralizing episodes in other parts of the world. For example, in South Africa's recent constitutional reforms, the largely white National Party (NP), once a strong partisan of centralized government, drastically altered its position, responding to electoral considerations:

[T]he NP discovered . . . that its traditional attitude to regional government made little sense if it was going to lose control of the centre. Since demographics offered the NP a strong prospect of controlling at least one region, the Western Cape, it became a keen advocate of federalism.[11]

The NP, in fact, did win a strong majority in the Western Cape. Electoral concerns have also led to the recentralization of power outside Latin America, with the Russian Republic providing an excellent example. In Putin's first days as president of Russia, he took strong moves to roll back the powers of regional governors. Putin won the presidency with strong support for his candidacy but without a strong party behind him; regional governors were seen as a threat to this power (Solnick 1999). Using decree powers, Putin "corralled the governors' 89 provinces into 7 new administrative districts, each overseen by a regional official who is answerable directly to Mr. Putin, and no one else" (Wines 2000), strengthening the center relative to the regions.

---

military) rule without a previous period of decentralized government. Though hard to categorize neatly here, decentralization in Mexico also appears heavily influenced by the electoral considerations of the PRI.

[11] This quotation is taken from R. Humphries, T. Rapoo, and S. Friedman, "The Shape of the Country: Negotiating Regional Government," in S. Friedman and D. Atkinson, eds., *The Small Miracle: South Africa's Negotiated Settlement* (Johannesburg: Centre for Policy Studies, Raven Press, 1994), quoted in Robinson 1995.

CONCLUSION

What does this analysis contribute to the larger questions raised at the beginning of this project about the quality of democracy and government efficiency? If one believes that decentralization improves democratic quality by deepening democracy and bringing democratic practice to local citizens, then understanding the forces conducive to bringing about decentralization is crucial to pushing decentralization forward. Likewise, for those who support the decentralization of government functions to subnational levels to improve efficiency in public goods provision, understanding the political forces that act on policy makers in the process of designing decentralization reforms provides insight into when and whether fiscal decentralization will occur.

For those who would promote greater decentralization in general, this project outlines the forces that must be examined in considering when decentralization is likely to occur. For those concerned with the particular shape that decentralization will take in different administrations, this project suggests the conditions under which decentralization will include both political and fiscal decentralization – effective decentralization – and when reforms of this type may create only partial decentralization along either the political or the fiscal dimension.

In a more general sense, this project points out the importance of examining the electoral motives of politicians at every stage in the crafting of decentralizing reforms. Politicians respond rationally to their incentives; when they perceive electoral advantages under decentralized systems, they are likely to push for decentralization. When their power is concentrated at the national level, they will attempt to recentralize power – to the extent possible – through attempting to change the formulae governing the mechanisms that distribute fiscal transfers to increase their control over resource disbursement. Understanding these incentives is crucial to those involved in these debates over quality and efficiency if they are to affect the outcomes of these political processes. In concrete terms, the analysis points out the importance of giving political parties a stake in the future, as demonstrated by the importance of parties' time horizons as they make decentralizing decisions. The analysis also suggests that parties with a more institutionalized base of support at subnational levels – particularly if they must compete closely for power at the national level – will be the most likely to implement real and lasting reform. Given that stable party support plays such an important role in encouraging parties to decentralize for long-term benefits, the de-institutionalization of several parties and party systems within the region – particularly in Venezuela and Peru – appears particularly troubling.

Today, the debates over decentralization's contribution to democratic quality and government efficiency remain inconclusive. Much recent research has questioned whether decentralized governments are in fact more efficient than centralized governments. One study (Stein 1999) analyzed the relationship between decentralization and government size (measured as expenditure as a percentage of GDP) and found a strong positive relationship between the two, suggesting that decentralized governments actually spend more than centralized ones. This study notes that this positive relationship is particularly strong in Latin American countries compared with OECD countries. In addition, there is a strong positive relationship between government expenditure and the degree of discretion in intergovernmental transfers, suggesting that soft budget constraints on subnational governments do make macroeconomic stability difficult. Thus it remains an open question whether it is decentralization per se that is in tension with government expenditure or whether it is, rather, its implementation that may harm overall government efficiency. A political perspective on the shortcomings of decentralization as it has been implemented in the region can shed quite a bit of light on the disjuncture between the theoretical promise that decentralization will improve the functioning of government and the reality that it has hindered government improvement in practice. If one understands decentralization as an attempt to improve democratic quality or economic efficiency, and it fails to do so, then the clearest explanation may seem to be incompetent implementation; if one understands how political concerns affect the crafting of these designs, however, then it is much easier to explain these failures without having to resort to charges of irrationality or incompetence.

In addition, researchers are questioning the relationship between decentralization and corruption (Tanzi 1994; Treisman 1999a and b; but see also Fisman and Gatti 2000). Proponents of decentralization often laud the potential for decentralization to reduce corruption by relieving the central government of many opportunities for rent seeking in local public goods provision. Recent work suggests that decentralization may merely move the level of corruption to lower levels, dispersing the graft rather than eliminating it. In addition, where intergovernmental transfers remain discretionary, central governments retain plentiful opportunities for corruption.

Despite these notes of caution, decentralization remains remarkably popular throughout the Andean region. Peruvians, denied the degree of decentralization they once enjoyed, have consistently fought to regain it (Delgado Silva 1995). The Popular Participation Law enacted by Sánchez de Lozada in Bolivia remains his most popular reform, although his administration enacted several major reform projects. In Colombia, despite the fact that guerrilla groups have targeted voters and candidates in each local election, support for decentralization remains high.[12] This support for decentralization can be seen in the high rates of participation in local elections. In countries that have experienced meaningful decentralization reform, abstention rates in local elections have declined relative to abstention rates prior to reform. Bolivia's 1993 local elections – held before the decentralization reforms of 1994 – saw participation rates of only 53 percent; the first election after reform saw a surge to 64 percent (Corte Nacional Electoral de Bolivia 1997). In Venezuela 43 percent participation rates in the 1989 local elections expanded to 55 percent in 1992, the first year in which mayors were popularly elected (Alvarez 1998). In Colombia, participation in local elections outstrips participation in national elections. In 1994, only 33 percent of eligible voters turned out to vote for the national assembly, while just under 48 percent voted to elect mayors in the same year (Hoskin 1998); in 1997, approximately 45 percent voted to elect mayors and 41 percent voted to elect governors (Querubin et al. 1998: 125). Despite heightened levels of violence – twenty-one candidates for local positions were killed during the campaign and another 100 or so withdrew under intimidation – regional and local elections in 2000 drew about half of the eligible voters in Colombia.[13] In Peru and Ecuador – the two most centralized countries at the end of the period studied – abstention rates for local elections are either higher

---

[12] A headline on cnn.com on October 30, 2000, just days after elections were held for regional and local posts, read: "Peaceful Colombia Vote Rejects Government, Armed Groups."

[13] Also from cnn.com article; see note 12.

(Peru[14]) than abstention rates in national contests or they are about equal (Ecuador[15]), and they are rising in both cases. Evidence from countries outside Latin America mirrors this trend: Decentralizing reforms in Bangladesh, Cote d'Ivoire, Ghana, and the state of Karnataka in India have all boosted participation significantly (Crook and Manor 1998).

Although there still remains much room for improving decentralization in each country that has adopted it, its popularity and staying power appear solidly entrenched throughout the region. Understanding the political bases on which decentralization's adoption and ultimate shape rests may help us to peer into the future of decentralization in the region, to determine where it might erupt next and also to predict where it may be in trouble.

---

[14] In the Peruvian case, Dietz (1998) notes that "abstention reached about 16 percent in the 1978 Constituent Assembly elections, and 19 percent in the 1980 presidential race, but it rose to 30 percent in the local elections of the same year. Throughout the decade of the 1980s abstention in presidential races generally ran between 10 and 20 percent, but it averaged well over 20 percent on the municipal level" (201–202).

[15] In Ecuador, abstention was 21 percent, 26 percent, and 22 percent in mayoral races held in 1978, 1984, and 1988, respectively. The relevant comparisons at the national level – in first-round presidential races – were 27 percent, 29 percent, and 22 percent in the same three years (Vjekoslav 1989).

8

Afterword

This book has focused on the Andean countries' experiences in the 1980s and 1990s; its statistical analysis ends with the administrations that governed through 2000. Not only was this a methodological choice – as the administrations elected in and around 2000 have not governed long enough for much to be written about this most recent period – but it has turned out to be a theoretically important bookend to the project, as well. As Latin America faced the new millennium, a sea change in political representation was under way. Where traditional parties were a major force in elections throughout the region during the period studied, they have ceased to be so in the last few years. Hints of this transformation can be seen even in the 1980s and 1990s, as Venezuela's two traditional parties lost favor in national elections and Chávez came to power trouncing all rivals in 1998 and as Fujimori and then Toledo triumphed over traditional parties in Peru.

This trend extends throughout the region. Lucío Gutiérrez won the presidency in Ecuador in 2002 after gaining national prominence as one of the leaders of the coup that ousted President Mahuad in 2000. Though Mahuad was expelled, power was restored to his elected vice president (Noboa), and Gutiérrez spent time in jail for his part in the coup. Still, his popularity vaulted him to the top of the polls when Noboa's replacement was contested in the next election. Less dramatically, Colombia elected Álvaro Uribe in 2002. Although he is nominally a Liberal, he did not have the party's endorsement in the presidential elections (Horacio Serpa was the official candidate); his election marks the first time a non-official Liberal or Conservative candidate has won the presidency since the beginning of the Liberal Front period, in the 1950s. Bolivia re-elected Gonzalo Sánchez de Lozada, the antagonist of much of Bolivia's decentralizing narrative; however, Goni was forced to step down from office and flee the country in 2003 in the midst of major uprisings over the management of the country's natural resources. He was replaced by his vice president, Carlos Mesa, who was a political novice when selected as Goni's running mate and who actively distanced himself from Sánchez de Lozada's unpopular policies. In short, not one of the Andean countries is presently governed by a president from a traditional political party.

In addition to the decline of traditional parties, instability in the Andean political systems has increased markedly, even among the non-traditional political leaders recently elected. Since 2000, Bolivia, Ecuador, and Peru have seen presidents ousted by popular protest, and though Venezuela's Chávez has survived, he has weathered both a coup attempt and a persistent campaign to force him to face a recall vote (which he won somewhat decisively). Current presidents in the region mostly face low approval ratings, including Toledo's approval rating of only 6 percent.[1] Only Colombia has endured this period unscathed, with Álvaro Uribe's approval rating the highest in Latin America (at 77 percent); there is also a movement afoot to allow him to stand for re-election in 2006.

Given the importance of political parties in the decentralization story of the 1980s and 1990s, recent political trends bode ill for decentralization's health in the region. Although I have argued that decentralization is hard to reverse, it is not difficult to weaken some of decentralization's key components, particularly through fiscal measures. As the region's governments come to be increasingly led by politicians who do not have strong linkages to decision makers at the subnational levels (forged through party alliances), many of the incentives for safeguarding decentralization will erode. It is always possible that some new mechanism may arise that will act – as I have suggested party alliances have

---

[1] According to *Latinnews Daily*, June 16, 2004.

acted – to align the preferences of those at the center and subnational levels in favor of decentralized policies. It is too early, however, to speculate as to what those mechanisms might look like. It is also too early to assess systematically how recent trends in political representation have affected decentralization in this unfolding era of political uncertainty in the Andean region.

Sources Cited

Albó, Xavier. 1999. *Ojotas en el Poder Local: Cuatro Años Después*. La Paz, Bolivia: CIPCA y Pader.

Alesina, Alberto, and Enrico Spolaore. 1997. "On the Number and Size of Nations." *Quarterly Journal of Economics* 112, no. 4: 1027–1056.

Alesina, Alberto, Roberto Perotti, and Enrico Spolaore. 1995. "Together or Separately? Issues on the Costs and Benefits of Political and Fiscal Unions." *European Economic Review* 39, no. 3–4.

Alesina, A., A. Carasquilla, and J. J. Echavarría. 2002. "Decentralization in Colombia." In *Reformas institucionales en Colombia: Una agenda reformista para los desafíos del nuevo siglo*, ed. Alberto Alesina. Bogotá: Fedesarrollo: Alfaomega.

Alvarez, Angel. 1998. "Venezuelan Local and National Elections, 1958–1995." In *Urban Elections in Democratic Latin America*, ed. Henry A. Dietz and Gil Shidlo, 243–278. Wilmington, Del.: Scholarly Resources.

Ames, Barry. 1987. *Political Survival: Politicians and Public Policy in Latin America*. Berkeley: University of California Press.

Andersson, Vibeke. 1999. "Popular Participation in Bolivia: Does the Law 'Participación Popular' Secure Participation of the Rural Bolivian Population?" Copenhagen, Denmark: Center for Development Research working paper 99.6.

Andolina, Robert. 1998. "CONAIE (and Others) in the Ambiguous Spaces of Democracy: Positioning for the 1997–98 Asamblea Nacional Constituyente in Ecuador." Paper presented at the Latin American Studies Association meeting, Chicago, September 24–28.

Angell, Alan, Pamela Lowden, and Rosemary Thorp. 2001. *Decentralizing Development: The Political Economy of Institutional Change in Colombia and Chile*. Oxford: Oxford University Press.

Angulo Perdomo, Oswaldo. 1997. *La Descentralización del Poder*. Ed. La Universidad de Carabobo. Valencia, Estado Carabobo: Donal Guerra Editor, S.A.

Archer, Ronald P. 1987. "Comportamiento Electoral y Posibles Consecuencias de la Elección Popular de Alcaldes." In *Colombia en las Urnas: Qué Pasó en 1986?*, ed. Carlos Valencia Editores. Bogotá, Colombia: Carlos Valencia Editores.

Archondo, Rafael. 1997. *Trés Años de Participación Popular: Memoria de un Proceso*. La Paz, Bolivia: Secretaría Nacional de Participación Popular.

Ardaya, Rubén. 1991. *Ensayo Sobre Municipalidad y Municipio*. La Paz, Bolivia: Instituto de Investigaciones y Desarrollo Municipal.

Ardila Duarte, Benjamin, and Alberto Camilo Suárez de la Cruz, eds. 1985. *Alfonso López Michelsen: Obras Selectas*. Ed. Cámara de Representantes, *Colección Pensadores Políticos Colombianos*. Bogotá, Colombia: Cámara de Representantes.

Bahl, Roy, and Johannes Linn. 1994. "Fiscal Decentralization and Intergovernmental Transfers in Less Developed Countries." *Publius* 24, no. 1.

Bailey, John. 1994. "Centralism and Political Change in Mexico: The Case of National Solidarity." In *Transforming State-Society Relations in Mexico*, ed. Wayne Cornelius, Ann L. Craig, and Jonathon Fox, 97–122. La Jolla: Center for U.S.–Mexican Studies, University of California, San Diego.

Bardhan, Pranab. 2002. "Decentralization of Governance and Development." *Journal of Economic Perspectives* 16, no. 4: 185–205.

Barkan, Joel D., ed. 1998. *Five Monographs on Decentralization and Democratization in Sub-Saharan Africa*. Iowa City: International Programs, University of Iowa.

Barr, Robert. 2001. "Parties, Legitimacy and the Motivations for Reform: Devolution and Concentration in Latin America." Paper prepared for the American Political Science Association meeting, San Francisco, August.

Base de Datos Políticos de las Américas. 1999a. "Colombia: Elección Presidencial de 1990." Georgetown University y Organización de Estados Americanos. Http://www.georgetown.edu/pdba/Elecdata/Col/pres90.html, accessed May 20, 2000.

———. 1999b. "Colombia: Elecciones Presidenciales 1994, Primera Vuelta, Resultados Regionales/Capitales Departamentales." Georgetown University y Organización de Estados Americanos. Http://www.georgetown.edu/pdba/Elecdata/Col/pres94_1a.html, accessed May 20, 2000.

———. 1999c. "Colombia: Elecciones Presidenciales 1994, Segunda Vuelta, Resultados Nacionales." Georgetown University y Organización de Estados Americanos. Http://www.georgetown.edu/pdba/Elecdata/Col/pres94_2.html, accessed May 20, 2000.

———. 1999d. "Colombia: Elecciones Presidenciales de 1998 (Primera Vuelta)." Georgetown University y Organización de Estados Americanos. Http://www.georgetown.edu/pdba/Elecdata/Col/pres98_1.html, accessed May 20, 2000.

_____. 1999e. "Colombia: Elecciones Presidenciales, Segunda Vuelta 1998." Georgetown University y Organización de Estados Americanos. Http://www.georgetown.edu/pdba/Elecdata/Col/pres98_2.html, accessed May 20, 2000.

Bates, Robert H. 1997. *Open Economy Politics: The Political Economy of the World Coffee Trade.* Princeton: Princeton University Press.

Bejarano, Ana María, and Andrés Dávila, eds. 1998. *Elecciones y Democracia en Colombia 1997–1998.* Bogotá, Colombia: Universidad de los Andes, Departamento de Ciencia Política.

Bell Lemus, Gustavo. 1998. "The Decentralised State: An Administrative or Political Challenge?" In *Colombia: The Politics of Reforming the State,* ed. Eduardo Posada-Carbó. New York: St. Martin's.

Bergquist, Charles. 2001. "Waging War and Negotiating Peace: The Contemporary Crisis in Historical Perspective." In *Violence in Colombia 1990–2000: Waging War and Negotiating Peace,* ed. Charles Bergquist, Ricardo Peñaranda, and Gonzalo Sanchez G. Wilmington, Del.: Scholarly Resources.

Besley, Timothy, and Stephen Coate. 2000. "Issue Unbundling via Citizens' Initiatives." National Bureau of Economic Research working paper W8036, December.

Betancur, Belisario. 1981. *Cambio, Cambio, Cambio: Planes y Propuestas del Movimiento Nacional.* Bogotá, Colombia: Ediciones Tercer Mundo.

Betancur, Belisario. 1982. "Sí Se Puede." In *Descentralización y Centralismo en Colombia,* ed. Alvaro Tirado Mejía, 105–119. Bogotá, Colombia: Editorial Oveja Negra.

Bird, Richard M. 1990. "Fiscal Decentralization in Colombia." In *Decentralization, Local Governments, and Markets,* ed. Robert J. Bennett. Oxford: Clarendon.

Bland, Gary. 1998. "Building Political Will: The Decision to Decentralize in Chile and Venezuela." Paper presented at the Latin American Studies Association conference, Chicago, September 23–26.

Blank, David. 1980. "The Regional Dimension of Venezuelan Politics." In *Venezuela at the Polls,* ed. Howard R. Penniman, 191–217. Washington, D.C.: American Enterprise Institute for Public Policy Research.

Blutman, Gustavo, ed. 1996. *Investigaciones Sobre Municipio y Sociedad.* Buenos Aires: Universidad de Buenos Aires, Oficina de Publicaciones.

Böhrt Irahola, Carlos. 2001. *La Descentralización del Estado Boliviano: Evaluación y Perspectivas.* La Paz, Bolivia: Fondo Editorial de los Diputados.

Boisier, Sergio. 1994. "Modernización y Gestion Regional: El Caso Chileno." Paper presented at the conference on "Regionalización y Cambio Económico: Una Visión Comparativa en Latinoamérica," Barquisimeto, Venezuela, November 18.

Boylan, Delia M. 2001. *Defusing Democracy: Central Bank Autonomy and the Transition from Authoritarian Rule.* Ann Arbor: University of Michigan Press.

Brewer-Carias, Allan R. 1984. *El Regimen Municipal en Venezuela.* Caracas, Venezuela: Editorial Jurídica Venezolana.

Buenahora Febres-Cordero, Jaime. 1991. *El Proceso Constituyente: De la Propuesta Estudiantil a la Quiebra del Bipartidismo*. Bogotá, Colombia: Pontificia Universidad Javeriana.

Buller, Eduardo. 1993. "Regionalización y Municipalización en el Proceso de Descentralización Administrativa: El Caso de Peru." In *Descentralización y Gobiernos Municipales*, ed. CORDES. Quito, Ecuador: CORDES: Corporación de Estudios para el Desarrollo.

Bunce, Valerie. 1999. *Subversive Institutions: The Design and Destruction of Socialism and the State*. Cambridge, U.K.: Cambridge University Press.

Bushnell, David. 1993. *The Making of Modern Colombia: A Nation in Spite of Itself*. Berkeley: University of California Press.

Cameron, John. 2000. "Municipal Decentralization and Peasant Organization in Ecuador: A Political Opportunity for Democracy and Development." Paper presented at the Latin American Studies Association conference, Miami, March.

Cameron, Maxwell A. 1997. "Political and Economic Origins of Regime Change in Peru: The Eighteenth Brumaire of Alberto Fujimori." In *Peruvian Labyrinth*, ed. Maxwell A. Cameron and Philip Mauceri, 37–69. University Park: Pennsylvania State University Press.

Camp, Roderic Ai. 1996. *Politics in Mexico*. New York: Oxford University Press.

Campbell, Timothy. 2003. *The Quiet Revolution: Decentralization and the Rise of Political Participation in Latin American Cities*. Pittsburgh: University of Pittsburgh Press.

Carrera Damas, Germán. 1988. *La Necesaria Reforma Democrática del Estado*. Caracas, Venezuela: Cavelibro.

Castro, Jaime. 1991. "La Elección Popular de Gobernadores." *Gaceta Constitucional*, June 15, pp. 6–7.

———. 1998. *Descentralizar para Pacificar*. Bogotá, Colombia: Editorial Ariel.

Centeno, Miguel Ángel. 1994. *Democracy within Reason: Technocratic Revolution in Mexico*, 2nd ed. University Park: Pennsylvania State University Press.

Cepeda, Manuel José. 1998. "Democracy, State and Society in the 1991 Constitution: The Role of the Constitutional Court." In *Colombia: The Politics of Reforming the State*, ed. Eduardo Posada-Carbó. New York: St. Martin's.

Cepeda Ulloa, Fernando. 1996. "La Crisis y la Reforma Política." *Revista Foro*, September, 67–75.

Cepeda Ulloa, Fernando. 1997. Interview, July.

Chang, Mota. 1985. *El Sistema Electoral Venezolano, Su Diseño, Implantación y Resultados*. Caracas, Venezuela: Consejo Supremo Electoral.

Colitt, Raymond. 1995. "Ecuador Reform Package Rejected." *Financial Times*, November 28.

Collier, Ruth Berins, and David Collier. 1991. *Shaping the Political Arena*. Princeton: Princeton University Press.

"Colombia: Local Elections Carried Out amid Violence." 1997. *Notisur*, October 31.

Conaghan, Catherine M. 1995. "Politicians against Parties: Discord and Disconnection in Ecuador's Party System." In *Building Democratic Institutions: Party Systems in Latin America*, ed. Scott Mainwaring and Timothy R. Scully, 434–458. Stanford: Stanford University Press.

Consejo Supremo Electoral. 1985. *Resultados Electorales 1958–1983*. Caracas, Venezuela: Consejo Supremo Electoral.

———. 1989. *Resultados Electorales 1988*. Caracas, Venezuela: Consejo Supremo Electoral.

———. 1995. *Elección de Gobernadores y Diputados a las Asambleas Legislativas, 1995*. Caracas, Venezuela: Consejo Supremo Electoral.

———. 2000. *Electoral Results*. Consejo Nacional Electoral (on-line resource), accessed September 26.

Coppedge, Michael. 1994. *Strong Parties and Lame Ducks: Presidential Partyarchy and Factionalism in Venezuela*. Stanford: Stanford University Press.

Cornelius, Wayne A. 1999. "Subnational Politics and Democratization: Tensions between Center and Periphery in the Mexican Political System." In *Subnational Politics and Democratization in Mexico*, ed. Wayne A. Cornelius, Todd A. Eisenstadt, and Jane Hindley. La Jolla: Center for U.S.–Mexican Studies, University of California, San Diego.

Corte Nacional Electoral de Bolivia. 1997. *Estadísticas Electorales 1985–1995*. La Paz, Bolivia: Corte Nacional Electoral.

———. 1998. *http://www.bolivian.com/cne*, accessed December 16.

Cox, Gary W., and Mathew D. McCubbins. 1993. *Legislative Leviathan*: *Party Government in the House*. Berkeley: University of California Press.

Crabtree, John. 1995. "The 1995 Elections in Peru: End of the Line for the Party System?" London: University of London, Institute for Latin American Studies.

Cramer, Marc. 1998. "The Bleaching of Bolivian Politics." *Bolivian Times*, December, 10.

Crook, Richard C., and James Manor. 1998. *Democracy and Decentralisation in South Asia and West Africa: Participation, Accountability and Performance*. Cambridge: Cambridge University Press.

Cumplido, F. 1992. "La Estructura Institucional del Modelo de Descentralización." Santiago de Chile: CEPAL.

Dahl, Robert A. 1971. *Polyarchy: Participation and Opposition*. New Haven: Yale University Press.

Dammert Ego Aguire, Manuel. 1999. *Desborde, territorial descentralista: Replanteando la reforma descentralista peruana: Territorios sociales, estado con regiones y municipios, impulso autonómico*. Peru: M. Dammert.

Dávila, Andres, and Ana Maria Corredor. 1998. "Las Elecciones del 26 de Octubre: Cómo se Reprodujo el Poder Local y Regional?" In *Elecciones y Democracia En Colombia 1997–1998*, ed. Andres Dávila and Ana Maria Bejarano, 77–116. Bogota, Colombia: Universidad de los Andes.

de la Calle, Humberto. 1997. Interview, August.

De la Cruz, Rafael. 1992. "La Estrategia de la Descentralización en Venezuela." In *Descentralización, Gobernabilidad y Democracia*, ed. Rafael de la Cruz. Caracas, Venezuela: Nueva Sociedad.

———. 1995. "La Descentralización en Venezuela: Alcances y Límites de un Proceso." In *Descentralizar en América Latina?*, ed. Sociedad Alemana de Cooperación Técnica/Programa de Gestión Urbana, 313–358. Quito, Ecuador: Sociedad Alemana de Cooperación Técnica/Programa de Gestión Urbana.

Delgado, Oscar. 1986. *Colombia Elige: Mitaca 84, Perspectiva 86*. Bogotá, Colombia: Pontificia Universidad Javeriana, Facultad de Estudios Interdisciplinarios, Programa de Estudios Políticos.

Delgado Silva, Angel. 1995. *Municipios, Descentralización y Democracia: Una Propuesta Democrática*. Lima, Peru: Servicios Gráficos.

Diamond, Larry. 1999. *Developing Democracy: Toward Consolidation*. Baltimore: Johns Hopkins University Press.

Dietz, Henry A. 1998. "Urban Elections in Peru, 1980–1995." In *Urban Elections in Democratic Latin America*, ed. Henry A. Dietz and Gil Shidlo, 199–224. Wilmington, Del.: Scholarly Resources.

Dietz, Henry A., and Gil Shidlo, eds. 1998. *Urban Elections in Democratic Latin America*. Wilmington, Del.: Scholarly Resources.

Dix, Robert H. 1987. *The Politics of Colombia*. New York: Praeger.

Domínguez, Jorge I., and Abraham L. Lowenthal, eds. 1996. *Constructing Democratic Governance: Latin America and the Caribbean in the 1990s*. Baltimore: Johns Hopkins University Press.

Downs, Anthony. 1957. *An Economic Theory of Democracy*. New York: Harper.

Dresser, Denise. 1994. "Bringing the Poor Back In: National Solidarity as a Strategy of Regime Legitimation." In *Transforming State-Society Relations in Mexico: The National Solidarity Strategy*, ed. Wayne Cornelius, Ann L. Craig, and Jonathon Fox, 143–165. La Jolla: Center for U.S.–Mexican Studies, University of California, San Diego.

Dugas, John. 1993. "El Desarrollo de la Asamblea Nacional Constituyente." In *La Constitución de 1991: Un Pacto Político Viable?*, ed. John Dugas, 45–76. Bogotá, Colombia: Universidad de los Andes, Departamento de Ciencia Política.

Dugas, John, Angélica Ocampo, Luis Javier Orjuela, and Germán Ruiz. 1992. *Los Caminos de la Descentralización: Diversidad y Retos de la Transformación Municipal*. Bogotá, Colombia: Universidad de los Andes, Departamento de Ciencia Política.

Duverger, Maurice. 1972. *Political Parties, Their Organization and Activity in the Modern State*, trans. Barbara North and Robert North, 3rd ed. London: Methuen.

Dyer, Geoff. 1999. "Halt Called on Debt Repayments to Brasilia." *Financial Times*, January 6, p. 6.

Eaton, Kent. 1998. "Political Obstacles to Decentralization in Argentina and the Philippines." Paper presented at the American Political Science Association meeting, Boston, September 3–6.

———. 2004. "Politics beyond the Capital: The Design of Subnational Institutions." Stanford University Press.

Ebel, Robert D., and Serdar Yilmaz. 2002. "On the Measurement and Impact of Fiscal Decentralization." World Bank policy research working paper 2809.

Echenique, Jorge, and Nelson Rolando. 1991. *Elecciones 1989 en el Campo.* Santiago: Agraria.

Elías Jiménez, Enrique Camilo. 1990. *Municipio entre Dictadura y Democracia.* Lima, Peru: CONCYTEC.

Ellner, Steve. 2001. "The Radical Potential of Chavismo in Venezuela: The First Year and a Half in Power." *Latin American Perspectives* 28, no. 5: 5–32.

Epstein, David, and Sharyn O'Halloran. 1999. *Delegating Powers: A Transaction Cost Politics Approach to Policy Making under Separate Powers.* Cambridge, U.K.: New York: Cambridge University Press.

Escalante Carrasco, Scarlet. 1997. "La Participación Popular y sus Efectos Sobre la Equidad." Manuscript, Unidad de Análisis Políticas Sociales, La Paz, Bolivia.

Escobar Navia, Rodrigo. 1997. Interview, August.

Escobar-Lemmon, Maria. 2003. "Political Support for Decentralization: An Analysis of the Colombian and Venezuelan Legislatures." *American Journal of Political Science* 47, no. 4 (October).

Escobar-Lemmon, Maria, and Erika Moreno. 2003. "Sub-national Elections and the Rise of Quality Challengers in Colombia and Venezuela, 1989–2000." Paper prepared for the Latin American Studies Association conference, Dallas, Texas, March.

Faguet, Jean-Paul. 2001. "Does Decentralization Increase Responsiveness to Local Needs? Evidence from Bolivia." World Bank policy research working paper 2516.

Ferrazzi, Gabriele. 2000. "Using the 'F' Word: Federalism in Indonesia's Decentralization Discourse." *Publius* 30, no. 2: 63–85.

Finot, Iván. 1990. *Democratización del Estado y Descentralización.* La Paz, Bolivia: ILDIS.

Fiorina, Morris P. 1977. *Congress, Keystone of the Washington Establishment.* New Haven, Conn.: Yale University Press.

Fiorina, Morris P., and Roger G. Noll. 1978. "Voters, Legislators and Bureaucracy: Institutional Design in the Public Sector." *American Economic Review* 68, no. 2: 256–260.

Fisman, R., and R. Gatti. 2000. "Decentralization and Corruption: Evidence Across Countries." World Bank policy research working paper 2290. Washington, D.C.: World Bank.

Fox, Jonathon. 1994. "Latin America's Emerging Local Politics." *Journal of Democracy* 5, no. 2.

Frank, Jonas. 2003. "Incentives for Fiscal Decentralization: Ecuador Case Study." Ph.D. dissertation, University of Potsdam, Germany.

Freidenberg, Flavia. 2000. "Cuestión Regional y Política en Ecuador: Partidos de Vocación Nacional y Apoyo Regional." Paper presented at the Latin American Studies Conference, Miami, Florida, March 16–18.

Friedman, Milton. 1953. "The Methodology of Positive Economics." In *Essays in Positive Economics*, ed. Milton Friedman, 3–43. Chicago: University of Chicago Press.

Gaitán Pavía, Pilar, and Carlos Moreno Ospina, eds. 1992. *Poder Local: Realidad y Utopía de la Descentralización en Colombia*. Bogotá: Tercer Mundo Editores.

Gamarra, Eduardo A., and James M. Malloy. 1995. "The Patrimonial Dynamics of Party Politics in Bolivia." In *Building Democratic Institutions: Party Systems in Latin America*, ed. Scott Mainwaring and Timothy R. Scully, 399–433. Stanford: Stanford University Press.

Gandhi, Ved P. 1995. "Intergovernmental Fiscal Relations and Economic Performance." In *Macroeconomic Management and Fiscal Decentralization*, ed. Jayanta Roy, 39–48. Washington, D.C.: The World Bank.

García-Guadilla, María Pilar, and Carlos Pérez. 2002. "Democracy, Decentralization, and Clientelism: New Relationships and Old Practices." *Latin American Perspectives* 29, no. 5: 90–109.

García Lema, Alberto Manuel. 1994. *La Reforma por Dentro: La Difícil Construcción del Consenso Constitucional*. Buenos Aires, Argentina: Grupo Editorial Planeta.

García Márquez, Gabriel. 1997. *News of a Kidnapping*. New York: Knopf.

García Peña, Daniel. 1999. "The Colombian Peace Process." Speech given at the Kennedy School of Government, Harvard University.

Garman, Christopher, Stephan Haggard, and Eliza Willis. 2001. "Fiscal Decentralization: A Political Theory with Latin American Cases." *World Politics* 53, no. 2.

Gastíl, Raymond. 1987. *Freedom in the World, 1987*. New York: Freedom House.

———. 1990. *Freedom in the World, 1989–90*. New York: Freedom House.

———. 1991. *Freedom in the World, 1990–91*. New York: Freedom House.

———. 2000. *Freedom in the World, 1999–2000*. New York: Freedom House.

Geddes, Barbara. 1991. "A Game Theoretic Model of Reform in Latin American Democracies." *The American Political Science Review* 85, no. 2: 371–392.

———. 1994. *Politician's Dilemma*. Berkeley: University of California Press.

———. 1995. "Initiation of New Democratic Institutions in Eastern Europe and Latin America." In *Institutional Design in New Democracies: Eastern Europe and Latin America*, ed. Arend Lijphart and Carlos H. Waisman, 15–41. Boulder, Colo.: Westview.

Golden, Miriam. 1997. *Heroic Defeats: The Politics of Job Loss*. New York: Cambridge University Press.

Gourevitch, Peter Alexis. 1980. *Paris and the Provinces: The Politics of Local Government Reform in France*. Berkeley: University of California Press.

Gómez Calcaño, Luís, and Margarita López Maya. 1990. *El Tejido de Penélope: La Reforma el Estado en Venezuela (1984–1988)*. Caracas, Venezuela: CENDES.

Graham, Carol. 1992. *Peru's APRA: Parties, Politics, and the Elusive Quest for Democracy*. Boulder, Colo.: Lynne Rienner.

————. 1994. *Safety Nets, Politics, and the Poor: Transitions to Market Economies*. Washington, DC: Brookings Institution.

Graham, Carol, and Cheikh Kane. 1998. "Opportunistic Government or Sustaining Reform? Electoral Trends and Public Expenditure Patterns in Peru, 1990–1995." *Latin American Research Review* 33, no. 1: 67–104.

Grindle, Merilee. 2000. *Audacious Reforms: Institutional Invention and Democracy in Latin America*. Baltimore: Johns Hopkins University Press.

Hao, Jia, and Lin Zhimin, eds. 1994. *Changing Central-Local Relations in China: Reform and State Capacity*. Boulder, Colo.: Westview.

Horn, Murray J., and Kenneth A. Shepsle. 1989. "Commentary on 'Administrative Arrangements and the Political Control of Agencies': Administrative Process and Organizational Form as Legislative Responses to Agency Costs." *Virginia Law Review* 75 (March): 499–508.

Hoskin, Gary. 1998. "Urban Electoral Behavior in Colombia." In *Urban Elections in Democratic Latin America*, ed. Henry A. Dietz and Gil Shidlo, 91–116. Wilmington, Del.: Scholarly Resources.

Huntington, Samuel. 1991. *The Third Wave: Democratization in the Late Twentieth Century*. Norman: University of Oklahoma Press.

Instituto de Investigación y Desarrollo Municipal. 1994. *Estadísticas Municipales 1994*. La Paz, Bolivia: INIDEM.

Instituto Nacional de Estadística y Censos. 1995. *Propuesta para Descentralizar las Rentas del Estado*. Guayaquil, Ecuador: INEC: Instituto Nacional de Estadística y Censos.

Inter-American Development Bank. 1994. *Economic and Social Progress in Latin America, Special Report: Fiscal Decentralization*. Baltimore: Johns Hopkins University Press.

————. 1997. *Economic and Social Progress of Latin America*. Washington, D.C.: Inter-American Development Bank.

International Monetary Fund. 1998. *International Financial Statistics Yearbook, 1997*. Washington, D.C.: International Monetary Fund.

Isaza Henao, Emiliano, and Darío Marín Vanegas. 1980. "Proyecto de Acto Legislativo No. 7 de 1980." In *Descentralización y Centralismo en Colombia*, ed. Alvaro Tirado Mejía, 233–235. Bogotá, Colombia: Editorial Oveja Negra.

Jones, Mark P. 1997. "Evaluating Argentina's Presidential Democracy 1983–1995." In *Presidentialism and Democracy in Latin America*, ed. Scott Mainwaring and Matthew Soberg Shugart, 259–299. Cambridge: Cambridge University Press.

Jones, Mark P., and Scott Mainwaring. 2003. "The Nationalization of Parties and Party Systems: An Empirical Measure and an Application to the Americas." *Party Politics* 9, no. 2: 139–166.

Jones, Mark P., Pablo Sanguinetti, and Mariano Tommasi. 2000. "Politics, Institutions and Fiscal Performance in a Federal System: An Analysis of the Argentine Provinces." *Journal of Development Economics*, 61, no. 2.

Jurado Nacional de Elecciones de Peru. 1997a. *Elecciones Generales 1995*. Lima, Peru: Jurado Nacional de Elecciones de Peru.

———. 1997b. *Elecciones Municipales 1995–1996*. Lima, Peru: Jurado Nacional de Elecciones de Peru.

Kay, Bruce. 1995. "Fujipopulism and the Liberal State in Peru, 1990–1995." Chapel Hill: Duke University of North Carolina Program on Latin American Studies.

Khemani, Stuti. 2001. "Decentralization and Accountability: Are Voters More Vigilant in Local Than in National Elections?" World Bank working paper no. 2557.

Kiewiet, Roderick, and Mathew D. McCubbins. 1991. *The Logic of Delegation: Congressional Parties and the Appropriations Process*. Chicago: University of Chicago Press.

King, Gary, Michael Tomz, and Jason Wittenberg. 1998. "Making the Most of Statistical Analyses: Improving Interpretation and Presentation." Paper presented at the American Political Science Association meeting, Boston.

Kirchheimer, Otto. 1966. "The Transformation of the Western European Party Systems." In *Political Parties and Political Development*, ed., Joseph LaPalombara and Myron Weiner. Princeton University Press. Pp. 177–200.

Klugman, Jeni. 1994. *Decentralization: A Survey of the Literature from a Human Development Perspective*. New York: United Nations Development Program.

Kraemer, Moritz. 1999. "One Decade of Decentralization – An Assessment of the Venezuelan Experiment." Washington, D.C.: Inter-American Development Bank.

Lalander, Rickard. 2002. "El Suicidio de los Elefantes? La Descentralización Venezolana entre la Partidocracia y el Chavismo." In *La Transición Venezolana: Aproximación al Fenómeno Chávez*, ed. Alfredo Ramos Jiménez. Mérida, Venezuela: Centro de Investigaciónes de Política Comparada, Universidad de los Andes.

Larrea, Carlos. 1986. "Crecimiento Urbano y Dinámica de las Ciudades Intermedias en el Ecuador (1950–1982)." In *Ciudades en Conflicto: Poder Local, Participación Popular y Planificación en las Ciudades de América Latina*, ed. Diego Carrión, Jorge Enrique Hardoy, Hilda Herzer, and Ana García. Quito, Ecuador: Editorial El Conejo.

León Velasco, Juan Bernardo. 1987. *Elecciones, Votos y Partidos: Evolución y Geografía de las Preferencias Electorales en el Ecuador*. Quito, Ecuador: CEDIME.

———. 1992. *Las Elecciones en el Ecuador: Concejales Cantonales 1978–1990*. Quito, Ecuador: CIESA.

López Maya, Margarita, Luís Gómez Calcaño, and Thaís Maingón. 1990. *De Punto Fijo al Pacto Social: Desarrollo y Hegemonía en Venezuela (1958–1985)*. Caracas, Venezuela: Fondo Editorial Acta Científica Venezolana.

López Murphy, Ricardo, ed. 1995. *Fiscal Decentralization in Latin America*. Washington, D.C.: Inter-American Development Bank.

Lowi, Theodore. 1969. *The End of Liberalism: Ideology, Policy and the Crisis of Public Authority*. New York: Norton.

Mainwaring, Scott, and Timothy R. Scully, eds. 1995. *Building Democratic Institutions: Party Systems in Latin America*. Stanford: Stanford University Press.

Malloy, James M., and Eduardo Gamarra. 1988. *Revolution and Reaction: Bolivia, 1964–1985*. New Brunswick, N.J.: Transaction.

Martínez, Federico. 1997. Interview, January.

Martner, Gonzalo D. 1993. *Descentralización y Modernización del Estado en la Transición*. Santiago: LOM.

Martz, John D. 1997. *The Politics of Clientelism: Democracy and the State in Colombia*. New Brunswick, N.J.: Transaction.

———. 1999–2000. "Political Parties and Candidate Selection in Venezuela and Colombia." *Political Science Quarterly* 114, no. 4: 639–659.

Martz, John D., and Enrique A. Baloyra. 1976. *Electoral Mobilization and Public Opinion: The Venezuelan Campaign of 1973*. Chapel Hill: University of North Carolina Press.

Matienzo, José Nicolás. 1994. *El Régimen Republicano-Federal*. Buenos Aires: Artes Gráficas Corín Luna.

Mauceri, Philip. 1997. "The Transition to 'Democracy' and the Failures of Institution Building." In *Peruvian Labyrinth*, ed. Maxwell A. Cameron and Philip Mauceri, 13–36. University Park: Pennsylvania State University Press.

McClintock, Cynthia. 1998. "Peru: Precarious Regimes, Authoritarian and Democratic." Paper presented at the American Political Science Association meeting, Boston, September 3–6.

McCubbins, Mathew D., Roger G. Noll, and Barry R. Weingast. 1987. "Administrative Procedures as Instruments of Political Control." *Journal of Law, Economics and Organization* 3/2 (fall): 243–277.

McCubbins, Mathew D., Roger G. Noll, and Barry R. Weingast. 1989. "Structure and Process, Politics and Policy: Administrative Arrangements and the Political Control of Agencies." *Virginia Law Review* 75: 431–482.

Medina García, Oswaldo. 1980. *Peru 1978–1980: Análisis de un Momento Político*. Lima, Peru: C'EST Editorial.

Menéndez-Carrión, Amparo. 1991. *Región y Elecciones en el Ecuador, 1952–1988: Elementos para el Debate*. Quito, Ecuador: FLACSO.

Mesa Gisbert, Carlos D. 1990. *Presidentes de Bolivia: Entre Urnas y Fúsiles*, 2nd ed. La Paz, Bolivia: Gisbert y CIA.

Miller, Gary. 1981. *Cities by Contract: The Politics of Municipal Incorporation*. Cambridge, Mass.: MIT Press.

Ministerio de Economía de la Provincia de Buenos Aires. 1996. *Estudio Sobre Finanzas Provinciales y el Sistema de Coparticipación Federal de Impuestos.*

Buenos Aires: República Argentina, Ministerio de Economía de la Provincia de Buenos Aires.

Ministerio de Planeamiento y Coordinación. 1993a. *Encuesta y Analysis Sobre la Descentralizacion Administrativa.* La Paz, Bolivia: ILDIS.

———. 1993b. *Hacia el Proceso de Descentralización.* La Paz, Bolivia: República de Bolivia, Ministerio de Planeamiento y Coordinación, Subsecretaria de Desarrollo Socioeconómico.

Moe, Terry M. 1990. Political Institutions: The Neglected Side of the Story. *Journal of Law, Economics and Organization* 6 (December): 213–253.

Molina, Sergio, and Iván Arias. 1996. *De la Nación Clandestina a la Participación Popular.* La Paz, Bolivia: CEDOIN: Centro de Documentación e Información.

Molina Monasterios, Fernando. 1997. *Historia de la Participación Popular.* La Paz, Bolivia: Secretaría Nacional de Participación Popular.

Molina Saucedo, Carlos Hugo. 1990. *La Descentralización Imposible y la Alternativa Municipal.* Santa Cruz, Bolivia: Editorial Cabildo.

———. 1994. "Las Reformas en el Regimen Municipal." In *Reflexiones sobre la Ley de Necesidad de Reforma de la Constitución del Estado,* ed. Juan Carlos Durán Saucedo. La Paz, Bolivia: ILDIS.

———. 1997. Interview, July.

Molinar Horcasitas, Juan. 1995. "Changing the Balance of Power in a Hegemonic Party System: The Case of Mexico." In *Institutional Design in New Democracies: Eastern Europe and Latin America,* ed. Arend Lijphart and Carlos H. Waisman, 137–159. Boulder, Colo.: Westview.

Montinola, Gabriella, Yingyi Qian, and Barry R. Weingast. 1995. "Federalism, Chinese Style." *World Politics* 48, no. 1: 50–81.

Montoya Retta, Rodolfo. 1990. *Las Transferencias Intergubernamentales en el Federalismo Mexicano.* Nuevo León: Universidad Autónoma de Nuevo León.

Moreno, Luis. 2002. "Decentralization in Spain." *Regional Studies* 36, no. 4: 399–408.

Munin, Helena. 1998. " 'Freer' Forms of Organization and Financing and the Effects of Inequality in Latin American Educational Systems: Two Countries in Comparison." *Compare* 28, no. 3: 229–343.

Musgrave, Richard A. 1959. *The Theory of Public Finance: A Study of Public Economy.* New York: McGraw-Hill.

Nickson, R. Andrew. 1995. *Local Government in Latin America.* Boulder, Colo.: Lynne Rienner.

Nielsen, Daniel L., and Matthew Soberg Shugart. 1999. "Constitutional Change in Colombia: Policy Adjustment through Institutional Reform." *Comparative Political Studies* 32, no. 3: 313–362.

Nohlen, Dieter. 1993. *Elecciones y Sistemas de Partidos en América Latina.* San José, Costa Rica: Instituto Interamericano de Derechos Humanos.

Oates, Wallace E. 1998. *The Economics of Fiscal Federalism and Local Finance.* Northampton, Mass.: Edward Elgar.

O'Donnell, Guillermo. 1994. "Delegative Democracy." *Journal of Democracy* 5, no. 1: 55–69.

Ojeda Segovia, Lautaro. 1993. "Las Políticas Sociales y de Gestión Local en el Contexto de la Modernización del Estado." In *Municipios y ONGs: Retos de la Descentralización y el Desarrollo Local en el Ecuador Actual*. Quito: Ciudad-Ficong.

O'Neill, Kathleen. 2002. "Decentralized Politics and Political Outcomes in the Andes." In *The Crisis of Democratic Representation in the Andes*, ed. Scott Mainwaring, Ana María Bejarano, and Eduardo Pizarro. Under review at Stanford University Press.

ONPE (Oficina Nacional de Procesos Electorales). 2003. Http://www.onpe. gob.pe/resultados2002, accessed Nov. 11, 2003.

Oporto Castro, Henry. 1998. *El Difícil Camino Hacia la Descentralización*. Edited by FES-ILDIS. Vol. 2: *Descentralización y Participación*. La Paz, Bolivia: EDOBOL.

Orjuela E., Luis Javier. 1993. "Aspectos Políticos del Nuevo Ordenamiento Territorial." In *La Constitución de 1991: Un Pacto Político Viable?*, ed. by John Dugas, 134–161. Bogotá, Colombia: Universidad de los Andes.

Osterling, Jorge P. 1989. *Democracy in Colombia: Clientelist Politics and Guerrilla Warfare*. New Brunswick, N.J.: Transaction.

Pachano, Fernando, ed. 1999. *La Ruta de la Gobernabilidad*. Quito, Ecuador: Corporacion de Estudios para el Desarrollo (CORDES).

Paredes Muñoz, Hernan. 1995. "Hacia un Proceso de Descentralización Integral." In *Descentralizar en América Latina?*, ed. Sociedad Alemana de Cooperación Técnica/Programa de Gestión Urbana, 59–130. Quito, Ecuador: Sociedad Alemana de Cooperación Técnica/Programa de Gestión Urbana.

Pastor, Manuel, and Carol Wise. 1992. "Peruvian Economic Policy in the 1980s: From Orthodoxy to Heterodoxy and Back." *Latin American Research Review* 27, no. 2: 83–119.

Pastor, Robert A., ed. 1989. *Democracy in the Americas: Stopping the Pendulum*. New York: Holmes and Meier.

Penfold Becerra, Michael. 1999. "Institutional Electoral Incentives and Decentralization Outcomes: Comparing Colombia and Venezuela." Ph.D. dissertation, Columbia University.

Peredo, Alberto L. 2000. "Fiscal Decentralisation under New Federalism in Mexico: Identifying the Sources of Reform." Paper presented at the Latin American Studies Association conference, Miami, Florida, March 16–18.

Pierson, Paul. 1996. "The New Politics of the Welfare State." *World Politics* 48 (January): 143–179.

Pinzón de Lewin, Patricia. 1989. *Pueblos, Regiones y Partidos: La Regionalización Electoral: Atlas Electoral Colombiano*. Bogotá, Colombia: CIDER Ediciones Uniandes.

Pírez, Pedro. 1986. *Coparticipación Federal y Descentralización del Estado*. Buenos Aires: Centro Editor de América Latina.

Prud'homme, Remy. 1995. "The Dangers of Decentralization." *World Bank Research Observer* 10, no. 2: 201–220.

Prud'homme, Rémy, Hervé Huntziger, and Sonia Guelton. 2000. "Decentralization in Bolivia." Paper prepared for the Inter-American Development Bank, draft version, August.

Przeworski, Adam, and Henry Teune. 1982. *The Logic of Comparative Social Inquiry*. Malabar, Fla.: R. E. Krieger.

Querubín, Cristina, Maria Fernanda Sánchez, and Ileana Kure. 1998. "Dinámica de las Elecciones Populares de Alcaldes, 1988–1997." In *Elecciones y Democracia en Colombia, 1997–1998*, ed. Andres Dávila and Ana Maria Bejarano. Bogota: Universidad de los Andes.

Quintero, Rafael, ed. 1991. *La Cuestión Regional y el Poder*. Quito, Ecuador: FLACSO.

Quintero, Rafael, and Erika Silva. 1991. *Ecuador: Una Nación en Ciernes*, 3 vols. Quito, Ecuador. Vol. 3.

Rangles Lara, Rodrigo. 1995. *Venturas y Desventuras del Poder*. Quito, Ecuador: Carvajal S.A.

Registraduría Nacional del Estado Civil. 1970. *Organización y Estadísticas Electorales, 1962–1968*. Bogotá, Colombia: República de Colombia, Registraduría Nacional del Estado Civil, 1970.

———. 1975. *Estadísticas Electorales, 1970–1974*. Bogotá, Colombia: República de Colombia, Registraduría Nacional del Estado Civil.

———. 1989. *Estadísticas Electorales, 1978–1988*. Bogotá, Colombia: República de Colombia, Registraduría Nacional del Estado Civil.

———. 1991. *Estadísticas Electorales 1990: Asamblea Constitucional*. Bogotá, Colombia: República de Colombia, Registraduría Nacional del Estado Civil.

———. 2001. *Election Results*. Registraduría Nacional Electoral de Colombia (on-line resource). Http://www.registraduria.gov.co, accessed January 1.

"Rewriting the Country?" 1997. *The Economist*, December 13.

Ribadaneira, Raul Gangotena. 1995. "El Proceso de Descentralización en Ecuador." In *Descentralizar en América Latina?*, ed. Sociedad Alemana de Cooperación Técnica/Programa de Gestión Urbana. Quito, Ecuador: Sociedad Alemana de Cooperación Técnica/Programa de Gestión Urbana.

Riker, William H. 1964. *Federalism: Origin, Operation, Significance*. Boston: Little, Brown.

Roberts, Kenneth. 1995. "Neoliberalism and the Transformation of Populism in Latin America." *World Politics* 48, no. 1: 82–116.

Robinson, Jenny. 1995. "Federalism and the Transformation of the South African State." In *Federalism: The Multiethnic Challenge*, ed. Graham Smith, 255–278. London: Longman.

Rodden, Jonathan. 2000. "The Dilemma of Fiscal Federalism: Grants and Fiscal Performance around the World." *American Journal of Political Science* 46, no. 3 (July).

Rodríguez, Victoria E. 1997. *Decentralization in Mexico: From Reforma Municipal to Solidaridad to Nuevo Federalismo*. Boulder, Colo.: Westview.

Roeder, Philip. 1991. "Soviet Federalism and Ethnic Mobilization." *World Politics* 43, no. 2.

Rojas Ortuste, Gonzalo. 1998. *Censura Constructiva, Inestabilidad y Democracia Municipal*, ed. Instituto Latinoamericano de Investigaciónes Sociales de la Fundación Friedrich Ebert Stiftung (FES-ILDIS). La Paz, Bolivia: Editorial Offset Boliviana Limitada (EDOBOL).

Rondinelli, Dennis A. 1989. "Decentralizing Public Services in Developing Countries: Issues and Opportunities." *Journal of Social, Political and Economic Studies* 14, no. 1: 77–98.

Rondinelli, Dennis A., John R. Nellis, and G. Shabbir Cheema. 1984. "Decentralization in Developing Countries: A Review of Recent Experience." Washington, D.C.: World Bank.

Rospigliosi, Fernando. 1994. "Democracy's Bleak Prospects." In *Peru in Crisis: Dictatorship or Democracy?*, ed. Joseph S. Tulchin and Gary Bland, 35–61. Boulder, Colo.: Lynne Rienner.

Rubinfeld, Daniel L. 1987. "The Economics of the Local Public Sector." In *Handbook of Public Economics*, ed. Alan A. Auerbach and Martin Feldstein. New York: North-Holland.

Saba, Raúl P. 1987. *Political Development and Democracy in Peru*. Boulder, Colo.: Westview.

Samuels, David. 2000. "Reinventing Local Government? Municipalities and Intergovernmental Relations in Democratic Brazil." In *Democratic Brazil: Actors, Institutions, and Processes*, ed. Peter Kingstone and Timothy Power. Pittsburgh: University of Pittsburgh Press.

Santamaria Salamanca, Ricardo. 1985. "La Reforma Política." *Economía Colombiana*, January.

Schady, Norbert R. 2000. "The Political Economy of Expenditures by the Peruvian Social Fund (FONCODES), 1991–95." *American Political Science Review* 94, no. 2: 289–304.

Secretaría de Hacienda. 1994. "Cambios Estructurales en la Relación Nación Provincias." Buenos Aires, Argentina.

Secretaría Nacional de Participación Popular. 1996. *Las Primeras Elecciones*. La Paz: SNPP/Unidad de Investigación y Análisis.

Serpa Uribe, Horacio. 1997. Interview, August.

Shah, Anwar. 1998. *Fiscal Federalism and Macroeconomic Governance: For Better or for Worse?* World Bank, Operations Evaluation Department, Country and Regional Relations Division.

Shirk, Susan. 1993. *The Political Logic of Economic Reform in China*. Berkeley: University of California Press.

Shugart, Matthew Soberg, and John Carey. 1992. *Presidents and Assemblies: Constitutional Design and Electoral Dynamics*. New York: Cambridge University Press.

Siavelis, Peter, and Arturo Valenzuela. 1996. "Electoral Engineering and Democratic Stability: The Legacy of Authoritarian Rule in Chile." In *Institutional Design in New Democracies: Eastern Europe and Latin America*, ed. Arend Lijphart and Carlos H. Waisman, 77–99. Boulder, Colo.: Westview.

Sivak, Martín. 2001. *El Dictador Elegido: Biografía no Autorizada de Hugo Banzer Suárez*. La Paz, Bolivia: Plural Editores.

Solnick, Steven L. 1995. "Federal Bargaining in Russia." *East European Constitutional Review* 4.

―――. 1998. "Gubernatorial Elections in Russia, 1996–1997." *Post-Soviet Affairs* 14, no. 1: 48–80.

―――. 1999. *Stealing the State: Control and Collapse in Soviet Institutions.* Cambridge, Mass.: Harvard University Press.

Sosa, Joaquin Marta. 1984. *Venezuela: Elecciones y Transformación Social.* Caracas: Ediciones Centauro.

Stein, Ernesto. 1999. "Fiscal Decentralization and Government Size in Latin America." *Journal of Applied Economics* 2, no. 2.

Stepan, Alfred. 1999. "Federalism and Democracy: Beyond the U.S. Model." *Journal of Democracy* 10, no. 4: 19–34.

―――. 2000a. "Brazil's Decentralized Federalism: Bringing Government Closer to the Citizens?" *Daedalus* 129, no. 2 (2000a): 145–169.

―――. 2000b. "Russian Federalism in Comparative Perspective." *Post-Soviet Affairs* 16, no. 2.

―――. 2001. *Arguing Comparative Politics.* Oxford, U.K.: Oxford University Press.

Stoner-Weiss, Kathryn. 1997. *Local Heroes: The Political Economy of Russian Regional Governance.* Princeton: Princeton University Press.

―――. 1999. "Central Weakness and Provincial Autonomy: Observations on the Devolution Process in Russia." *Post-Soviet Affairs* 15, no. 1: 87–106.

"Stuck." 1995. *The Economist*, January 28.

Suberu, Rotimi T. 2001. *Federalism and Ethnic Conflict in Nigeria.* Washington, D.C.: United States Institute of Peace Press.

Subsecretaria de Desarrollo Regional y Administrativo. 1994. *El Proceso de Descentralización en Chile: 1990–1993.* Santiago: LOM.

"Supermodel Angst." 1999. *The Economist Newspaper Limited*, July 3.

Tanaka, Martín. 2003a. "La Dínamica de los Actores Regionales: El Despertar del Letargo?" Manuscript, Instituto de Estudios Peruanos, Lima.

―――. 2003b. "El Gobierno de Alejandro Toledo: Una Oportunidad Perdida?" Manuscript, Instituto de Estudios Peruanos, Lima.

Tanzi, V. 1994. "Corruption, Governmental Activities, and Markets." IMF working paper 94/99. Washington, D.C.: International Monetary Fund.

Tarrow, Sidney. 1974. "Local Restraints on Regional Reform: A Comparison of Italy and France." *Comparative Politics* 7, no. 1: 1–36.

―――. 1995. "Bridging the Quantitative-Qualitative Divide in Political Science." *American Political Science Review* 89, no. 2: 471–474.

Tendler, Judith. 1997. *Good Government in the Tropics.* Baltimore: Johns Hopkins University Press.

Thedieck, Franz, and Eduardo Buller. 1995. "Descentralización de la Administración en el Peru." In *Descentralizar en América Latina*, ed. Sociedad Alemana de Cooperación Técnica/Programa de Gestión Urbana, 195–236. Quito, Ecuador: Sociedad Alemana de Cooperación Técnica/Programa de Gestión Urbana.

Tiebout, Charles M. 1956. "A Pure Theory of Local Expenditures." *Journal of Political Economy* 64, no. 5: 416–424.

Tocqueville, Alexis de. 1843. *Democracy in America.* Trans. Henry Reeve. 2nd ed. London: Saunders and Otley.

Tomz, Michael, Jason Wittenberg, and Gary King. 1999. "CLARIFY: Software for Interpreting and Presenting Statistical Results, Version 1.2.1." Harvard University, Cambridge, Massachusetts.

Treisman, Daniel. 1999a. *After the Deluge: Regional Crises and Political Consolidation in Russia.* Ann Arbor: University of Michigan Press.

————. 1999b. "Decentralization and Corruption: Why Are Federal States Perceived to Be More Corrupt?" Paper prepared for the annual meeting of the American Political Science Association, Atlanta, Georgia, August.

Tribunal Supremo Electoral. 1978. *Resultados de las Elecciones del 16 de Julio de 1978.* Quito, Ecuador: Tribunal Supremo Electoral.

————. 1979. *Resultados de las Elecciones del 29 de Abril de 1979.* Quito, Ecuador: Tribunal Supremo Electoral.

————. 1980. *Resultados de las Elecciones del 7 de Diciembre de 1980.* Quito, Ecuador: Tribunal Supremo Electoral.

————. 1984. *Resultados de las Elecciones del 29 de 1984.* Quito, Ecuador: Tribunal Supremo Electoral.

————. 1986. *Resultados de las Elecciones del 18 de Junio de 1986.* Quito, Ecuador: Tribunal Supremo Electoral.

————. 1988. *Resultados de las Elecciones del 31 de Enero de 1988.* Quito, Ecuador: Tribunal Supremo Electoral.

————. 1990. *Resultados de las Elecciones del 17 de Junio de 1990.* Quito, Ecuador: Tribunal Supremo Electoral.

————. 1992. *Resultados de las Elecciones del 17 de Mayo de 1992.* Quito, Ecuador: Tribunal Supremo Electoral.

————. 1994. *Resultados de las Elecciones del 1 de Mayo de 1994.* Quito, Ecuador: Tribunal Supremo Electoral.

————. 1996. *Resultados de las Elecciones del 19 de Mayo de 1996.* Quito, Ecuador: Tribunal Supremo Electoral.

Tsebelis, George. 1990. *Nested Games: Rational Choice in Comparative Politics.* Berkeley: University of California Press.

Tuesta Soldevilla, Fernando. 1994. *Peru Político en Cifras, Elite Política y Elecciones*, 2nd ed. Lima, Peru: Fundación Friedrich Ebert.

Urdaneta, Alberto, Leopoldo Martínez Olvarría, and Margarita López Maya. 1990. *Venezuela: Centralización y Descentralización del Estado.* Caracas, Venezuela: CENDES.

Urenda Díaz, Juan Carlos. 1998. *La Descentralización Deficiente.* Santa Cruz, Bolivia: Talleres Gráficos de Imprenta Landivar S.R.L.

Urioste Fernández de Córdova, Miguel. 2002. *Desarrollo Rural con Participación Popular.* La Paz, Bolivia: Fundación Tierra Editores.

Valenzuela, Arturo. 1977. *Political Brokers in Chile: Local Government in a Centralized Polity.* Durham, N.C.: Duke University Press.

Van Cott, Donna Lee. 1998. "Constitution-Making and Democratic Transformation: The Bolivian and Colombian Constitutional Reforms." Ph.D. dissertation, Georgetown University.

———. 2000. *The Friendly Liquidation of the Past: The Politics of Diversity in Latin America.* Ed. by Billie R. DeWalt, Pitt Latin American Series. Pittsburgh: University of Pittsburgh Press.

———. 2003a. "Bolivia's 2002 Election: From Exclusion to Inclusion." *Journal of Latin American Studies* 35, no. 4 (November).

———. 2003b. "From Movements to Parties: The Evolution of Ethnic Politics in Latin America." Manuscript, University of Tennessee, Knoxville.

Velásquez, Fabio. 1995. "La Descentralización en Colombia: Antecedentes, Desarrollos, y Perspectivas." In *Descentralizar en América Latina?*, ed. Sociedad Alemana de Cooperación Técnica/Programa de Gestión Urbana, 237–311. Quito, Ecuador: Sociedad Alemana de Cooperación Técnica/ Programa de Gestión Urbana.

Véliz, Claudio. 1980. *The Centralist Tradition of Latin America.* Princeton: Princeton University Press.

Verano de la Rosa, Eduardo. 1991. "Respuesta a los Centralistas y Opositores de la Region." *Gaceta Constitucional*, June 18, pp. 7–8.

Verdesoto Custode, Luis. 1996. *Temas para una Sociedad en Crisis.* Quito, Ecuador: Fundación Esquel.

Vice-Ministerio por Participación Popular y Financiamiento Municipal, Gobierno de Bolivia. 2000. *Municipal Results.* Vice-Ministerio por Participación Popular y Financiamiento Municipal (on-line resource). Http://www.vppfm.gov.bo, accessed October 3.

Vjekoslav, Darlic Mardesic. 1989. *Estadísticas Electorales de Ecuador, 1978– 1989.* Quito, Ecuador: ILDIS.

Weingast, Barry. 1995. "The Economic Role of Political Institutions: Market-Preserving Federalism and Economic Development." *Journal of Law, Economics and Organization* 11, no. 2: 1–31.

Williamson, John, ed. 1994. *The Political Economy of Policy Reform.* Washington, D.C.: Institute for International Economics.

Willis, Eliza, Stephan Haggard, and Christopher Garman. 1999. "The Politics of Decentralization in Latin America." *Latin American Research Review* 34, no. 1: 7–56.

Wines, Michael. 2000. "Putin's Move on Governors Would Bolster His Role." *New York Times*, May 22.

World Bank. 1990. *Argentina: Provincial Government Finances.* Washington D.C.: World Bank.

———. 1993. *Chile: Subnational Government Finance.* Washington, D.C.: World Bank.

———. 1996. *World Debt Tables.* CD-Rom. Washington, D.C.: World Bank.

———. 1997. *The World Development Report.* Washington, D.C.: World Bank.

———. 2000. *The World Development Report.* Washington, D.C.: World Bank.

Yañez, José, and Leonardo Letelier. 1995. "Chile." In *Fiscal Decentralization in Latin America*, ed. Ricardo López Murphy, 137–188. Washington, D.C.: Inter-American Development Bank.

Yashar, Deborah. 1996. "Indigenous Protest and Democracy in Latin America." In *Constructing Democratic Governance: Latin America and the Caribbean in the 1990s – Themes and Issues*, ed. Jorge I. Domínguez and Abraham F. Lowenthal. Baltimore: Johns Hopkins University Press.

Zafra, Gustavo. 1997. Interview, August.

Zas Friz Burga, Johnny. 1998. *La Descentralizacion Ficticia: Peru 1821–1998*. Lima, Peru: Universidad del Pacifico, Centro de Investigacion.

Zegada, Maria Teresa. 1996. *Democratización Interna de los Partidos Politicos en Bolivia*. Ed. ILDIS, Debate. La Paz, Bolivia: Artes Gráficas Latina.

———. 1998. *La Representación Territorial de los Partidos en Bolivia*. Ed. ILDIS, Debate. La Paz, Bolivia: EDOBOL.

Index